A DREAMER'S JOURNEY

MORRIS R. COHEN, 1943

Bust by Ann Wolfe

A DREAMER'S JOURNEY

The Autobiography of

MORRIS RAPHAEL COHEN

1949

Trade Edition · THE BEACON PRESS · Boston, Mass.
Text and Library Edition · THE FREE PRESS · Glencoe, Ill.

ACKNOWLEDGMENTS

The publishers wish to express their gratitude to the following holders of copyright for permission to quote excerpts from books and articles by Morris R. Cohen:

To *Commentary*, for "Jewish Studies of Peace and Post-War Problems," *Contemporary Jewish Record*, IV (1941), 110.

To The Dryden Press, Inc., for the foreword to *Legal Claims Against Germany* by Siegfried Goldschmidt, 1945.

To The Open Court Publishing Company, for *Meaning of Human History*, 1947.

To The University of Chicago Press, for "Legal Theories and Social Science," *International Journal of Ethics*, XXV (1915), 469.

TABLE OF CONTENTS

BOOK FOUR

THE VALLEY OF HUMILIATION (1900-1912)

BOOK FIVE

MY CAREER AS A TEACHER OF PHILOSOPHY

BOOK SIX

THE DEVELOPMENT OF MY PHILOSOPHY

BOOK SEVEN

JEWISH SOCIAL STUDIES AND AMERICAN DEMOCRACY

BOOK EIGHT

WHAT LIFE HAS MEANT TO ME
(FRAGMENTS)

LIST OF ILLUSTRATIONS

FOREWORD

Dear Gene Maura:

Your father and mother knew my parents who were of that heroic generation that tore up their roots in their old homeland, and unaided and with no equipment other than their indomitable faith and courage, built new homes in this land and raised up children who have made invaluable contributions to the life of this country in the fields of art, science, industry, education, and philanthropic work. I need not give you any list of these. It would be too long and would omit too many distinguished names. I will merely mention one friend of your grandfather's, Justice Felix Frankfurter, as representative of that second generation, who, even though themselves technically immigrants, brought here old enough to remember the Old World, still had their American careers made possible for them by the wonderful devotion of their parents. But now, even that second generation is facing its declining years. And when you grow up to young womanhood many of them will no longer be here. If you will then wish to understand the background of your splendid American-born parents and whence they sprang, you will have to read books like the following.

I have told the story of a life that cannot be said to have bubbled over with sweetness and joy. But it is a life that has had worthy moments, because actuated by efforts after things that are of perennial value, efforts which have proved sustaining in dark hours and which I think will strengthen human hearts in the future, as they have in the past.

Brief is the life of man, and of uncertain duration is his handiwork, be it ships, houses, governments or laws. But the echoes from soul to soul will go on so long as human life lasts.

Your devoted grandfather,

MORRIS

BOOK ONE

THE OLD WORLD

MY PEOPLE—
HOW THEY CAME TO RUSSIA

THE COHENS are today the oldest priestly family known to history. When the Temple at Jerusalem was destroyed and Talmudic scholars became the leaders of the Jewish people, the hereditary priesthood did not completely lose all of its privileges and obligations. The ceremony of blessing the congregation on solemn holidays remained the hereditary office of the *Cohanim;* and the Orthodox still consider it a duty to redeem the oldest son by paying a fee to a Cohen. To this day, whenever the Torah is read, the first to be called up for the reading must be a Cohen if there is one in the congregation. Of the old code of priestly purity there still remain the rules that a Cohen may not marry a divorced woman, and must not come within a certain distance of a dead body.

According to the Biblical account, all the rightful priests of Israel were descended from Aaron, the brother of Moses; and during the Second Commonwealth they traced their descent from Zadoc, the companion of David, who became the first priest of Solomon's Temple. In any case, when the Temple was rebuilt, after its first destruction by the Babylonians, the strictly hereditary character of the office of Cohen was definitely established through the influence of the prophet-priest Ezekiel and the Priestly Code of the Pentateuch.

In my youth I would not have mentioned this, for I then joined in the romantic and uncritical disparagement of all priesthoods to extol the revolutionary or reforming prophets. But as I grew older, I began to recognize that while the inspiration of the prophets is necessary to prevent the hard cake of custom from choking off all growth and adaptation to new conditions, men cannot live on revolutions

3

alone. The preaching of prophets would be merely an emotional in-
dulgence if it did not find embodiment in some law, custom, or
ritual to make smooth and channelize our daily life. Priests are essentially the guardians of the ancient and hallowed ways of the common
man's life cycle from birth to death, and reforms or revolutions can be
justified only if they bring about forms more congenial to human life.
Certainly the Jews could not have held together through their many
vicissitudes without the legal system that grew out of the Priestly
Code, just as the teaching of Jesus could not have spread without well-
organized churches.

I may here also record the fact that I have never been ashamed of
being born among people who, like the Greeks, English, or Americans,
did not take the rooted plant as their ideal of life but deliberately
chose to change their habitat in the course of time.

The light of common intelligence makes it clear that since we
cannot control the deeds of our remote ancestors, we cannot be held
responsible for them and therefore deserve neither credit nor dis-
credit on that account. But we humans are generally born into social
groups whose language, social customs and traditions are among the
first things that we acquire and that thus mold our nature. While,
therefore, the history of a people cannot fully explain the lives of its
individual members, it helps us to understand them. Particularly is
this true of a people with a recorded history of three thousand years,
the Biblical and other portions of which enter into their daily prayers
and into all ceremonial occasions.

Even before the destruction of their Commonwealth by Ves-
pasian and Titus, the Jews spread to various provinces of the Roman
Empire. As early as the time of Cicero and Horace, the number of
Jews in Rome was sufficiently large to cause considerable notice of
them; and we find Jews in Germany in the early centuries of the present era. For centuries they there maintained their religious and cultural institutions, and made their great contributions to scholarly
studies. Yet the extent of their intercourse with the German people
is shown by the fact that to this day the vast majority of the Jews, scattered throughout the world, speak a German dialect, and refer to it
as Yiddish (that is, the language of the Jews).

The spirit of the Crusades, which led to the expulsion of the
Jews from England, France, and later from Spain, did not leave Ger-

many untouched. Many German-Jewish communities were utterly destroyed, and thousands of men, women and children were slaughtered. The harassed survivors turned their faces to the East, and some of them found a haven of refuge in Slavic Lithuania and Poland.

The great influx of Jews, however, into these lands came in the middle of the thirteenth century, after the Mongol invaders had devastated Poland and left it with an impoverished peasantry and a handful of nobles. To protect the land against future invasion by building up strong towns and to develop the economic life of the country by providing an artisan and a mercantile population, German Jews were invited to come in and they did so as legally protected communities. Thus it came to pass that the industrial and trading classes, and many of the cities of that part of Poland that Russia acquired in 1753 were up to the end of the nineteenth century predominantly Jewish. Even in the first quarter of this century not only were a number of Polish industries entirely Jewish but, though the Jews constituted only a tenth of the population, they had a preponderant number of skilled artisans. The close association between their religion and learning, which made the Jews a predominantly literate people, caused them to be in great demand as economic administrators for the great Polish estates.

This position naturally created hostility towards them on the part of the peasantry and the clergy, especially in regions such as the Ukraine where a Roman Catholic nobility ruled over a Greek-Orthodox population. In the Chmelnitsky Rebellion in 1648, some calculated that more than half of the Jewish population of the world was destroyed. The degradation of Polish Jewry followed that tragic event. They soon lost their political autonomy, and their opportunities in the economic field became more and more restricted. Even their Talmudic learning suffered decay, to revive only in the latter half of the eighteenth century under the influence of Elijah, Gaon of Vilna.

Then came the partition of Poland and Russia acquired the main portion of Polish Jewry.

In the reaction against the Enlightenment, the Russian Government under Czar Nicholas I adopted the program of crushing the Jews by compelling at least a third of them to leave the country, another third to give up their religion and communal association (by adopting Christianity) and the remaining third to be crowded into a small

territory where extreme poverty would gradually lead to their ex-
termination. As part of this plan children of Jews were forcibly
taken away from their parents, put into the homes of *moujiks* (peasants) until they became of age, and then forced to serve in the Czar's
army for twenty-five years.

The Russian defeat in the Crimean War discredited the general
fanatical policy of Nicholas I, and some relief came to the Jews
through the relatively mild or liberal regime of Alexander II. But
the assassination of the latter in 1881 brought about an extremely
reactionary attitude in all fields of Russian life. The Jews were huddled together in cities, and the occupations from which they could
draw a livelihood were more and more restricted. Riots against them
were encouraged by the Russian Government and their lives made
harder by all sorts of special laws designed to degrade them. This
was the cause of the great exodus which forced several million Jews
to leave Russia in the next twenty-five years and made the Jewish
population of the United States rise from an estimated 200,000 in
1880, to between four and five million fifty years later.

MY PARENTS

My father was born in the town of Kletsk in the government of
Minsk in White Russia. I never knew his father or mother. They
had died some years before my birth, and my father seldom spoke
about them or even about his own past. It seems that in those rare
intervals of life when he could find work my paternal grandfather
was a tailor. But most of the time he read the Psalms. In the long
evenings this was done by candlelight, and the drippings of the
candle left their marks on every page of the book. One incident related by my mother gave me a vivid picture of my father's background.
His father in his poverty could not do much for his children, and
so his eldest daughter, when she came to be about twelve years of
age, had to leave the paternal home to take service with a family in
some distant town. In the course of time my grandfather lost all
trace of her whereabouts. (This is not at all strange when we remember that girls were then as a rule illiterate, and that money for post-
age and for hiring a letter-writer was not generally available to a
servant girl.)

Bessie Farfel Cohen (1848-1936)

Abraham Cohen (1847-1934)

A number of years later when my grandfather was on a journey and stopped at some wayside inn he thought that the mistress of the house looked familiar to him. He got into conversation with her and found that she was his long-lost daughter. I do not know whether they kept up any correspondence after that accidental meeting. But my Aunt Eshka, then a young girl, did receive, after that event, several dresses from her older sister.

My father's education along pious Orthodox lines could not have been a prolonged one, for very early in his teens he became a tutor to the children of Jewish farmers. This opportunity he probably owed not only to what scholarship he possessed but perhaps even more to his great abilities as a general handy man about the farm. Throughout his life there were few mechanical tasks which he hesitated to undertake or which he failed to carry through skillfully.

In 1867 at the age of twenty he married my mother with the usual understanding that my maternal grandfather would maintain the newly-wedded couple for a year during which my father could learn or find the way to support a household of his own. After a few weeks, however, my grandfather found that he had not sufficient food to maintain his daughter and son-in-law, so they were invited to shift for themselves. Through my mother's great ingenuity they were able to obtain a room and start a grocery store. My father tried his hand at various occupations, principally acting as agent for those who bought up the rye and wheat which peasants brought to town. His territory encompassed the entire district. When he succeeded in inducing a peasant to sell a wagonload of such grain, he would receive three, or sometimes five, groschen (1½ to 2½ cents) from the purchaser. People generally thought that my maternal grandfather had done well in securing a "hustler" for a son-in-law. But when my mother was confined in her first childbirth the grocery store was robbed, all the goods and the few fixtures taken out, and the young couple and their child (my brother Tom) left high and dry.

After the unfortunate incident of the grocery store, my mother went to work as a seamstress in the home of Mr. Levine, a brewer, in the town of Mir. She had great skill in sewing and she was a wonderful seamstress. Her wit and charm enabled her to become well-liked in the house. She was thus able to secure a position for my father as a general handy man. His scrupulous honesty, trustworthiness, and general ability to do all kinds of odds and ends of jobs made him a very useful servant, so that Mr. Levine resisted for a number of years the pressure of relatives who were scandalized that a stranger should have such a position (paying 75 cents a week). He was sent out on all sorts of errands, especially those requiring the carrying of funds.

It was characteristic of my mother that she remembered the help that the Levines had been in time of distress, and she kept up a friendly correspondence with the family for many years.

The days in Mir could not have been a happy chapter in my father's life, for he was not only deprived of all opportunity for continuing his studies but given little personal consideration of any kind. A characteristic incident occurred when my mother went back to her parents at Neshwies to give birth to her second child, my brother Sam. My father naturally wanted to see his wife, and in accordance with the pious practice of the Jews, to be present at the *b'rith* (the rite of circumcision) of his second son, but such leave of absence was not granted.

His labors were at times not only hard but even dangerous. One wintry night he was sent to deliver some goods to a distant town and he had to sit on a loaded sleigh. On the way he fell off and before he could shout for help, the sleigh had moved too far ahead for him to be heard. He got up and tried to run along the snowy road to overtake his party or to make his shouts heard. But after some hours of this he fell down in the snow, exhausted. It was only when the peasants arrived at their destination that they noticed the absence of the "young teacher," as my father was called. They turned back and found my father barely conscious, almost frozen to death in the snow. It was weeks before he recovered from the exposure. This illness reduced his value as an employee, and after he had recovered his health, the constant pressure of his employer's relatives finally prevailed, and my father was discharged just as my mother was giving birth to another child. Again my father found himself without any means of supporting his family.

In those days rumors reached Mir of an extensive fire in the city of Minsk and of a consequent opportunity for carpenters. Minsk was already the junction of the Moscow and Vilna railroads, and as the headquarters of an army corps it attracted a good deal of miscellaneous business. So my father decided to try his luck there. He gathered together a few belongings, made a bundle of them, and after saying good-bye to my mother went to seek his fortune in Minsk. He had not a cent in his pocket, and he knew not a single soul in the whole of that relatively large city. He had had no food that day, and his mind was troubled about the condition of his wife and youngest infant. He started to walk towards the center of town without any clear idea whither to direct his steps. Finally, tired from walking and from hunger, he sat down on a stone by the roadside. One man who passed by, noticing his disconsolate appearance, approached him and in a friendly tone asked him the reason for his despair. When my father explained his situation to the kind stranger he was invited to his home for supper. He made such a favorable impression that he was at once engaged as an assistant to his host, who was a boss carpenter named Elje. Hard work, efficiency and frugal living soon enabled him to earn enough to bring over his wife and children to live with him in Minsk.

My mother was born in Neshwies, a town near Kletzk, in the year in which Europe saw so many revolutions — 1848. Her father, who later proved the determining influence in my life, was a tailor, Hirsh Farfel, popularly known as Hirshel Shleimeh Malieh's. (Shleimeh was his father's name and Malieh his mother's.) Despite the religious subordination of Jewish women, a man was often designated as his wife's husband, so that my great-grandfather was referred to as Shleimeh Malieh's.

My grandfather was one of ten children, all except one of whom grew up to raise large and respectable families. The exception was one brother who was taken away from home as a boy by the army, and after being kept in a Christian establishment until the age of eighteen, served his twenty-five years in the army of Czar Nicholas I. After his discharge from the army he was allowed to live in St. Petersburg, where he became a pawnbroker and later a banker. He married but never had any children.

When my mother was a young girl, this rich uncle of hers became a widower, and my grandfather sent her to St. Petersburg in the hope that uncle and niece might hit it off and marry. The journey was a series of adventures, and her brief stay in the Russian capital provided a good deal of an education. But another niece prevailed and my grandfather was keenly disappointed. In 1887 this banker brother died rather suddenly, leaving everything to the young wife without any mention of his poor relatives in the will. But my grandfather faithfully continued to say *Kaddish* (the prayer for the dead) for a whole year.

Ugly rumors told unkind things of the young widow who soon thereafter married a young man. About twenty-two years later I heard that their children turned revolutionists and disowned their parents.

Like the others of his father's children my grandfather was turned loose from the parental home when he was about twelve years old. For years he was an itinerant tailor, walking the long distances from village to village carrying a heavy pressing iron as part of his equipment. Ultimately he managed to acquire enough money to set himself up in his parental home as a tailor and even employed his father and another man as his helpers. In the days of his prosperity he also built an addition to his father's house, which brought him some rent.

There was a neighboring monastery of Polish monks belonging to the order of St. Bernard (whence the street in which my grandfather's house was situated received its name). The monks liked to converse with the highly intelligent Jewish tailor and also to buy liquor from him to allay their troubled spirits. After some years, however, the Russian Government closed down the monastery. When this happened, its funds, to escape confiscation, were entrusted to my grandfather. He was later rewarded for his fidelity in scrupulously retaining them by a generous gift. But the money did not last long. There followed a period of dire poverty.

My mother remembered the hard times when food was only occasionally seen in the house — such food consisting almost entirely of stale bread discarded or sold for next to nothing by certain warehouses. Often my mother as a child would cry for food until she fell asleep from fatigue. With that invincible courage which has enabled the Jews to survive unprecedented calamities for over three thousand years, my grandfather kept up his dignity as well as his trust in God. When he had no bread in the house, he would walk in the street with a toothpick in his mouth to give the impression that he had eaten meat. Naturally, continued calls on the endurance of hardships did not make him soft. He learned to make a virtue of necessity, and to find various reasons to glorify coarse bread, wooden spoons, and similar forced economies. Life was certainly not easy for my grandmother or for my mother, the only girl in the household.

My mother and a baby boy were twins, but she alone survived the first week. She was undersized but that did not prevent her from being over-worked. She had an older brother, my Uncle Elias, who, as a boy and the heir apparent, was regarded as entitled to the best of everything available, while she had to help her mother with household work and the care of the four other boys who came in subsequent years. At the age of eleven she was hired out as a field worker picking potatoes and carrying heavy sacks of them. Even so, her first employer had some quarrel with my grandfather and refused to pay her. Despite her stunted growth and overwork she had a great deal of spirit and a beautiful face framed in flaming red hair and illumined by penetrating eyes, whose lustre eighty-eight years of life could not quench.

As a cavalry regiment was stationed near my grandfather's house, he was afraid that some officer or soldier would seduce his daughter, and he sometimes spoke as if he intended to cripple her to prevent such a calamity. Believing implicitly in every word of the Bible, he was thoroughly convinced that he who spares the rod spoils the child; one day he beat my mother so that out of sheer humiliation she ran out to the pond and jumped in to drown herself. Some monks rescued her and forced my grandfather to promise that he would never beat her again.

Though that promise was kept, my mother's lot was not a happy one. She became an expert seamstress, but her earnings went to her father. Occasionally she did get a kopeck to buy something to eat with her bread. This she saved in order to pay a woman to teach her how to write. Though my grandfather, who had some scholarly pretensions, could read, he never learned to write. Reading prayers and sacred books was for men a religious virtue, but writing was a luxury — especially for women — and so in that effort my mother was ultimately defeated. But she made up her mind that when she had children she would do her utmost to see that they had the opportunity to learn to write as well as to read. I owe the privilege of a college education in large part to that resolve of hers.

Marriage came to her not as a result of any romance (hardly

known in those days to children of her circle), but in the regular way through a marriage broker who brought the parents together. My mother's hard common-sense realism is best reflected in her story of what had happened when she first met my father. She was in charge of a booth at an annual fair, selling some linens, when my father, his father and the marriage broker approached and pretended that they wanted to buy some of the things that she was selling. She realized what they were after and said to my father, "What is the use of pretending? I know why you came. Do I please you?" My father was a tall handsome young man with an unusually sweet expression on his face. But my mother told me that she would have married a Tartar to be released from the domination of her father. I have no hesitation in repeating this story because of the moral that may be drawn from the sequel. Despite the fact that my father and mother were of diametrically opposed temperaments in most respects, they lived together in mutual devotion and absolute fidelity for sixty-seven years. The love that grows out of devotedly living together in common efforts proved at least in their case more enduring than the romantic love that is often only temporary attraction.

When my parents established themselves in Minsk, my mother began to find more room for her energies and talents. At first she helped to increase the family revenue by taking in sewing of diverse kinds. But after they accumulated a little money she began a small pawnbroker business, pawning the pledges at a lesser rate of interest, so that her small capital went a long way. Difficulties with a defaulting army officer made her finally discontinue that business. But with the several hundred rubles that she had thus managed to accumulate, my father was able to purchase a plot on a relatively new street and build a house. This they soon sold at a handsome profit and built a much larger one farther up the street — indeed a double one divided into apartments calculated to bring in some revenue through rent. But prosperity did not last. The building boom in Minsk subsided, and there came a general business decline after 1881 with new hardships for Jews. In 1883 the situation became quite hopeless, and it was decided that my father should go to find work in America. Thereupon, my older brother was apprenticed to a shoemaker, my brother Sam to a tailor, and my father left for America, leaving my mother with myself and my sister, who was barely six months old.

When my father arrived in New York he had, besides his little bundle containing prayer shawl, phylacteries and some underwear, eighty-five cents in his pocket. He did not know a single person on this side of the Atlantic, and he had no address of any Jewish institution. The landing place of immigrants in those days was Castle Garden, a building which later housed the Aquarium. He waited for a long while for something to turn up, and sure enough, after an hour or so, a man came along and offered him some work. In those days, immigrants were in demand in the clothing sweat shops and agents made it their business to engage these immigrants. My father found a position, but as he had never been a tailor, he did not do well in his new trade. He managed to find a synagogue on Norfolk Street, and some one directed him to a family that took in boarders. Then began the checkered career of trying to find an occupation by which he could make a living.

Whether there were too few Jewish carpenters in those days or for some other reason, he could not continue here the kind of work he had done in Minsk, nor did he succeed better when he tried his hand as a glazier. Then some one advised him to turn peddler.

Before the days of the automobile, rural free mail delivery, parcel post, and mail-order houses, the peddler was in much demand in places where a visit to the store in town could not be a daily event. The Yankee peddler was once a familiar figure throughout rural America. The German Jews who came here after 1848 turned in considerable numbers to that occupation, and many of those who subsequently became storekeepers and later great merchants began their careers by carrying large packs on their backs and walking many miles a day from house to house in rural regions to sell their goods. The Russian Jews who came here after 1881 followed them in this respect. Several stores on the East Side specialized in providing peddlers with goods, sometimes at liberal credit.

My father, therefore, turned hopefully to that occupation. But alas! it was a great mistake. Despite his inordinate capacity for hard and persistent work, his abstemious and ascetic habits, and his open honest countenance, which inspired confidence, he was bound to fail. He did not have sufficient command of English, and his forthright honesty prevented him from being a good salesman. Nor was he well advised as to the vicinity to choose for his route. After suffering a great many mortifying and heartbreaking experiences, often not being able to find a night's lodging, he saw his hopes defeated.

However, he finally found fairly steady work in Rochester, New York, as a presser of boys' jackets. Out of about five dollars per week that he thus earned, he was able not only to save a little money to send home but also to lay aside a sum to enable him to return to Russia to rejoin his wife and children, after a painful absence of more than three years.

CHAPTER ONE

A PROBLEM CHILD

PRESSED BY VARIOUS official requests for the exact date of an event that I cannot possibly remember and of which I have no record, I have always given July 25, 1880, as my birthday. I confess to have had little qualms of conscience in regard to asserting this resolution of mine as if it were the statement of an historic fact. For I not only had to do this under *force majeure* when I first entered the New York public schools, but I have thus avoided a great deal of annoyance to officials who would have been much embarrassed to have on their documents such answers as "Yes! I must have been born. But I don't know when." Moreover, it would be useless for any historian to search the official records of the city of Minsk where my parents lived at the time. For, to take advantage of the peculiarities of the Russian law regulating the military draft, the records of the births of male children used to be manipulated so as to create the most favorable legal position for evading the hideous hardships of service in the Czar's army.

I was a fifth or sixth child (though only two brothers survived at the time of my birth), and my arrival was not the most memorable event in the life of my hard-driven parents. In the summer of 1893 they held a conference as to when I was to become *Bar-mitzvah* (that is, attain my religious majority which comes on reaching the age of thirteen). There was some uncertainty as to whether 1880 or 1881 was my natal year. In deference to my mother's superior memory, and to put me on the safe side in regard to wearing phylacteries at morning prayers, the decision was in favor of 1880. So I was called to read the Torah on the next Saturday, which was the Sabbath of Comfort,

15

that is, the Sabbath on which the Haftorah or prophetic portion begins "Comfort ye, Comfort ye my people" (Isaiah 40). This circumstance and some remarks of my father would lead to the conclusion that I was born on the ninth day of Ab, the fast day which commemorates the destruction of the Temple and the beginning of the Exile (Golus). But as the ninth day of Ab is, according to certain traditions, also the appointed day on which is to be born the Messiah who will release the Jews from bondage and lead them back to the Holy Land, I have concluded that my birthday must be on some other date. I chose July 25 because on that, or on some other day in the summer of 1892, my mother, my sister and I reached the harbor of New York and a new chapter of my life began.

The dawn of consciousness must have come to me very early, for my memory goes back to events which could not have happened after I was two years old. I remember vividly the time when I could not yet walk, but crawled on my hands and knees. I remember being carried in my father's arms into the open street on a warm spring day and receiving the fresh and vivid impression of the out-of-door earth and sky. In front of our house men were digging a drainage trench, and Russian policemen with swords hanging at their sides were shouting and scolding. It was some time later that, still unable to walk, I crawled out of the house on all fours into our yard and was terrified by a pig licking my hand — a terror that I have never forgotten.

Unforgotten also is the cradle where I spent the first years of my life and where I received the sugar cookies which my father used to bring for me when he came home from work. I remember also being waked up in my cradle once by the glare of the Friday night candles, an unusual hubbub in the house and my mother kissing me. This occasion I later learned was connected with the fatal burning of our neighbor's child through the upsetting of the Sabbath candles.

I was a little over two years of age when my sister was born, and I remember my mother's groans and the midwife stumbling over me as she hurried to her assistance.

Almost as soon as I learned to walk, I managed to get lost. I have no direct recollection of that incident, but my mother frequently referred to it as one of the most trying experiences of her life. It was a hot July day, and I had only a child's chemise on when I crawled away from the house, while my mother was doing some marketing.

When my mother came home, she could not find any trace of me. Anxiously she inquired of all the neighbors, but found no clue. After hunting for me for four or five hours under a blazing sun she was caught in a sudden summer downpour and had to seek refuge in the home of a Christian family. They told her that a child had wandered into their home earlier in the day, and that when they recognized it as Jewish they took it over to their Jewish neighbor. It was over a mile from our home at the edge of the city near the cemetery. Thereafter I was not encouraged to leave the house.

I was a very sickly child, and, according to my mother, had all the children's diseases usual in those days, including scarlet fever, malaria and dysentery. My life was despaired of on several occasions. My mother frequently told of a time when every one thought that the end had already come, and she put a feather to my nose to test whether any breath of life was left in me. She had been making a pumpkin compote, and some of the mashed vegetable was still clinging to her finger. As she touched my lips, I licked the pumpkin, whereupon they not only pronounced me alive but gave me a little of the delectable food, which I ate with avidity to the great improvement of my health. My mother frequently told the story to point out the dangers of undernourishing sick children, and to illustrate the cruel ignorance of those days as to the care of children. It was not then customary among our people to call in doctors when children were sick, for few in our neighborhood could afford it. Indeed, the poverty was so great that many were too poor to buy caskets, so that the beadle could be seen in the street carrying the lightly-clad bodies of dead infants to the cemetery. But when I was about five or six years old and suffered from malaria, my mother did call a doctor. The fact that he came in a carriage, that he had no beard, and that his name was Polak, has stood out in my memory as vividly as have the horribly bitter quinine powders which I was forced to swallow.

With the amount of work that a Jewish housewife had in those days, and with the large number of children that were born, it is a wonder that any of them survived. For, in addition to the household work familiar to us, the women then had to chop wood for the oven, bake the bread, go considerable distances to draw water from some well, and carry it up hill even when the streets were covered with slippery ice. Worst of all, underwear, linen sheets, table cloths, and the like, had to be washed in the river nearly a mile away, even in the wintry months when the washing had to be done through a hole in the ice. To press the water out of the wet things a kind of wooden hammer had to be carried, in addition to the wooden board. It was indeed a heavy load to carry home.

In the winter of 1883-84, when my father left us to seek in America a more secure way of earning a living for himself and his family, my two brothers were apprenticed to a shoemaker and a tailor respectively, and my mother went to work peddling apples, rolls, etc. As she had to leave the house very early in the morning, before my sister and I were awake, she used to leave a pot of cooked potatoes for our nourishment. But my oldest brother, who did not get much food from his shoemaker master living nearby, used to come home and help himself to the precious potatoes. Hunger was thus our fairly steady companion, especially vivid when we saw other people eat.

In this connection one incident stands out in my memory. I was walking along with my young sister and we passed a house where people in the front room were having their midday meal, at which I looked longingly. I was ashamed to ask for anything, but I turned to my sister and inquired, "Friedke (Florence), are you hungry?" The mother of the family gave each of us a piece of bread dipped in soup and launched into a tirade against my mother for leaving us alone all day and not providing us with sufficient food. But the delightful taste of the food prevailed over my indignation at the disrespect to my mother.

Despite all our difficulties the days generally ended pleasantly. When mother came home in the evening she would prepare some warm supper. Often she brought us fruit, sometimes even rare ones, such as oranges. Once she brought us a watermelon!

On Fridays mother would come home earlier to do the cooking and cleaning in preparation for the Sabbath. And on Saturdays she would be with us all day. The savory Sabbath Tcholent (a baked dish of meat and potatoes), the white bread, and the tzimis (a compote of turnips and carrots) were the green oases in the desert of our early life. When I grew older I also enjoyed my mother's reading aloud the weekly portion of the Tzenou V'renou, a popular Yiddish free translation of, and commentary on, the Five Books of Moses. The book from which she read had old quaint pictures such as the angel with a sword chasing Adam and Eve out of Paradise, and Abraham about to sacrifice his son Isaac. In the long Sabbath twilight before the appearance of the stars allowed the lighting of lamps or candles, my mother would sing folk songs on Biblical themes.

Just before recitation of the *Havdoleh* (the Hebrew prayer which divides the week days from the Sabbath) my mother used to chant a Yiddish prayer beginning, "God of Abraham, Isaac and Jacob," asking God's mercy for the week to come. I can never forget its plaintive notes, nor resist the flow of tears when I hear any echo of it.

A few years after my father left for America, my mother's youngest brother, Abraham Farfel, came to live and work in Minsk, and he used to come regularly to our house on Saturdays. My mother was always a protecting angel to all relatives who came to Minsk, and a peculiarly sweet and mutually helpful relationship grew up between her and my uncle. In fact, my mother arranged for his marriage. In later years I grew to admire his remarkably clear-headed wisdom. Though some illness had made him look prematurely old and grayish, he was youthful in spirit, and he and some other young men and women would dance and sing in the afternoons. Once in a while my mother herself would perform an elaborate mimetic dance called "The Robber" to the great delight of the company. But I never could take to dancing.

The house in which I was thus brought up stood in the New Romanova, which was then a relatively new street in Minsk. Like most houses, ours was built of partly planed logs with moss between them; but unlike other houses, it had wooden floors instead of hardened earth. Perhaps it would be more accurate to say that it was a combination of two houses, each with its own oven, but with a covered shed (called a forehouse) between them, which contained a common entrance door. This common shed was also a storeroom for such things as wood, and in winter it prevented cold blasts of air from coming in when one opened the door of either house. The front house looked out on a very large field. Beyond it the earth and sky seemed very much closer together, so that often I felt sorry for the people who lived there. The remembrance of that feeling has helped me to understand why so many others who see the zenith over their heads find it hard to realize that those living far away also have the highest point of heaven over their heads.

After my father left for America and my brothers had been properly apprenticed, my mother, my sister and I moved into a room of the rear house and rented the rest of it to a drayman who also used the stable. Our new home looked out uphill, on a seemingly endless series of vegetable gardens sloping down to our house. That winter I first noticed the double windows, with white cotton and a splash of red paper ribbons between them. The outstanding memory of the period was my sitting by the window on Saturdays and watching the number of boys standing close together on a wooden board sliding down on the hard-packed snow toward our house. This was repeated for several winters. At first it never occurred to me that I might have the privilege of joining them, but when I was almost seven years old my brother Sam invited me in and took me under his protection. Even so, I got some snow down my neck and did not venture out again.

Whether because of illness, undernourishment or absence of proper care, I was a listless child, unusually clumsy in all physical undertakings. Indeed, the latter trait has persisted throughout my life. If I ever tried to climb a ladder I invariably fell off, and when I handled a fragile cup it generally dropped out of my hand and broke. In regard to the latter I remember a curious incident. Tired of seeing me break every cup that I handled, my mother brought me one that was supposed to be unbreakable. Indeed, when it fell out of my hand the first time it did not break. This interested me very much, and I wanted to find out at what height I could thus safely drop it. I held it high above my head and dropped it without any damaging effect. This intrigued me so that I climbed up on a chair, dropped it, and lo! it broke. A flood of chagrin then swept over me as I realized the foolishness of my procedure.

My shyness and backwardness in participating in the usual boys' adventures was to some extent reinforced by an incident of which I cannot think to this day without shuddering. I was walking through the street one day when I saw a man driving a buckboard loaded with sand and allowing a number of children to jump on and sit in the sand. I tried to do the same, but fell off, and the rear wheel of the wagon passed over me — fortunately over the part of my body that had most fleshy padding — so that no serious injury resulted. But I realized even then how narrow was my escape from being crippled or killed.

I cannot recall any childhood games that I ever played with other children. When I occasionally ventured out into the street some child or other would manage to hurt me so that I would run crying into the house. With my general inactivity, however, there went a certain intensity of memory. I never forgot a blow or other grievance, and my consciousness was certainly very vivid in the interminably long wakeful hours when, troubled with sores on my body, I used to try to catch the moment which separates waking from sleeping.

Outer listlessness caused me to be regarded as decidedly feeble-minded. The common appellation by which I was known was *Kalyéleh*, which seems to have denoted a helpless half-wit. Sometimes a kind neighbor would remonstrate with my mother that she should not allow me to respond when people said, "*Kalyéleh*, come here." But with great self-assurance my mother would reply proudly, "Never mind, some day they will all be proud that they have talked to my Meisheleh" (the Yiddish diminutive of my Hebrew name). It has been one of the great satisfactions of my life that my mother did live to feel that her prediction was fulfilled. But in those early years I did little to support her faith and hope in me. She certainly had a very long and seemingly fruitless struggle before she could get any comfort from me.

In front of our house, some boards covered the open drainage trench to enable wagons to pass from the street to our stable. In rainy weather I used to love to crawl under the boards and splash my naked feet in the running water, though the rain came in over my head through cracks between the boards. That experience stood out as a blissful feeling in those drab days, and I could not understand why kind neighbors used to drag me away in disgust as if I had committed some terrible sin. But when my mother came home on Friday afternoons to give me my weekly washing, the accumulation of dirt on me could not be removed with altogether gentle means. Hence I used to run away and she used to run after me through the street accompanied by the pitying glances and comments of the neighbors. She naturally felt humiliated.

It was then the custom of Hebrew schoolmasters to send toys to those prospective pupils that were beginners. The school year began immediately after Passover and the gift was sent on the previous Purim, a day on which people generally exchanged presents. When, therefore, I received a *dreherl* (a wooden mechanism which when turned on its axis made a noise, customary in the synagogue whenever the name Haman occurred in the reading of the book of Esther) I knew that I was soon to go to *cheder* (school) and I looked forward to the new life, especially to the prospect of walking to a distant part of the city with a teacher's assistant to guard against anyone teasing or hitting me. But the actual experience was somewhat disappointing. I had heard that on the first day that a Jewish boy begins to learn his ABC's an angel drops him a coin, and so when on that morning I opened my mother's drawer and found a large copper coin — I think it was five groschen — I helped myself to it without informing any one. When I reached school and was allowed to go into the yard I bought a piece of candy and was agreeably surprised at the amount of change I got. But the sequel was not so pleasant. The transaction was reported to the *rebbeh* (teacher) who, either because he suspected that the money did not come into my possession quite legitimately or because he was angry that I did not make my purchase in his wife's store nearby, administered the usual *a posteriori* punishment with the official strap and confiscated the change which he gave to the assistant to return to my mother. The latter seems never to have done so. My mother missed the coin but did not directly ask me whether I took it. After the whipping I had not the courage to tell her.

For the rest of the year life and I continued to find each other dull and uninteresting, for the instruction we received was not calculated to stimulate young minds. We were taught nothing at first but to recognize the letters of the alphabet with their vowel points. After an interminable time of this we were taught to read (that is, to pronounce) the words of the Hebrew prayer book, words whose meaning we were not told. This I later found was not merely a basis for future education but an immediate primary objective for most pupils, for it enabled them as good Jews to fulfill their religious duty of reading or reciting their daily prayers and the longer ones on Saturdays and holidays.

Nor were the physical conditions of the schoolroom markedly pleasant. It was crowded, noisy, unventilated, and conducted without any apparent rule or order. Our *rebbeh* was a consumptive who coughed and spat extensively and occasionally shivered: in fact, he died the next year. Though we were in school practically all day, instruction was only occasional. The rest of the time we were either in the yard or sitting or walking about and talking in the classroom without any particular plan.

As we did not return home until very late in the day, we were given some food for our midday meal. The wealthier children had some liquid food which their mothers put in uniform vessels strung together by straps and carried by the *rebbeh's* assistant. Like the more plebeian boys I had only a piece of bread along, which I carried in my pocket and which I ate whenever I was so inclined. Sometimes in the middle of the day a woman would come with a large earthen pot of freshly baked, steaming, soft chick peas and sell a measure of it to the aristocrats who had a groschen. It never occurred to me to ask my mother for money to obtain that delicacy. But the recurrent sight of these peas did make my mouth water. And while I accepted the fact that I was not one of those to the purple born, it did not add to my happiness. I remained listless and indifferent.

Thus, while I made normal progress in learning to read the Hebrew prayer book, the lack of proper washing and other care showed itself in my general bearing. And when I developed scalp trouble my mother felt herself defeated. But the fortunate turn of events which enabled my father to earn more money enabled her to form the plan of sending me to her parents in Neshwies to take better care of me and incidentally, by paying three rubles a week for it, to help to support the old people, whose income was running very low.

In the spring of 1887 my father came back from America, intending to remain in Russia. But the absence of any opportunity soon made him change his mind, and a few weeks later he took my two brothers and left for America. Their apprenticeships were leading nowhere and America offered much better prospects. My brother Tom's master, the shoemaker, threatened to denounce him to the authorities as intending to escape military service, but he was bought off. After a week of double baking, so that the bread would not get moldy on the journey, my father and my brothers thus provisioned left for America. Why the rest of us did not accompany them I did not understand at the time. Nor did I understand why we did not accompany my father a year or so later, when, after a brief visit, he again returned to America with three relatives. In later years my mother explained it as due to my father's fear that America would offer little opportunity for a woman of her talents, and his hope that he might save enough money by hard work in America to enable him to return and set up some business in Minsk. Events proved that his fears were well founded but his hopes vain.

A few days before Passover my grandfather came and took me with him to Neshwies. We left in the evening in a *droshky* (buggy) and then we boarded the train. That was the first time in my life that I saw one. I soon fell asleep, but early in the morning I was awakened. We got out as the train stopped at Horodjeh. We climbed into a wagon and, after what seemed an interminable ride through the forest, we landed in Neshwies.

CHAPTER TWO

NESHWIES (1887-1890) — THE OLD PIETY

ANYONE ACCUSTOMED to the American standard of living who might have come to Neshwies in those days and walked through its unpaved and unlighted streets, looked into its small, unventilated and often overcrowded wooden houses, devoid of all plumbing or the simplest precautions against contagious diseases of an epidemic character, would have pronounced the town unbelievably poor, dirty, criminally ignorant as to hygiene and altogether lifeless. Indeed, he would have wondered how its six to eight thousand inhabitants managed to live at all. But while outwardly correct, he would thus have reckoned without its inner life and religious devotion which ennobled its joys and sorrows and provided strength and dignity for meeting the tasks and perplexities of the day.

At any rate, people did manage to keep alive, to raise large families, to give their children a pious education, to build and rebuild their wooden houses and synagogues, and to send out to the world renowned writers, scholars and other distinguished men. Nor did Neshwies forget that it had been the home of Solomon Maimon, the greatest Jewish philosopher since Spinoza, of Reb Isaac Elkhanon, one of the great rabbis of the nineteenth century, and of Shomer (M. M. Shaikewich), the Dumas of modern Yiddish literature.

About the dirt and material poverty of the town there could be no doubt. It was miles from the nearest railway station. There were no factories or large industries to sustain its economy. So far as any one could tell, the town lived on trade with the peasants who brought to its markets their wood, potatoes and grain and took back salt, nails, kerosene, and sometimes linen goods, shoes and other "luxuries," besides a little money to help pay their taxes. The stationing of a cavalry regiment must have added to the commerce of the town, though the military supplies came in wagons from the outside world, and the officers and soldiers did not seem to have very much money to spend.

A very serious handicap was the meager water supply from the few wells. There was a pond at the outskirts of the town. But as the stables of the cavalry regiment bordered on it, people did well not to drink its water, except after boiling. They supplemented the amount they bought from water-carriers by gathering in the rain in simple primitive ways. Thus, every time it rained, pots and pails were put out to catch the water that came over the massive buttresses of the military barracks.

This lack of water made people helpless against the frequent fires which in the summer would sweep away many houses — none of them insured. I remember that every time that the weekly portion of the Pentateuch began with Numbers, chapter 8, "Thou shalt kindle," we expected a fire. In one of these, the young son of a former neighbor of ours and his blind grandfather whom he was leading through a street were caught and burnt to death. When such fires broke out we used to pack up our belongings in a few bundles, carry them to a nearby field, and wait between hope and fear. One year our synagogue was burned, and later a volunteer fire company was organized. But the scant water supply limited its usefulness, and the town was almost wiped out a few years after I left. Still, even if there was no running water in any house, people never ate without previously washing their hands. There were no theaters, dance halls, or other places of public games or amusement. But there were numerous joyous occasions, besides holidays and the weekly Sabbath. There was music, and the seven days of festivities with every marriage, and every birth was likewise a joyous celebration. A rich intellectual life prevailed in the synagogues where men would foregather in their plentiful leisure, either to study or to engage in general discussion, and where an occasional *Magid* (lecturer on sacred themes) would hold his audience spellbound for hours with his animated discourse. For the less intellectual there were the frequent colorful parades of the soldiers.

Though there was a sizable minority of non-Jewish folk in the town, and its main business was with peasants and with the military, relatively few Jews knew the official language of the country. It was considered a point in favor of selecting Reb Lippe as *rov* (judge of Jewish law) in succession to Reb Heshiel that he could speak Russian.

My grandfather's other house was tenanted by a semi-genteel Polish widow, her sister and her two sons, one of whom was some sort of official, and the other a pathetic failure who did the chores around the house and subsequently drowned himself. Outside of the town there was a Polish nunnery, and I suppose that there must have been a few more people of that nationality to give some color to the successful claim in 1920 that it was a Polish town. But I met few Jews other than my grandfather who spoke Russian fluently.

The land of the town and for many miles around belonged to Prince Radzivil. His palace or chateau could be reached from the town by a causeway and a small bridge across a pond. I once actually entered it with a relative of my grandfather, but all I saw was the chancellery room where the business of adjusting ground rent was transacted. I never heard of any complaint against the *ducas* (duke) as the Prince was called.

In the summer the Prince, his wife and his young son frequently passed our house in an open carriage. My grandfather would always take off his cap and the Prince would graciously bow in turn. Some time in the late nineties the son was married here in America and the New York Mutual Benefit Association of Neshwies sent him a telegram of congratulation to which he responded with some donation to its treasury.

When Grand Duke Vladimir, the brother of Czar Alexander III, visited Prince Radzivil, the order was issued by the police that every owner of a corner house must put up a lamp post with a lantern. This cost my grandfather almost the whole of a ruble and was regarded as a calamity. Moreover, the people generally were disappointed because they never got a chance to see what the Grand Duke looked like. He came at night and our lamp post lantern did not sufficiently illumine the scene to make the persons in his carriage visible.

As the majority of *Goyim* (Gentiles) whom one met in Neshwies were peasants or poor city dwellers, some of them former serfs, few of them literate, the Jews generally regarded them as an inferior race. I remember that among us children there was a separate set of words to characterize the life cycle of non-Jews. Since, in our eyes, they did not have the proper religious ceremony, they did not marry; they mated. Their children, according to our manner of speech, were not born; they were brought into the world the way cattle are. So, too, they did not die; they passed out like the beasts of the field.

In later years I had occasion to note the paradox that the Russian Jews, who were then poor and horribly persecuted, confidently regarded themselves as the superiors, while the more affluent and better educated German and other Jews regarded their Gentile fellow citizens as the superiors to be imitated.

An incident which illustrates the prevailing attitude toward Christianity occurred in my last year in Neshwies. I went into a neighbor's house one Saturday afternoon and found a Hebrew translation of the Gospel of St. Matthew. I assumed, of course, that *Goyim* did not know or accept our Bible, and I had never heard that they had sacred books, much less that those books could be in Hebrew, which we always called the "sacred tongue." I therefore naturally accepted the Gospel stories as part of Jewish history; indeed, I was fascinated by the figure of Johanon (John) the Baptist preaching repentance like the older Hebrew prophets. Naturally, I was quite captivated by the story of Joshua (the Hebrew name of Jesus), the flight of his parents to Egypt and his deeds and preaching. Incidents such as those with Satan were quite in the familiar tradition, and I was especially impressed by the scene of young Joshua in the Jordan, the dove descending upon him, and the voice announcing, "This is my beloved son."

I must have spent over an hour intensely absorbed in the book. When my grandfather came in and saw what I was reading, he tore the book out of my hands and threw it on the floor with the utmost disgust, to my complete amazement. I could not understand why a book written in the sacred tongue and about such pious characters should be so treated, but my grandfather explained that this book was written by men who were *Meshumodim* (apostates), and was translated into Hebrew by those who wished to mislead the Jews into deserting their religion. I soon accepted my grandfather's explanation. A few months afterwards when missionaries came to Neshwies, hired a store and began to distribute free copies of the New Testament in Hebrew, I joined the procession which took the books and immediately tore the pages in front of the distributors, thus littering up the street. We did that with great enthusiasm, but I could not understand then and do not understand now the motives of those who kept on distributing these copies when they saw what we did with them. I suppose they were paid for it and didn't care what happened. In any case, the proceedings did not impress me with the intelligence of these missionaries.

The day that I arrived in Neshwies every one was talking of the dreadful event of the previous night when soldiers of the cavalry regiment attacked the Jewish inn on the outskirts of the town and brutally killed all of its inhabitants. So far as I can recall that talk did not arouse any fear in me. Nor, I must confess, was I markedly homesick. The new surroundings interested me, and my grandmother was very kind to me and made considerable fuss over me. I was much attracted by the pretty wine cups and the Passover food, such as the *Matzoth* (unleavened bread) baked with eggs and the fragrant wine. To this day I treasure an old colored wine glass of my mother's so much like the one out of which I drank at my grandfather's that it seldom fails to stir the pleasant memory of my first Passover in Neshwies. It was only after almost three years of life in that town that I felt any urgent desire to go back to Minsk.

As none of their children or grandchildren were then living in Neshwies, my grandparents were naturally glad to have me with them. My grandmother, although she generally attended to the daily cooking and washing, was a good deal of an invalid and spent a large part of her time in bed. I got more attention from my grandfather. He belonged to the stern old school that did not encourage the outward expression of affection. I think, however, that he was drawn to me and developed considerable pride when I began to distinguish myself in my Hebrew studies. Thus, when I asked my *rebbeh* why Laban is called a son of Nahor (Genesis 29:5) when he had previously been referred to as a grandson, my grandfather boasted about it all over town even in my own hearing. And though as a pious Jew he had too active and relentless a faith in the Biblical warning against sparing the rod, I did not at first harbor any resentment. It was only later that the injustice of some of his too hasty punishments did rankle in me. Life in Neshwies was a vast improvement over my previous existence, and the companionship of my grandfather was the central feature of it. His humble antecedents and low economic status did not prevent him from being regarded as one of the leading citizens of the town. And I was filled with pride when he was once selected as the community's representative on some mission to Minsk.

As soon as the first Passover was over I was put into a *cheder* where I was taught to translate the Bible into the vernacular — Yiddish. This was a great joy, especially when we came to the narrative portions of the Book of Genesis and later to those of Judges, Samuel, and Kings. These were my first story books as well as my introduction to history, and to this day the Biblical stories have an inexhaustible liveliness for me, as if I had actually lived through them.

My first *rebbeh* in Neshwies was exceedingly poor, had four children and was very much harassed. In his irritation, he omitted the usual ritual of deliberate punishment, the letting down of the trousers and the application of the strap. Instead he lashed out his blows at the least provocation, and sometimes as in my case even without provocation, since I generally knew my lessons and had little energy for mischief. However, pleasant features were not absent. The *cheder* was located on a quiet street, and the long rectangular back yard was covered with grass. I remember especially one late afternoon as the long shadows were fading with the setting sun, I ran around in the yard with a feeling of great elation. When we were called in I lingered until I was alone, enjoying an experience the memory of which always brings a fragrance of peace and happiness. I suppose it was the first exhilarative experience of a hitherto parched soul responding to healthy exercise in the open air.

In the winter, we had to stay in the *cheder* until after dark and so had to light our way home by carrying lanterns. For a long time the possession, the cleaning, and the carrying of the lantern, appealed to me as a thrilling adventure.

For the rest there were few organized games among us inside or outside of the classroom; and my natural timidity kept me from participating too actively in the more adventurous outdoor activities of my classmates. This tendency to isolation was strengthened by the teachings of my grandfather, who constantly warned me against boys' mischief. As I advanced in my studies I was generally respected and left alone except by one boy, who took delight in pummeling me until his father was told about it by my grandfather. The only one of my classmates with whom I could be said to have been especially friendly was one of the *rebbeh's* sons.

After two years in my first *cheder* I was sent to another *rebbeh*, Reb Nehemiah, who was a *maskil*, that is, one who believed in bringing some of the beauty of Western learning into Hebrew studies. Indeed, he gave private lessons in grammar to advanced pupils who came to his house late in the afternoon or evening. One of these was Dr. Nissem Tourov, who subsequently did a great deal to develop modern Hebrew as the vernacular of Palestinian Jews and later became Professor of Education at the Hebrew University. But we, the regular pupils, were taught nothing but the traditional curriculum, the Pentateuch with the Commentary of Rashi and a few other books of the Bible. Only in an occasional comment would our *rebbeh's* learning open up for me glimpses of the great outside world of geography and history. I remember particularly his explanation of the origin and evolution of boats and of the Franco-Prussian War of 1870. One remark of his which later grew on me was his observation on the rich clothes and fine living of those who collected the charity money in the tin boxes dedicated to Reb Meier of the Miracle and found in every pious home.

The boys in the new *cheder* came from somewhat more aristocratic families than those of the previous one. And at first they laughed at some of my ways, such as shaking my head when intoning the Hebrew texts according to the cantilation marks (tropes), but Reb Nehemiah recognized my superior attainments in the way of miscellaneous knowledge which I had acquired under my grandfather, and his respect communicated itself to my fellow students.

My mother, who never forgot her disappointment at not having succeeded in her ambition to learn the art of writing, was determined that I should not be similarly handicapped. So she had a letter written to her father that he should see to it that I receive instruction in the art of writing Yiddish. To this my grandfather replied, "My dear daughter, I am giving your son Torah — the substance of life. The trimmings can come later." Under the conditions of life in which he lived, that came very near the truth, for he did not know how to write himself and did not feel the lack of it very seriously. But my mother, living in the large city of Minsk, insisted and prevailed. An old man was engaged to teach me and a neighboring boy how to write. I remember that a good deal of my practice writing was done with my finger or with a thin stick on the surface of a box of sand to save the cost of paper. That is perhaps the reason why to this day writing to me is still associated with the easily erased impression on sand. When I did graduate to the use of paper I remember that after filling several sheets of writing I could exchange them for a fresh sheet at the store. The old sheets were used for wrapping paper. I must confess that after learning to write I had relatively little occasion for using that art. I could write to my mother only on those occasions when my grand-father wished to communicate with her. For he had to supply the paper and the precious stamp, which cost several kopecks.

My main education, however, came from my grandfather. Certainly most of my memories of those three years center about him. It is not altogether easy to reconcile this with the fact that I went to *cheder* for six days in the week and, except for Friday when we were dismissed a little earlier, the school day began at eight in the morning and lasted certainly after six.

And there were relatively few vacation days in the year, practically none except the holiday weeks of Passover and Succoth (the harvest festival). Yet I cannot doubt the memory of many days spent with him when I practiced writing, which could not have been on Saturdays and holidays.

Nor can I be mistaken about the frequent visits of our water-carrier, an old man who had been a soldier under Czar Nicholas. He had been taken away from home as a very young boy, kept in some sort of non-Jewish institution until he was eighteen and then served twenty-five years in the Russian army, his regiment participating in the Crimean War. After his discharge he returned to Neshwies, married, and on his meager earnings as a water-carrier, brought up two adopted children of whom he frequently spoke. Whenever he came to the house to deliver water, he and my grandfather would exchange stories — often the same ones — but I listened with rapt attention to the discussion between the two old men in regard to former days — the incidents of the Crimean War, of the Polish uprisings of 1832 and 1863, of the Turkish War of 1878, and what happened to the Jews during these and other days. Equally informing was it to listen to my grandfather's conversation with other people in the synagogue or with an occasional visitor to our house. He frequently spiced his talk with an apt quotation from the Bible, some proverb or picturesque fable, or with recondite learning that he had picked up not only in the synagogue but also in his travels, and in his dealings, in earlier years, with the monks of the neighboring Bernardine monastery. I remember that it was from my grandfather's lips that I first heard of Aristotle as well as Maimonides, and of Napoleon's campaign in Russia, of which some monuments in the form of earthworks were still visible outside of the town.

He also took me along with him whenever he went to any festive occasion, such as a betrothal, a wedding or a *b'rith*. He always gave me a portion of everything he ate or drank. He had a quaint idea of giving me a sip of any brandy he took on such occasions. And as it usually irritated my throat he put the glass on my head to keep the fumes down, as he explained.

Every Friday afternoon we would walk over the bridge across the pond to the town bathhouse. On the way he would explain to me the workings of the flour mill that was run by the falling water, and the activities of the peasants who were cutting grasses in the neighboring fields or marshes.

The men's bathhouse had no pool, tubs, or showers. It was a room heated by steam which came from water poured by a *moujik* over heated stones. The men whipped themselves with soft brooms and then poured pails of water over themselves. As the heat was more intense in the upper part of the room, there was in the center a series of platforms of different heights to accommodate different tastes. I distinctly did not aspire to the heights in this respect. Indeed the steam heat which made the room misty was altogether highly unattractive to me. But the stimulation to the skin resulting from throwing cool water over oneself had a refreshing effect. In later years I wondered why many of us, especially the older men, did not catch dreadful colds coming out from the heat into the bitter winter air, but perhaps some did and I never heard of it.

In the summer my grandfather, on the way home, would often let me bathe for a few minutes in the pond, and the activity of splashing around in the water was most welcome. Since those days I have bathed in cleaner, less sleepy and inherently more attractive lakes. But in contrast with the steam-clouded, over-heated, crowded and noisy bathhouse, the balmy open air and the peacefully spacious sunset view of the spreading water and distant fields developed in me a sentimental attachment for the pond. Often, on summer mornings, when I was sent there to fetch some water for cooking purposes, I would stand still suffused with delight. The warm air tingled and everything glistened in the golden sunlight. Those moments have stood out as jewels that brightened the drab natural scenery of my childhood.

The center of life was of course the Sabbath which began on Friday night. After the services in the synagogue which included a chant of welcome to the spirit of the Sabbath in the quaint language which envisioned her as a bride, we came home to find everything tidied up — *challoh* (white bread) and fresh tablecloth and the candles lighted. Then followed the *kiddush* (blessing) over the white bread. The proper order of the Friday evening meal was fish, meat, and soup. But though the fish was seldom there, the potatoes were always called fish-potatoes.

The almost inevitable fly in the ointment of human happiness took the form of a violent distaste for the noodle soup which came with monotonous regularity. At first my grandfather tried to induce me to like it by promising me a groschen. But after a while he resorted to threats, and when these also failed he used actual force. This entirely defeated his noble purpose, for it induced an anti-peristaltic reflex embarrassing to all concerned. This resulted in an adamant distaste for that good food, which lasted for forty years. And as my grandmother took my part, my grandfather reluctantly abandoned his effort and let me have clear soup without any noodles.

Saturday morning we would get up very early and before any breakfast go to the synagogue, where my grandfather would read some sacred book before the regular services. After I learned to understand Hebrew I did likewise. But even before that I would accompany him and just sit in the synagogue, sharing the feeling of elation of being in a pious place. It did not detract from this enjoyment that the synagogue was more pleasantly lighted and heated than my grandfather's house. I confess that I often got hungry before the long Saturday morning services ended. But still I gladly stayed with grandfather to hear Reb Joseph Ber read the Midrashic commentary on the weekly portion of the Pentateuch. The legends and the homilies excited and thrilled me. When we came home, grandfather greeted grandmother with a recitation of the portion of the Book of Proverbs beginning "The Virtuous Woman." (The original Hebrew really means "The Woman Who Is a Host in Herself.") It was regarded as a tribute to the woman of the house, and I never thought of it as a form of exploitation of woman's labor. Then there followed the second Sabbath meal of *Tcholent* and the complete relaxation after it.

Yet most things happened on Saturday afternoons, especially in summer. There were the usual walks on the causeway to the Radzivil's Palace and sometimes in open fields at the other end of the town. In the summer I used to go to *cheder* for some time in the afternoon to read the only homiletic tractate of the Talmud, The Sayings of the Fathers. And always there were a few hours of the afternoon in the synagogue reading the Psalms or some pious book. And at home we had a copy of Yosiphon (a medieval Hebrew epitome and extension of Josephus), which I devoured in my tenth year and which gave me a taste for history that I have never lost.

Despite what may seem a crowded calendar I often visited one of the two relatives of my grandfather.

Of all his father's ten children my grandfather's youngest sister and he were the only ones who continued to live in the town of their birth. This great-aunt of mine seemed to me then, and still seems to me in memory, one of the most beautiful women that I have ever seen. She was very kind to me when we called on her, but I do not recall her ever coming to see us. She married a man who had a store on the market square where he sold nails, lubricants for wagons and other commodities to the peasants. They had three handsome children, two sons and an older daughter who was married to a *rayfeh* (Hebrew for healer), a sort of secondary physician. In 1888 my father took one of these boys with him on his return to America, and later the granddaughter and her uncle also came to America. I believe that uncle and niece ultimately married.

The only other house that we ever visited was that of a niece of my grandfather's, by the name of Zivieh. Her husband was away working as a shoemaker in a Russian town where he had no legal right to reside, and I imagine that they must have had a hard time to support themselves and their two children — both girls. Grandmother always brought them a large part of the Saturday cake which I confess I somewhat begrudged them.

Zivieh was the daughter of my grandfather's sister who had lived in Warsaw and who, despite a tragic marriage, had been successful in her heroic struggle to bring up her four children, of whom Zivieh was the oldest. Ultimately she and all her children came to America. She frequently visited my parents and was always affectionately known as the *moomeh* (aunt). The only other relative of my grandfather's that I met was a nephew of his by the name of Abraham who came to Neshwies to report for military service. He stayed with us for some time, and he and I shared the top of the oven as our sleeping quarters. But after a while he was sent to Minsk, where my mother greatly helped him.

Despite my general acceptance of life in Neshwies and the attachment that I developed for my grandfather, a feeling of lonesomeness began to grow on me. I craved the companionship of a near relative of my own age. At the end of the three years my grandfather could not tell me anything new, and in the *cheder* it was the old routine. I was disappointed that I was not being taught the Talmud, the crown of Jewish education. While I was not at that time fully conscious of it, a certain cumulative resentment against the unjust punishments which I endured from my grandfather may have been a factor in the situation. I was, I think, an unusually docile child, but resented injustice bitterly.

My first offense occurred the first week that I spent in Neshwies. I took an apple from the pantry without asking permission, probably under the impression that such permission would not be granted. When this was discovered, my grandfather took down the Bible and sternly showed me the passage, "Thou shalt not steal." That made a profound impression on me. Months later I found on the floor a thin ivory tube for holding needles, and I could not resist the temptation to put it into my pocket. It appealed both to my sense of sight and to that of touch, and I was loath to part with it when my grandfather missed it. Ultimately he found it in my pocket. I received a whipping and reluctantly recognized that it was due me. But later on when my grandfather again lost that needle container, he at once assumed that I had taken it. He refused to accept my insistent protestations of innocence, and repeatedly whipped me with considerable vehemence until my mild grandmother who seldom raised her voice began to protest.

The next incident that stands out in my memory with ever-enduring vividness occurred once when my mother and sister were visiting us. We were having a Sabbath midday meal and in the enjoyment of the unusual pleasure of my mother's company I became a little hilarious. All at once my grandfather slapped my face with a force that almost stunned me. But more than the pain, I felt the humiliation before my mother and sister, and as soon as I could manage it, I left the house and told my sister that I would drown myself. I had once before thought of doing so on account of some petty incident in which my grandmother displeased me, but on the way to the pond my ardor had cooled and I did not reach my intended destination. This time, however, I did not go to the distant pond but hurried to a neighbor's well. The walls of the well were somewhat high and I had to stand on my tiptoes to look into it. Inability to see the water caused some hesitation. As I was thus standing I heard the voices of my grandfather and my mother, so I hastily hid under a pile of boards. Soon I saw my grandfather, my mother and my sister coming straight to the well. They looked into it, and after a while my grandfather pronounced definitely that I was not in it. But as I had been seen entering the yard, they began to search for me and soon found me. My grandfather looked somewhat sheepish. My mother said not a word, but affectionately took me by the hand and walked with me back to the house. Never in my life has the expression of affection given my heart a more soothing and sweeter happiness than this simple act of my mother's. It was like almost everything she did, simple, direct and full of understanding. To my dying day the memory of her will always be entwined with the picture of that walk hand-in-hand.

That incident did not change my grandfather's philosophy of education, and towards the end of my stay in Neshwies he did something which raised my resentment to the point of rebellion.

There was in Reb Nehemiah's *cheder* a grandson of one of the most prominent Jews of Neshwies. He was an attractive boy and the *rebbeh* paid him unusual attention. One day he went out for a walk and some boy hit him. When he came back he claimed that I had set the boy on him. I protested my complete innocence, but in vain. Down I went on the bench and the regular punishment was administered before the whole class as an admonitory example to all. My blood boiled at the outrageous injustice of it, but there was nothing that I could do about it.

Within half an hour or so my grandfather came to visit us, and the first thing that greeted his ears was Reb Nehemiah's story that I had arranged with an outside boy to beat up his darling. Without giving me any chance to say a word of denial, my grandfather ordered me to be whipped again. This time I struggled so frantically that it required both men to get me down. But even before the punishment was completely finished and before the back part of my trousers was rebuttoned I slipped out of their clutches and ran out of the house. My grandfather came after me, and I ran far out to an unfamiliar part of the town. When I was exhausted and stopped running my grandfather came up, took me by the hand and, realizing that he could not drag me to the *cheder*, walked home with me.

It took three days before my indignation cooled down. My grandmother was scandalized that I had been so unjustly dealt with and supported my resolution not to go back to the *cheder*. My grandfather seemed abashed and said not a word. It was, however, regarded as a sin and a calamity for a boy of my age not to go to *cheder*, and so at the end of three days another *rebbeh* was sent for. I talked with him and he professed to be charmed by the ease with which I quoted apt Hebrew expressions from the Bible. But I was ever averse to any changes if I could avoid them, and so I decided to go back to Reb Nehemiah for the remainder of the term, which was not very long. No one teased me about the affair or said a word about it. Indeed I felt relatively little indignation against Reb Nehemiah in comparison with my resentment at my grandfather's action. Reb Nehemiah was by far the most inspiring *rebbeh* that I had ever had. After I was in Minsk for a year I wrote to my grandfather that in the whole of that large city there was no *rebbeh* like Reb Nehemiah.

A final incident that made me wish to leave Neshwies was the death of my brother Isaac. At the end of the summer of 1889 my mother came to Neshwies with my recently born baby brother. She had developed a bad breast which prevented her from nursing him herself, and she wanted a wet nurse. A niece of my grandmother's was hired and we all felt that he would thus be well cared for. I used to dream of the days when he would grow up and we two would be companions. He thus grew to mean a good deal in my life. But he did not receive adequate care. When he became seriously sick, no doctor was called. One Saturday early before dawn my grandmother took me to see him. By the light of a dim Sabbath lamp he looked to me wonderfully beautiful in repose, free from all pain; but my grandmother shook her head dolefully in hopeless resignation. That afternoon after reading The Sayings of the Fathers in the *cheder* and playing a bit with the boys, I again went to see my brother and was shocked to hear that he was dead. It was my first meeting with the work of the Grim Reaper and it darkened the rest of my days in Neshwies. I regretted that as a Cohen I could not follow his corpse to the graveyard.

The Sabbath before Passover is known as the Great Sabbath, and I conceived the idea that I must be in Minsk on that occasion to hear some great rabbi preach. My grandfather somewhat resented my haste, but I insisted.

A young man, not of the best reputation, who lived in Minsk, happened just then to be passing through Neshwies on the way to his home, and I was entrusted to his care. He showed that he deserved his ill repute. First he tried to pocket the money given him for my railroad ticket by making me crawl under a bench when the conductor came to collect the tickets. The ruse did not succeed, and he made some sort of deal with the conductor. He also tried to sell a little basket of eggs which my grandmother entrusted to him to give to my mother. But I looked at him sharply and he realized that he had underestimated my intelligence, and so he delivered the eggs to my mother.

When I left Neshwies my mind was full of anticipations of what I would do in Minsk. But it was not long before I realized my great good fortune in having been sent to my grandfather in those crucial years of my life. Without that opportunity I could not have acquired the moral and intellectual interests which have been controlling in the course of my subsequent life.

As I reflect on it now, life in Neshwies illustrates the familiar hedonistic paradox that people attain happiness more readily when they do not strain to attain it. In the mind of my grandfather, and of the pious people whom I met, the accepted view was that life on this earth is an expiation, a corridor to the life beyond, and the only worthwhile activity in this corridor is to acquire merit for what is to come. Nothing, therefore, was considered of real importance, except as it bore on religion, the prescriptions of which were generally known. Only occasionally did we have to go to the *Dayin* (judge) to settle a point of ritual. Hence followed the great paradox that this life, despite its lack of material resources and outer graciousness, still harbored not only a sustaining peacefulness but also a sense of superiority to those who cared for worldly goods. Renunciation led to fulfillment.

Though I later came to reject my grandfather's ascetic philosophy as intellectually inadequate, I have never been able to deny its outstanding merits, and it has influenced my temperament even more than my philosophy. Nor could I forget the wisdom of not accustoming ourselves to luxuries of which fate may deprive us at any moment. I have also found it worth while to remind others of the wisdom of my grandfather's saying that the weak but yielding grass survives the storm that breaks the strong and resisting tree.

CHAPTER THREE

MINSK (1890-1892) — THE BEGINNINGS OF THE ROMANTIC ENLIGHTENMENT

WHEN I ARRIVED in Minsk I found hardly any physical change in the old city. The house in which I had lived up to my seventh year had, to be sure, been sold to a family named Fisher. But my mother and my sister continued to live in it in a room rented from the new owners. The latter were the only new people in our old neighborhood. Despite all that, however, I soon realized that I was coming into a new world.

I had left Minsk in 1887 a little animal and I came back an Orthodox pietist. But Minsk was a large metropolitan city, and while the binding character of Jewish religious law was generally recognized by its Jewish inhabitants the strict religiosity which characterized the old men of Neshwies did not prevail among those with whom I came in contact. Thus in Neshwies it was considered an act of piety to let the *payess* (forelocks) grow in front of the ears. But when I came home in that condition everyone laughed at it. Even my sister, as well as the young daughter of the senior Mr. Fisher, teased me about my queer ways. A grandson of Mr. Fisher, a year or so older than myself, who attended a Russian school, very soon began to pal with me and with the hunchback and his cousin, the orphaned son of a chimney sweeper, who lived in the house next to ours. But at first he could not resist the temptation to ridicule my ways. My mother realized the situation and, despite my mild protest, cut off my *payess* and obtained clothes for me more like those worn in Minsk. But this did not altogether remove a chasm which continued to exist between me and the less piously indoctrinated boys of the neighborhood. It was not so much the things they did but their talk and gen-

41

eral attitude which made me often say (though not always aloud), "This is not in accordance with the Torah."

In that part of the town where we lived there were located a number of houses of ill fame patronized mainly by soldiers. All the good families naturally drew in their skirts, but the existence of "the social evil" could not be hidden from us children who played in the streets. Indeed, while we took the procession of soldiers to these houses for granted, some of my playmates would raise derisive cries when a visitor looked like, or was suspected of being, a divinity student. One of my playmates, a little older than myself and a student at a Russian school, made me uncomfortable by the frequency with which he spoke gloatingly of sex and future gratification. It all seemed to me so contrary to the Sacred Law of the Torah. In my three years in Neshwies I had heard of only one open public defiance of the Law. A married man deserted his wife and lived with a loose woman who had a child by him. They occupied a house in the yard of a Mr. Talpay whose wife kept a grocery store. Good people looked askance at one who would rent his house to such immoral persons. One day in Minsk a beggar entered our house — it was not then the custom to knock before entering — and I recognized the beggar to be Mr. Talpay. I was quite unprepared to hear mother say "How do you do" to him and invite him to a visit and a meal with us. When he hurriedly left in obvious confusion I was inclined to see in his fate God's punishment. But my mother mildly rebuked me by saying that many pious people in Neshwies were reduced to the same sad fate.

When my father came home for the Passover, he brought me several presents that were the envy of all my playmates. I also enjoyed the walks that on Saturday afternoons he, my mother, my sister, and I would take to the Governor's Park outside the city. Despite the years of hard work my father was still tall and handsome, and my mother looked resplendent in a beautiful shawl that my father had brought her from America. The picture of the green lawns in the park and the lights in the stores as we went back in the evenings stands out in my memory.

My relations with my father were not on the whole happy, for my strange ways grated on him after he had lived nearly seven years in America. It went against his grain to see me doing such things as going barefooted to school with nothing but a huge piece of bread.

Moreover, as he became absorbed in business, he could give me little time and never spoke to me about my studies. Hence the fear of him that I had acquired in his previous two visits only increased.

One afternoon he uttered an unusually severe derogatory remark about me which made me decide to run away from home. I went to the yard where the principal synagogues were located and after walking disconsolate about the city for hours, I could not form any idea of where else to go. So late in the evening I finally turned my steps home. As I cautiously opened the door I heard my father and others in Mr. Fisher's room laughing. It seemed to me that they were all laughing at me and I felt bitterly humiliated. But not knowing what else to do, I crawled into my bed. My mother came in and offered me some supper, but, fatigued and mortified, I cried myself to sleep.

The *cheder* to which I was sent with the hunchback and the young chimney sweep did not mean much in my intellectual or spiritual life. We continued the study of the Pentateuch, with the commentary of Rashi, and we read the Prophets Isaiah, Jeremiah, and Ezekiel, but the *rebbeh* was not much of a scholar and gave me no new insight or vision. Intellectual stimulus came to me from a different source. Nor was the physical life of my *cheder* more satisfactory. The *rebbeh's* house was situated in a part of the city popularly called the *Blotte* (the Mud). It was a small house with low ceilings and small windows that were seldom opened. Its only advantage was its nearness to the river where we were allowed to swim without any supervision. Once, however, I nearly drowned by allowing myself to float on a current which carried me beyond my depth so that I managed to return only after considerable difficulty.

The *rebbeh*, like most of those who followed his calling, was financially harassed and was frequently away from his pupils. He was a small, powerfully built man, rather sensible but narrow in his outlook. He administered punishments with his walking stick instead of his fist or strap. One day I stole the cane and was taking it to throw it into the river, but a few of my fellow students decided to return it. But if the *rebbeh* was not particularly interesting, one of his sons was. He was a clerk in some store and was taking up with the growing Socialist Movement, to the great fear and horror of his parents. That was the first time I heard of socialism and I remember that I was rather undecided as to whether my attitude to this young rebel was sympathetic or not. His opposition to the Czar, the head of our oppressors, seemed to me natural and commendable, but I was not sure whether the rebel was sufficiently pious. His preference for Russian words raised doubts on this point.

After two or three terms (that is, half-years) in this *cheder* I was put into a more satisfactory one. My second *rebbeh* was a more cultivated person and more modern in his views of education. He showed me unusual personal consideration, talking to me about what I heard from my father in America, what I was reading outside of school, and urging me to read more Hebrew rather than Yiddish books. But I did not find Hebrew books, with their stilted metaphors and heavily allusive, indirect style, interesting. As a matter of fact he himself lent me a Yiddish manuscript treatise on arithmetic written by his brother of which I copied out a large part.

My new *rebbeh* did not rely on the traditional method of maintaining some order by corporal punishment. He was deterred from the latter by his easy-going temperament and by an unfortunate physical defect. Instead, he had a system of rewarding achievement and good behavior by marks, and an elaborate system of honors based on them. It was understood that the one who had the highest marks for a whole term would receive a chart written by him containing astronomic diagrams and other miscellaneous information. According to the marks and all the canons of fairness I was entitled to receive it. But, whether because of some disagreement with my mother or for some other reason, it was awarded to the son of a wealthy family to the surprise and general indignation of the whole class. Several, indeed, threatened to waylay the recipient and snatch the chart from him. My own indignation was decidedly mild, though I was naturally anxious to get the information in the chart. But my predominant feeling was of gratitude to the *rebbeh* for enabling me to obtain what I had desired in vain for several years — an opportunity to study Gemara. We had an old Talmudic scholar teach several of us the Tractate Baba Kama, while others were taught Russian by a young man. After the Passover my mother hired a young Talmudic scholar who was living in a nearby synagogue and waiting for a call to serve as a *rov* to help me continue my Talmudic studies. I enjoyed that immensely, but probably more from pride at attaining the heights of pious study rather than because of any inherent interest in the minutiae of the Law of Divorce.

Before I came to Minsk all of my reading had been of sacred books and, with the exception of the Yiddish part of Kav Hayosher, in Hebrew. But one day as I passed the large synagogue on the Shoolhof of Minsk I saw two men in the archway with bundles of books which served as a lending library. One of them had a Yiddish translation of the Yosiphon, which I had read in Hebrew in Neshwies. My mother lent me a ruble to serve as a deposit for the return of the book, and I paid for the loan of it out of my pocket money which my mother, considering her limited means, generously allowed me. Very soon, however, I found a simpler scheme of paying for the books I borrowed to read. My mother used to give me a number of *beigles* (unsweetened doughnut-shaped rolls), and I sold several of them. After a while I persuaded my mother to let me buy the *beigles* myself, and as I bought half a dozen for five kopecks and sold them for one kopeck apiece, I had adequate means to finance my reading.

I reread with ardent enthusiasm especially the heroic story of the Maccabean Revolt against the Syrians and of the unsuccessful but still heroic defense of Jerusalem against Titus. When I returned this book, I took out one about Jacob Diradia, the leader of a group of Marranos who escaped from Spain and Portugal to found a Jewish community in Holland. As I recall it now, it was full of absurdly impossible exploits, such as the defeat of Spanish battleships by the refugees. But having been brought up on Biblical miracles, such incidents did not seem to me unbelievable or even strange. In any case, I was deeply stirred. It was in that book, I believe, that I first read of Shakespeare, the performance of his *Merchant of Venice* and of the struggle of Elizabethan England against Spain.

Less stirring but not less interesting was the story of Shabsheh Zvi, the Turkish Jew who represented himself as the Messiah and who raised tragically false hopes among the Jews who had hardly yet recovered from the terrible catastrophe of the Chmelnitsky Rebellion.

But the story that gripped me most of all was that of Bar Kochba, the leader of the final Judean Revolt against Roman oppression. The story of the suffering of the Jews and how in defense of their holy religion a handful of them successfully resisted the whole Roman Empire for three years fired my imagination to an unusual degree. For some days I carried a flat piece of wood under my coat picturing it in my mind's eye as a sword with which I, too, might some day fight

the armies of our persecutors. Those who discovered me carrying this
piece of wood and made fun of my strange foolishness had little realization of what fantastic dreams were associated with it. They saw the
wood but not its symbolic meaning to me. To this day, I cannot read
the story of the martyrdom of Rabbi Akiba which occurred in connection with that rebellion without being moved to tears.

The transition from sacred books to secular romances was remarkably easy — in fact, imperceptible. But it might be dated from
my reading the Yiddish translation of a Hebrew novel by Abraham
Mappu called *The Love of Zion*. It had a highly artificial plot and a
series of melodramatic incidents without much character delineation
other than the simple division between the good and the bad, but I
did not at that time notice any of these traits. It peopled for me the
Biblical scenery, and it was sweet to live in imagination in the Holy
Land in the period of the pious King Hezekiah and feel the fragrance
of its sacred fields. Naturally I was deeply moved to sympathy for
the suffering of its faultless hero and heroine.

Still disinclined to read any book that had other than a pious
purpose I once picked up a volume entitled *The Cohen* by Shomer.
At that time I did not know that Shomer was a famous Yiddish
writer who came from Neshwies, but the fact that the book was
about a Cohen made me feel that it was proper reading. The story
began with a moving description of a forlorn wanderer who is saved
from cold and starvation when he declares himself to be a Cohen on
an occasion when one is needed for a religious ceremony. I was
entranced by the account of his subsequent adventures, and my heart
was also wrung by the tragedy which in the end comes to his son who,
under the impression that as a Cohen he cannot marry the divorced
woman whom he loves, commits suicide. Too late does his father
confess that he is really not a Cohen but that he had represented
himself to be one in order to get some relief.

This book opened a door for a host of longer and shorter novels
by Shomer and others. Having no guide, my reading was most
miscellaneous and of diverse values. I picked up Jewish translations
of the romances of Beauvais, of the Niebelungen and of other world
classics. But the book that gripped my imagination most was a Yiddish
translation of the *Arabian Nights,* especially the "Adventures of
Sinbad." I also remember vividly an historic romance of the life of

Empress Eugenie. It centered about three heroes, one of whom was called Olympios, and the heroine, Dolores. Together with many weird, hair-raising adventures I got something of the history of the Spanish Civil War and the history of France from 1848 to 1871. These larger books were interspersed with shorter "penny dreadfuls," some of which however were quite amusing. Curiously enough, the one story of that group which has stood most tenaciously in my memory in a most intriguing way, is a thin booklet called *The Polish Boy* (not the large and famous book of the same title by Linetsky). It began with a picture of a small boy who leaves his house in the evening to attend to the window shutters outside and comes back fifty years later. It has haunted me ever since.

One of the most impressive books that I read in those days was *The Dobbin,* an allegory of the suffering of the Jewish people written by Mendele Mocher Sforim. This made me read two other books by the same author, *Die Takse* (The Tax) and *Fishke, der Kroomer* (Fishke, the Lame One). Both of these books were from a literary point of view a little above my previous reading. They had no thrilling adventures in them. But their social lesson sank into my consciousness and influenced me considerably in my subsequent attitude toward Jewish affairs. *Die Takse* was an exposé of the abuses and injustices in the way in which Jews raised revenue for their communal purposes. It made me understand why in the principal synagogue of Neshwies, where the *rov* himself prayed, there were occasional protests taking the form of men preventing the reading of the Torah until the redress of grievances was promised.

Fishke, der Kroomer dealt with life among Jewish beggars. It was quite slow and unromantic. But meeting beggars every day one could not but become somewhat interested in their life. Moreover, a particular experience about that time gave me a special interest in the problem. One day a beggar entered the house and, finding that I was the only one present, sat down and told me he was very tired. Partly out of sympathy and partly because I did not know what else to do, I sat down too and watched him so that he should not steal anything from our house. Very soon another beggar entered and the two held a long conversation. Their talk showed them to be pious and refined men, and I was interested in their comparison of the difficulties of their lives, the trudging from house to house, the relative generosity of different people, and the problem of finding lodgings. Their conversation so interested me that I told them of the system of treating beggars in Neshwies. Good people like my grandfather would buy from the *rov* stamped pieces of paper, I think four for a kopeck, and give them out to beggars who came to their houses. When these pieces of paper were redeemed, the beggars had a little money and there was thus some check on the amount that each received. They told me that this was not feasible in Minsk and that was why they went with bags, hung from their shoulders to the side, in which they put the pieces of bread that they received. But some people, they said, gave them regular money.

In the winter of 1891-92 I became acquainted with what might be called general Yiddish literature through the reading of the first two volumes of the *Volksbibliothek,* a miscellany edited by Sholem Aleichem, who referred to himself as a (spiritual) grandson of Mendele Mocher Sforim. Each of these volumes was a collection of sketches of Jewish life, historical narratives, literary criticism, and one long novel. I found the non-fictional and the non-historical parts of these volumes not very exciting. Even the two novels *Stempenu* and *Yosele Solovei* were somewhat slow. *Stempenu* was a study of a temperamental musician. But fine psychological observations passed over my head. *Yosele Solovei* interested me more because it was mostly the story of a boy, but apart from the description of a boy's solitude, which appealed to my own love of daydreaming. I do not remember its contents.

There was in these volumes a good deal of rather harsh criticism of Shomer which I naturally resented. As I reflect on it now, that criticism may have been just, from a purely literary point of view, but it missed the fact that despite the cheapness of Shomer's novels he had a powerful educational and liberating influence on the Jewish people.

In those days relatively few read Hebrew literature. Almost all women and most men lacked adequate training for the understanding of Hebrew. The language that every one acquired from his mother was Yiddish or, as we called it (not knowing the etymology of the word), "jargon." Hence Hebrew literature had no roots in daily life, and its limited vocabulary made it resort to highly artificial metaphors giving the whole of it a decidedly stilted form. Shomer's stories were read with avidity by hundreds of thousands of men and women who had never read anything before. And despite the impossible romances and highfalutin language, the moral tone of his writings still seems to me to have been high and serviceable for its time. The general attitude was that of the *Haskalah,* or Enlightenment. He ridiculed the absurdities of the old superstitious fanaticism, and his young heroes and heroines who had taken up modern thought and education, were always superior personalities. My judgment in this respect was confirmed when some years later Shomer died in New York, poor and, it seemed, completely forgotten; yet when the papers announced his funeral, more than one hundred thousand Yiddish-speaking men and women turned out to follow his bier to the grave. He had meant something in their lives.

Still, the reading of the *Volksbibliothek* did educate or elevate my literary taste.

One of the more literary novels that I read about this time and that made a deep impression on me was the *Stone of Stumbling* by Jacob Dinneson, a heart-rending story of an orphan, a young girl whose father dies early in life. Years later I read another story by the same author which dealt with the unrelieved suffering of a boy whose father is sickly and who is almost constantly the victim of cruel injustice. The latter reminded me of many incidents in my own life, especially in *cheder,* but this excessive harping and concentration on the pathetic became distasteful to me in later years. It seems to me that that kind of literature like Hardy's *Jude the Obscure* ignores the truth of Shelley's lines:

> Many a green isle needs must be
> In the deep wide sea of misery,
> Or the poor mariner, worn and wan,
> Never thus could voyage on.

My devotion to secular Yiddish literature was shared by one of my classmates, Shmuel (Samuel), the son of a pocketbook-maker. Shmuel was the strongest boy in the *cheder* on the *Blotte* and naturally dominated it, but like myself he began to devour many books in Yiddish and we became bosom friends. Every day we would narrate to each other what we had read the previous day, and we continued to see each other even after we ceased to attend the same *cheder.* When I left Minsk for America I gave him a notebook and we swore never to forget each other. That oath I have kept. But in my early years in America I did not have the wit or ability to keep up any correspondence with him and so we lost touch with each other. I would give a good deal to find out what became of him.

My memory of the stories I read must have been remarkably good. Once I told a story to Shmuel in his father's house and one of the women remarked that my narrative was practically word for word as it appeared in the sixteen-page booklet in which it was printed. Others, on the other hand, commented on my inability to get away from the text so as to condense the story in telling it. Still I was in considerable demand as a narrator of stories, especially on summer evenings. In front of our house was a *prisha* (a seat of compressed earth), set against the wall and protected from disintegration by being enclosed on its other three sides by boards. Here the boys of our neighborhood would crowd me in and demand that I tell them stories, which I gladly did.

While I was thus reading and telling various stories and romances, a struggle of epic proportions, at any rate of the kind that Balzac would have delighted to describe, was being carried on by my parents.

When my father came back from America, he brought with him a little money which he had saved up from his poor earnings as a presser, and my mother had sold our house at an advantageous price to the Fishers. With the capital thus acquired through their long years of labor, they hoped to start some business in which they could sustain themselves. The plan which they finally adopted was to buy a plot of ground on the street known as the Nyemieh and build on it a brick building to be used as an inn. The lot chosen was bought from the Hassidic synagogue and was adjacent to it. When the two-storied brick structure was finished, it looked big in comparison with the one-storied Hassidic *stübel* (little house). But very soon a bigger building was erected on the lot adjoining ours on the other side and this made ours look puny. Worse than that, when the foundation of the adjoining building was dug, the walls of ours were not adequately supported and a crack or fault in our house resulted.

My parents were entirely inexperienced in the kind of enterprise in which they had thus entered and they naturally underestimated the amount of money needed to complete their operation. Moreover they encountered more difficulties than they expected in procuring a mortgage. In this state of affairs they were too harried to sue their neighbor for the damage done to their building by the carelessness of his contractor who dug his foundation.

Other difficulties arose from the fact that the man who owned the house to the rear of our yard claimed that he, rather than the Hassidic synagogue, was the true owner of the ground on which our inn was erected. Not being able to prevent my father from proceeding with the operation of the building he succeeded however in venting his spleen to our great damage. His house was on a higher ground than ours which sloped down to the Nyemieh. When, therefore, city water was installed in his house, he allowed a continual flow of it to go down, which threatened to undermine the wall of our stable in the rear of the yard. As we could not get relief through the intolerably slow proceedings of the Russian courts, we had to break a hole in the stable wall to make a channel to let the water through. But in the winter this made our yard full of ice and seriously affected the use of the stable for the purposes of the inn. Here also the tortuous legal procedure of the Russian courts gave us no relief.

As the rent we received from the inn-keeper turned out to be less than expected and as my father could find no suitable work in Minsk, there was no alternative to his going back to America, leaving the rest of us in Minsk until mother could succeed in selling our new house. The latter operation was complicated by new and unexpected troubles and took a year and a half before it was completed and we could rejoin him in New York.

When my father left Minsk in the fall of 1888 he travelled on what was known as a government passport, on which there was a tax of ten rubles. To save the return tax he came home in an illegal way. When he was preparing to leave Russia again in the fall of 1890, there were rumors of serious mishaps to those who tried to steal over the boundary and so he thought it more prudent to try again for a government passport. But, unable to wait until his application was granted, especially as he was taking my aunt to rejoin her husband Abraham Farber in New York, he left in the usual underground way in which most emigrants left in those days. In the Passport Bureau, however, they soon discovered from the record that he must have come back from America in an illegal way. The police came to summon him, and not finding him made an inventory of our goods with a view to levying a fine on his property. My resourceful mother went to the police headquarters and used her unusual persuasive power to enable us to get off with a moderate fine which she paid. Meanwhile, however, a worse difficulty developed.

The Registry of the Army discovered that my brother Tom had failed to report for military service and the usual fine of three hundred rubles was clapped on the family. As my mother did not have any such sum, there was danger that our real property — that is, the brick building — would be sold at auction and the savings of more than twenty years of toil thus completely wiped out. My mother, however, rose to the occasion. Going from office to office she finally persuaded the Governor of Minsk to allow the fine to be paid in a series of installments. But the payment of these installments was no easy matter; and various subordinate officers, seeing that she was in trouble, put all sorts of difficulties in her way in order to have their palms oiled. On one occasion she paid an installment to the captain of the police who promptly lost it that very night at cards. To protect himself he tried to make the record of the case appear as if he had not yet received the money. This put my mother in a desperate plight. For a Jewish woman to impeach a police captain in the Russia of those days was unthinkable. By a series of pleadings and threats and some gratuities to various officials she managed to straighten the matter out. But the trouble she had to endure was terrific. The police would knock at our windows in the middle of the night, wake us up and demand payment or else that mother go at once to police headquarters.

After the fine of three hundred rubles was paid, mother turned her attention to the problem of selling our brick building.

Real estate values at the time promised to rise with the indications that, as the city of Minsk was modernizing itself, its industries and business would expand. The most striking of these indications was the introduction of city water and the horse car.

When running water was first installed in our brick house, people came from considerable distances not only to fill their pails but also to see the wonder of it. Indeed it seemed truly magical to turn a faucet and have as much water as you wanted. Curiously enough, the horse car was even more of a seven-day wonder. People from villages around came to see it and many of us boys forewent our meals to save five kopecks in order to take a ride.

My mother thus realized that if she held on to her property for some time she would get a better price for it. But the trouble with the police had so embittered life that she decided to leave Russia as soon as possible to reunite the whole family in America.

As mother's anxiety to sell became generally known, prospective purchasers tried to take advantage of it to reduce the price below the actual cost of the building. But by persistent effort she found a cashier of Brody's Bank who agreed to a reasonable price. However, after the contract was signed he refused to go through with the purchase on the ground that the crack in the building was not mentioned in the agreement. There then followed more negotiations lasting many weeks. My mother discovered technical Hebrew and Russian legal difficulties in the purchaser's case and unusual ways of compelling him to go through with his undertaking. Thus, without resorting to litigation that would have taken years, she finally forced a compromise and the house was actually sold.

During this period my mother suffered serious health difficulties which were aggravated by the condition of the house in which we lived. When the inn was completed, my parents built on a part of the yard a small brick house as our own residence. It was near the end of the summer when we moved into it. The winters in Minsk are rather long and severe and no one ever thinks of keeping any windows open. Houses were heated by burning wood in a brick oven and to keep the heat the chimneys were closed. The result was that in winter nights the oozing moisture from the cement in our walls and the various gases from the oven brought fainting spells on my mother and myself. This became so serious that we had to move out, and mother hired a room in the house of a Mr. David Engineer. With the advent of spring we returned to our little brick home; and while the next winter's conditions were somewhat better, my mother and I were constantly suffering from severe headaches.

One winter morning the door of our little house got frozen in so that we could do nothing to open it. We knocked and made noises to attract the people in the inn, but no one came to our rescue. It was only after several hours had passed that the increasing warmth of the day thawed the ice and enabled us to go out to purchase some needed food for breakfast.

Beside the inn our brick building had a store which was at first rented out to the wife of a *Hassid* (follower of a sect of Jewish mysticism) who was separated from her husband. She could not make her little business very successful, and after she was arrested for some infraction of the complicated law that no one understood except the police, she moved out. My mother then formed a partnership with an old woman who used the store for the sale of fruit. The old woman also rented from her the room which, before my father's departure, had been used as his and my mother's bedroom. It was amazing to see how my mother was able to make people buy all sorts of apples and pears which the old woman, experienced in the business, did not think at all saleable. By this means, and from the earnings of my father, she managed to raise the three hundred rubles to pay the military fine and support herself and her two younger children.

I ought not to conclude my reminiscence of Minsk without a word about our Hassidic neighbors. I often found it convenient to pray in the Hassidic *stübel* right next door instead of going a considerable distance to a *Misnagid* synagogue (that is, a synagogue devoted to learning rather than mysticism). The difference turned out much less than I expected. It is true that the *Hassidim* danced around more during services, but the text of the prayers was the same except for one minor rearrangement. I also found that the few young Talmudic students in it behaved very much the same as others — they turned with avidity from the Gemara to read any Yiddish romances which I brought them. The distinctive institution of the *stübel* was the Saturday afternoon meal. On Friday each member of the congregation would bring a white roll to be cared for by the beadle's wife. On Saturday afternoon they would make a repast of these rolls, and their leader (I do not recall whether he was called a *rov*) would discourse to them. I found those discourses very dull, nor did I find any of their books very attractive.

One of their books, the Kav Hayosher, I had read in Neshwies to the great detriment of my peace of mind, since it aroused all sorts of horrible fears as to what *sheidim* (devils), especially the female kind, could do to me when I was asleep. In the light of the more modern and rationalistic Yiddish books that I had been reading in

Minsk it seemed to me a superstitious and low moral view to assign to devils so much influence in the life of innocent men and women. I also began to doubt the magical power supposed to be possessed by those who could pronounce the four letters JHVH which constitute the proper name of God (generally written "Jehovah" in English and supposed by modern scholars to have been pronounced anciently "Jahveh").

Many years later, when I read various essays about the *Hassidim* and what their emphasis on enthusiasm meant in brightening the lives of hundreds of thousands living under outer conditions of misery, I was prepared to believe it. And I suppose that when the Dark Ages settle again on the European scene as they threaten today, Hassidic joys and piety will enable many to survive where those accustomed to a more intelligent and sensitive life will perish. Indeed on reading Peretz's stories depicting the inner simplicity and spirituality of *Hassidim* I have frequently been moved to admiration. Nevertheless, I have never been able to respect those who, on the basis of ultra-modern romantic obscurantism, have tried to idealize the Hassidic combination of ignorance and superstition. That has always seemed to me to be a form of intellectual decadence and corruption.

CHAPTER FOUR

NESHWIES REVISITED
AND THE JOURNEY TO AMERICA

BEFORE LEAVING for America my mother took my sister and me for a farewell visit to her parents in Neshwies. I had now become quite sentimental about the small town where my intellectual life had begun to sprout, and I was deeply touched when in the bright morning air I again saw from our wagon the high spires of the Radzivil Castle.

After the hustle and noise of the busily growing city of Minsk, Neshwies now seemed a deserted town. It had indeed, in the two years since I left it, lost a large part of its population through emigration, and the absence of the cavalry regiment from the grounds and barracks opposite my grandfather's house emphasized the stillness. But I also found more traces of modernism and emancipated views than I had previously been able to see when I had been tied, as it were, to my grandfather's apron strings. I was rather amused to learn that a *Yeshiva* (college or academy) student who used to eat at our house in Minsk and who had been proposed by a *shadchen* (marriage broker) to a young woman in Neshwies was refused by her on the ground that he was not sufficiently modern.

We stayed in Neshwies about four weeks, and during this period my Talmudic education was crowned by my getting a chance to study with Reb Joseph Ber, who conducted a small *Yeshiva* in the Butcher's Synagogue. The method of study in a *Yeshiva* was different from that of the *cheder*. Instead of reading a text with the *rebbeh* and having him explain it as we went along, we had to read and unravel its meaning by ourselves and then translate it before the head of the *Yeshiva*. The text assigned to us then was Kadushin. At first I was somewhat at a loss, but I soon got the hang of it and had the satisfaction of having Rabbi Joseph tell my grandfather that I was a good student.

During this period I saw a few of my former classmates and found that they were all still studying the same things and following the same method pursued two years before when I left Neshwies. One of my meetings, however, was with the two sons of my first rabbi. They had been my closest friends and what they told me, and especially their tone, made a deep and lasting impression on me. Their father had died in prison where he was put because he had signed some papers which helped a neighbor's son to escape from military service, and their mother died soon thereafter of grief. I can never forget the sad tone in which the older one recounted what had happened.

After some deliberation mother decided to go to America by way of Minsk. We took a wagon not to Horodjeh, the nearest station on the railroad, but to Steibsk which was farther away and which thus gave us a chance to be for a while longer with grandfather who accompanied us in the wagon. The wagon ride for hours through dirt roads in the forest was not very enlivening, and though I was thrilled when we crossed the famous Niemen River by a sort of floating bridge directed by a rope — an arrangement which I had never seen before — I fell soundly asleep as soon as we reached an inn in Steibsk. When the time came for us to board the train for Minsk, I was awakened by my grandfather kissing me good-bye. I was overcome with keen anguish that never, never would I see him again. The tears rolled down my cheeks before I knew it. Compared to my mother, he had been a hard taskmaster. But he had been the center of my life during three formative years of young boyhood and I realized even then, as I have more fully since, that he had laid the foundation not only of my intellectual development, but of that inner superiority to worldly fortune which is the essence of genuine nobility, spirituality, or, as I prefer to call it now, the truly philosophic life.

The subsequent history of my grandparents was tragically sad, and it has been one of the great regrets of my life that I did nothing to lighten it.

When I returned to my parents in 1890 and the three rubles per week for my maintenance was cut off, my grandfather found it increasingly difficult to support himself and his invalid wife. Though he was then past seventy, he was still physically able to ply his trade as a tailor; but he could find no work. He never bought a sewing machine and could not compete with the younger men for the little business obtainable, so he sold his house and went to Theodosia, Crimea, to live with his oldest son. Most of the money that he thus received went to my uncle Yankel (Jacob) who was the only one of his sons who had served in the army, and in consideration for this service had been given a note to be cashed on the sale of the parental home. When, therefore, my grandparents came to Theodosia, they had very little money left. As it was unfitting for the dignity of my uncle Elyeh, who was a scholar and a *shochet* (a ritual slaughterer of animals), to have his father work as a tailor, the two old people had to pack up their scant belongings and go to Kishenev where my uncle Yankel lived as a fairly prosperous tailor. Their remaining years constituted a sorrow's crown of sorrows, for my grandmother could not get along well with her daughter-in-law. And after the death of my grandfather, my grandmother was reported to have committed suicide.

I could not have helped them financially — my parents did their utmost along this line. But possibly I might have written to them more often. Even that, however, was not so easy. Very soon after I came to America I lost my interest in Talmudic studies, and I did not want to distress my grandfather by writing him about my new interests. When in 1895 I wrote him that I had received a gold medal for the highest standing in the college entrance examination in my school, he wrote back chiding me that unlike myself gold does not change its nature. Later he was reported to have said to a friend in Kishenev that for one thing he expected to be punished in the hereafter and that was for letting me go to America. But when I think of what probably would have been my career had I remained in Russia and what little I could have accomplished there, it certainly seems very fortunate that I was able to come to these blessed United States where I have been able to develop a career of some usefulness and to lighten the burdens of my parents for many years of their old age.

When we came back to Minsk we stayed about two weeks in a room in the inn which had been ours. Naturally I saw my old playmates, and when they pressed me as to why we returned I thought it would be a good joke to tell them that we had been sent back when we had tried to cross the Russian boundary line. It is characteristic of those days that the rumor soon spread, so that it reached my father in New York before we got to America.

Instead of going to America on a government passport my mother made arrangements with an agent who sold her a combination ticket from Minsk to New York, and this included an arrangement for the illegal crossing of the boundary into Germany. So many people were going to America that way that the enterprise was quite standardized.

We boarded the train at Minsk in the evening and passed through Vilna the next morning. Vilna was a city where almost all the books that I had read had been printed, and I viewed it as the center of Jewish learning. Though our train stopped there about an hour all I saw of that famous city was a beggar boy who wrung my heart by his tale of woe, probably through his professional competence. When we were approaching Kovno in the afternoon, all the Russians on the train would point to our group as America-bound emigrants. Why the conductor of the train and other Russian officials did not know what everybody else knew I did not understand.

Either in Kovno or in some subsequent railroad station our group left the train and we were distributed among a number of Jewish homes. Late at night we were called out and travelled in a sort of covered wagon for the rest of the night and the next day. This time I noticed that we had gravel roads. The going was not very smooth, but at least we did not get stuck in the mud. At night we were distributed again. My mother, my sister and I slept in some garret on straw. The next morning we were collected again and crossed the boundary near Memel in what was outwardly the legal way. A soldier appeared, read an official roll of those entitled to pass, and each of us in turn answered "Yes" to names which we had never heard of before. After that we were allowed to pass and soon were on German soil. I heard the driver explain the tariff that he had to pay to the soldier and to every one else on the way. He complained that little was left to him despite the hard and dangerous character of his business.

At Memel we left our baggage to be inspected by German customs inspectors, and were taken to an inn run by a Jew who spoke our familiar Yiddish instead of German. I was even more surprised that the peasants who came to the inn spoke Russian instead of German. I remember that my mother left a bottle of brandy in her valise, and I was afraid it would be confiscated by the young German officer in a spiked helmet, who paid little attention to it.

We spent most of the day at the inn and took a train in the evening. We travelled in cars which were marked "Fourth Class." They might have been cattle cars, for there were no seats. We sat on the floor and slept by reclining our heads on our bundles. In the morning and in the afternoon when the train stopped at stations, mother or I would go out and purchase some hot water which, with the hard bread and a few other things, served as our meals.

At one station my mother was almost left behind because I was delayed in coming back and she went out to look for me. In the evening our train arrived at Berlin. I remember vividly the covered station and the fact that our car was switched to a side line where we were treated to coffee and white rolls. It must have been the work of some philanthropic society wishing to help and refresh the weary travelers. I remember that when I misbehaved in some way or other one of the women attendants, a social worker, I suppose, slapped my face.

The next morning we arrived at Bremen and were told that there was some delay about boarding the ship which was to take us across the Atlantic. Again we were distributed, three families and ourselves being assigned to an inn on the outskirts of the city run by a young German couple who seemed at the time to have no other guests. The young wife was pretty and aloof but the young host was jolly, and he and my mother had no difficulty in communicating with each other on all sorts of topics.

I was amazed at the amount of liquor he consumed and especially by the fact that whenever he had to take a walk he took some along. We must have stayed in Bremen for a week or so. I do not know who paid for our maintenance, certainly my mother did not. But the meals were, under the circumstances, very skimpy. My mother made inquiry for a Jewish restaurant, and I remember our entering one and seeing a number of people eating, none of whom seemed to me like the kind of Jewish people I had ever seen before. They were indistinguishable from other Germans. But the trip was in vain because the prices of meals in that restaurant were, to my mother, prohibitive.

I remember that on a Saturday morning I decided to explore the town in the company of several young people in our group. As we walked through, children would greet us derisively as *Juden,* but no violence was offered us. I was most amazed by seeing cars going on tracks without engines or horses. I had not at that time heard of electricity, and I could not, for the life of me, understand how the motion was effected.

When we got to the river that runs through Bremen the rest of our party decided to hire a boat, but I walked home by myself. It was not easy to find my way back through the strange town, and I hated to approach any one and ask the way. But I managed to get home without serious embarrassment. A day or two later I was surprised to learn that Bremen is not a port, but that we would have to take a train to reach Bremerhaven, where we boarded the "Darmstadt."

The character of the "Darmstadt" may be indicated by the fact that it took about fourteen days to reach New York. We were huddled together in the steerage literally like cattle — my mother, my sister and I sleeping in the middle tier, people being above us and below us as well as on the same level. Naturally, we could not eat the food of the ship, since it was not kosher. We only asked for hot water into which my mother used to put a little brandy and sugar to give it a taste. Towards the end of the trip when our bread was beginning to give out we applied to the ship's steward for bread, but the kind he gave us was unbearably soggy. The hardships of the trip began to tell on my mother, so that she took sick and developed a fever, but the ship's doctor did not think it was serious and prescribed some bouillon for her. As the law regulating kosher foods does not apply to medicines my mother took it, but I wouldn't touch it.

More than the physical hardships, my imagination was occupied with the terror of ships colliding, especially when the fog horn blew its plaintive note. A woman next to my mother was always harping on the danger of collision between boats at night or in a fog. One morning we saw a ship passing at what seemed to me a considerable distance, but our neighbor said that we were lucky, that at night we escaped a crash only by a hair's breadth. After a few days on the boat, we saw land and I was puzzled. It could not be America, and yet I thought we should have passed the Channel within the first day or two. It was probably Ireland.

During the last two days we ate up the last piece of our own bread so we had to resort to dipping the crust of the ship's soggy bread in hot water, producing a most distasteful effect. It was therefore with great joy that one morning we heard the news that we were approaching America.

As we passed Quarantine Island and the immigrant inspectors examined every one of us, my mother was rather anxious lest, as a result of the unsanitary conditions under which we had passed the two weeks, some defect would be found in me and I would not be allowed to land, but I encountered no such difficulty. I was also fortunate that in those days immigrants were not cross-examined as to their beliefs. And so we soon found ourselves on land in Ellis Island. My brother Tom and my father came to take us over to the house of my uncle Abraham — not, however, before we were treated to bananas which, despite their novelty, we ate with avidity.

A ferry boat took us from Ellis Island to Bowling Green, where we boarded a Second Avenue Elevated. Despite the fact that the Elevated cars then were drawn by steam locomotives, the whole arrangement seemed to me amazingly strange. But I was naturally glad to enter our uncle's apartment on the fourth or fifth floor of a house on Orchard Street. There we were regaled with fresh rolls, of which I ate a plenty.

For several days the three of us joined by my father stayed in the three-room apartment which housed my uncle, his wife and their two infants, until mother found living quarters — a three-room apartment on the corner of Broome and Norfolk Streets — and bought furniture and kitchen equipment. Then, after the long years of separation, our family — parents, brothers, my sister and myself — were at last reunited.

BOOK TWO

YOUTH ON THE EAST SIDE (1892-1900)
SOCIALISM AND PHILOSOPHY

WHAT I FIRST SAW of America did not come up to the high expectation which popular accounts of its unlimited wealth and radical difference from the Old World had led me to entertain. Almost all the people I met in the street and in the stores, with the exception of some children, spoke Yiddish; and though their dress had a somewhat different tone from the one to which I was accustomed, it did not seem much richer in quality. Grand Street, which at that time was the great business thoroughfare of the East Side, and still had department stores such as Ridley's and Lord and Taylor, did not seem so much grander than the great mercantile streets of Minsk, such as the Franciscaner.

The most marked outer difference was the uniformity of the many-storied houses and the absence of any wooden ones. Though in those days there were still some private residences on the East Side, the streets presented solid fronts, with no gardens or vacant spaces between the houses. I was also impressed with the fact that the roofs of houses were flat rather than slanted. But I soon found out the advantage of a roof on which one could sleep on hot summer nights.

Our first home in New York was a three-room apartment on the corner of Broome and Norfolk Streets. After a few months in our first American home we moved into an apartment with somewhat larger rooms on Suffolk Street near Rivington and there we lived until the end of September, 1893.

Of course there were the wealthy people in the neighborhood and their style of living did not answer to this description, but they constituted a different community from that of the foreign and the poor. It took some time before the separate communities began to have sufficient intercourse to influence each other.

The pioneer of the humanizing influence on the East Side was Charles Stover, who had a penchant for public service and devoted himself to it with religious ardor. The first task he set himself was to get rid of the slums. After much agitation the city was persuaded to adopt a program of slum clearance. Many of the old rickety houses situated on Stanton Street, Houston Street, Rutgers Street and neighboring streets were torn down. At first, no homes took their place but soon the ruins were replaced by fountains and other decent buildings. Some people complained that the city refused to put up a fountain because the donor was Mr. Schiff, a philanthropic Jew. But that was only a matter of delay for the progress was inevitable. As the income of the people of the East Side increased, the housing improved. There were some hindrances: many pious Jews were opposed to the installation of facilities for athletics — an old prejudice which goes back to the struggle against Hellenism in the days of the Maccabees.

Some of the improvements had to be privately financed and Mr. Stover found little encouragement. I remember his enthusiasm when Mary Ryshpan promptly paid for some tickets which were sold to raise the necessary funds for gymnasium facilities.

On the inner side of life, the chief characteristic difference was the greater intensity and hurry. At six o'clock in the morning the alarm clock would wake us all up. My mother would prepare breakfast, my father would say his prayers and after a hurried meal my father and my brother Sam would leave the house so that they could begin their work at the moment when the clock struck seven.

I had occasion to visit my father's "shop" and I was impressed with the tremendous drive which infiltrated and animated the whole establishment — nothing like the leisurely air of the tailor shop in Minsk where my Uncle Abraham had worked and where the men would sing occasionally. Sometimes my father and another presser would start a competitive drive to see who could press the largest number of jackets during the day. We all knew by his appearance that this had happened when he came home at seven o'clock in the evening. It was hard to dissuade my father from engaging in such drives, for he was paid according to the number of jackets pressed.

I soon understood why the unions were fighting so hard for a weekly wage to take the place of payment for piece work. That experience made me realize what later my friends educated in economics could not see, namely, the wisdom as well as the humanity of some limitation of output. For, in the long run, excessive work diminishes the effective life span and thus reduces the chief productive power of the nation. Even a machine cannot be economically run if it functions always at maximum speed. What good is it to a nation to increase the number of its commodities if it exhausts and brutalizes its human beings?

When later I learned of the large profits that the manufacturers were making and how lavishly they spent their money, I could not dismiss as mere rhetoric the complaint against the harsh injustice of the distribution of wealth under capitalism. But at first I knew only that my father worked in a "shop" in the rear building of a yard on Ridge Street, and that his boss, a certain Mr. Riemer, received the cloth all properly cut, ready to be sewed up into garments, after which it was returned to the manufacturers, who were referred to as "the warehouse" and who sold the product to distributors. Mr. Riemer, as the boss, was an Olympian figure to us. He was the one who paid my father. But the Sampters, who paid Mr. Riemer, were dim figures whose magnitude I had no opportunity to measure. (Little did I dream that some years later the daughter of one of these would sit at my feet in a philosophy class at my home.)

One of the great conveniences which made life simpler for my mother in this country was the availability of gas for lighting and especially for cooking purposes. No more need for chopping wood, for making a fire in the oven or sweeping out the ashes. Just by lighting a match the business of cooking could be quickly achieved. At first my father raised religious objections against lighting matches and using gas on Saturday. And though my mother's clever answers did not satisfy him, she prevailed, so that we did not face the question of getting a *Goy* (Gentile) to come in to light the fire for us on the Sabbath. In all other respects the old ritual observances remained in force.

On the religious side there was at first much less difference than I had expected. All the people that I knew (with the exception of my brother Tom who was a clerk in a shoe store on the Bowery) refrained from working on Saturdays, and all the stores in our immediate neighborhood were closed on that day. On Friday nights, on Saturdays and on holidays I would accompany my father to a hall on Broome Street where the Neshwieser Verein held religious services in the regular Orthodox manner. It differed from a regular synagogue in the old town only in not having daily services, a library of sacred books, or any rabbi to preach and expound the Torah after the prayers were finished. At these services on Broome Street I found myself in Neshwies again. There were not only two of my uncles, who had changed their names from Farfel to Aronson and Jackson respectively, but three of my former classmates at my first *cheder* in Neshwies. Two of them were brothers at whose house I had often stopped on my way home. I met another of my former classmates only once. But he had an evil reputation. He was reputed to have helped the Russian secret police, and sensing the unfriendly atmosphere he never showed up again. I also met Dr. Perlman who had lived on the same street with me in Neshwies and in whose house I believe I took my lessons in writing.

The Neshwieser Verein was an important institution in the life of its members and typical of a class of organizations that helped the immigrant to overcome the difficulties of life in the new land and adjust himself to its demands. Some time at the end of the eighties a group of immigrants from Neshwies met in the store of one of their members and decided that it would be very helpful if they formed a society for mutual assistance. The initial dues were ten cents per month. The society grew and by 1892 it had several hundred members. It offered the latter the necessary opportunities for religious services. The majority of the members were workingmen who had to go to work early in the morning and came home so late that few could afford to come to daily prayers. Besides, it was doubtful whether the Verein could afford to pay rent for the whole week. The renting of a meeting hall for Friday night and Saturday of each week and for the traditional holidays met the most pressing needs of the group. The Verein owned a burial ground and had a special group to attend to funerals, as well as a committee to visit the sick and the needy. The hall on Broome Street not only served as a house of prayer, but was also a place where the business of the society was transacted on Saturday nights.

Though my father was a native of Kletsk and lived in Neshwies only a short time, he became, through my mother, associated with the Neshwieser Verein almost from its beginnings and was a faithful member of it for over forty-four years. Though there were times when there was no bread in his house, and there was no money for rent, he never applied for relief. My mother inherited her father's dignity and extraordinary capacity for good household management. Today the bodies of both of them lie in the Neshwieser Cemetery, after sixty-seven years of married life together. No one ever accused my father of a base deed or ever heard a foul word cross his lips. Nor did anyone ever hear my mother utter anything foolish. For all its poverty and lack of modernity Neshwies was a noble nursery of men and women.

The society, which later became known as the Progressive Brethren of Neshwies, grew and later it built a synagogue on Henry Street, acquired extensive plots in three cemeteries, and helped to start other societies of folk from Neshwies in the Bronx and Browns-ville. Finally it contributed considerably to the welfare of the people in Neshwies itself — though it seemed to me that so many had come here that there could hardly be any left in the old town.

I continued to attend religious services with my father up to 1899 although I had drifted away from my religious Orthodoxy long before that. In the first place there was no incentive and little opportunity for me to continue my Hebraic and Talmudic studies. There were no suitable books in our house and no one urged me to continue such study. It was taken for granted that in a few years I would join my father in some phase of tailoring, for I had no desire to become a rabbi. I did, indeed, once go to the synagogue on Norfolk Street where I found some tractates of the Talmud, but I lacked the ardor to engage in such study by myself long enough to surmount the difficult places.

A more important factor, however, in my drift from religious Orthodoxy, was provided by a conversation which I overheard between my father and a certain Mr. Tunick, in the fall of 1892. Mr. Tunick's brother had been a neighbor of ours in Minsk, and my father had helped him to come to this country. Our visitor challenged my father to prove that there was a personal God who could be influenced by human prayers or deeds, or that the Jewish religion had any more evidence in favor of its truth than other religions. To this challenge my father could only answer, "I am a believer." This did not satisfy my own mind. And after some reflection I concluded that in all my studies no such evidence was available. After that I saw no reason for prayer or the specifically Jewish religious observances. But there was no use arguing with my father. He insisted that so long as I was in his house I must say my prayers regularly whether I believed in them or not.

Such is the Orthodox conception. I had to conform to it until I was in a position to refuse to obey and tell my father I would leave his house if he insisted. This occurred in the fall of 1899.

Though my father respected my independence it came as a heavy blow that I should desert the only intellectual life we had ever shared. To him the synagogue meant a great deal. He would go to services every morning and in addition would attend the class in Mishnah on Saturday afternoons. He was a devout believer in all the teachings of Orthodox Judaism and conformed to all its laws in most faithful fashion. In later years the synagogue at Bensonhurst became almost the center of his life. He had no doubt about a life after death but was not certain as to what punishment would be accorded to his son who was morally good (according to his view) but religiously an infidel.

My abandonment of Judaism as a religion was later reinforced in my mind by my scientific, historical and philosophical studies. Although I never abandoned my interest in the history and in the welfare of the Jewish people, I ceased to read Hebrew, so that after many years it became almost a foreign language to me.

A similar change took place in regard to my knowledge of Russian. In Minsk my mother had for a while hired a tutor to instruct me in the reading and writing of that language. Our removal from the old house and other factors forced a discontinuance of these lessons but I managed to read some Russian fairy tales by myself and my mother served as a dictionary, since she could speak Russian very well although she had never learned to read it. However, my absorbing interest in Yiddish books caused me to neglect the reading of Russian and after I came to this country I had no occasion whatsoever to read it, so that in the course of the years I almost completely forgot what little of it I ever learned.

Most of my intellectual life now became distinctly less intense. It was some time before I could read English books in the library, and there was very little of Yiddish literature at home.

My school attendance during the first year meant nothing to me except as an opportunity to hear English spoken.

In September, 1892, my sister and I were sent to public school. In those days there were no special provisions for older and more advanced immigrant children unfamiliar with English; and so I was

THE COHEN FAMILY, ABOUT 1895

Seated, from left: Florence, Abraham Cohen, Bessie Farfel Cohen; *standing, from left:* Sam, Morris, Tom.

put into the beginners' or ABC class. I do not recall that I was particularly embarrassed by being placed among small children, but I was dazed because I understood little of what it was all about. Despite all that, in the course of a few weeks I was promoted several times from one class to another — probably to make room for new entrants. Thus I soon reached the third grade. (In those days the classes in public school were numbered not according to the progress of the pupil, but in the reverse order so that the final or graduating class was called the first.) The teacher of this grade seemed sympathetic and showed considerable patience at my inability to answer in English.

After a month or two, the principal, Miss Byrnes, came in, wrote a problem in subtraction on the blackboard, and asked how many could solve it. I volunteered to do so, and together with several others, I was again promoted in the middle of the term.

My new teacher was younger and decidedly "uppish." At any rate, she showed marked displeasure at the new addition to her class, as well as a general repugnance to all her pupils, who, it must be admitted, were poorly dressed and not too carefully washed and kempt. But I never caused any disorder and in February, 1893, at the end of my first term in the New York public schools, I found myself in the first grade of Primary School 92. The teacher, Miss Z. Choate, boasted of being a niece of Rufus Choate. She was strict but sympathetic and decidedly competent. Using the system of rewarding us with good marks, she kept perfect order in the classroom. Everyone sat up straight, immobile as statues, the typical ideal of discipline in those days. With her guidance, I began to learn and make progress in the reading and writing of English. (The elementary arithmetic lessons were too easy for one who had a year before mastered fractions by himself.)

In the spring of 1893, there was an exhibit in the Grand Central Palace, sponsored by the Press Club, of the work of the New York public schools. Miss Choate had asked us to write a composition on Columbus, which was to be sent to the exhibition. She was greatly pleased with mine and placed it on the top of those that she submitted and invited me to visit the exhibition after classroom hours. Here she not only paid my carfare but also treated me to some popcorn. The many and different things that I saw were somewhat bewildering, and I did not think of thanking her for her kindness. The next week she invited a girl member of the class whose composition was second to mine and the following day she commended her during class for having been thoughtful enough to say "thank you." She did not look at me when she made that comment, but I got the point. However, I must confess that on many subsequent occasions I have omitted the expression of thanks even when I felt deeply grateful.

At the end of the term, the principal of the grammar school to which the graduates of our primary school had to be admitted came to examine the class. Miss Choate promised a prize — a book — for the one who made the best showing and I received a copy of *Jack Wheeler*, a story of the Far West in the days of Indian fighting. I do not recall whether I thanked her or not at that time.

My intellectual life before I could read English books with understanding would have tapered off to nothing, had it not been for the stimulus of the little Yiddish literature at home which I devoured as one famished for food. My brother Sam had copied from some book, in his own handwriting, the story of the various attempts to kill the Czar of Russia; and I was moved to intense admiration for the heroic devotion of the Nihilists who thus labored and sacrificed their lives in order to help overthrow the people's oppressors. Sam had bought a series of paper-bound booklets which constituted a Yiddish translation of Gaboriau's *Monsieur Lecoq* ("For the Honor of a Name"). Another such series which I read with avidity told the story of Napoleon. For years I could not overcome the highly favorable attitude toward Napoleon which the author entertained. But even more thrilling, indeed possibly the most thrilling story that I ever read, was a Yiddish translation of the first part of Dumas' *Monte Cristo*, published as a serial in a journal called *The House Friend*, of which we had a bound volume. The story of the persecution of Edmond Dantès, his education by the Italian *abbé*, his marvelous escape, and finally his possession of the treasure, was a rare delight. The rest of the story was not printed and I did not miss it.

But for intellectual stimulus I turned every week to the *Arbeiter Zeitung*, the Jewish organ of the Socialist Labor Party. In its columns I read translations of Flaubert's *Salammbô*, and of Smolenskin's *Kevuras Hamar* (disgraceful burial). The former stirred me by its military narratives, the latter by the revelations of the chicanery and corruption of the old fanatical leaders of Jewish communities. I was, moreover, seriously interested in the news of the week and in Abraham Cahan's articles on socialism, which were in the form of addresses like those of the old Hebrew preachers. The early numbers of the Socialist monthly *Die Zukunft* also gave me much mental nourishment.

In Minsk, when we lived in the house of Mr. Engineer, I had listened to the reading of the news of the week in the Hebrew weekly *Hazfirah,* published in Warsaw by Nahum Sokolow, who later became president of the Zionist organizations of the world. And in that house I heard some rumblings of the coming Russian Revolution. I remember that a young man gave a vivid representation of a Talmudic student who is told to report for military duty, and who asks in innocence, "How does the Czar know me? I never saw him. How does he even know my name?" Then changing the role somewhat the young man sang a heart-rending song describing the horror of Russian military service and the lack of justice for those who served the Czar. Meetings of this sort were my first introduction to the temper which created a strong socialistic movement among the Jews in Russia in the years immediately following 1892. Socialism was almost entirely resentment against the injustices of the Czarist regime.

But now socialism began to mean to me something more than opposition to the Czar's oppression. Seeing the hard labor which my father and my brothers had to undergo in order to earn their livelihood, and reading about the luxury in which the rich profiteers were living, I began to see the reality of class oppression and the consequent class struggle. *Die Arbeiter Zeitung,* in its incisive comments on politics and world affairs, always stressed the significance of the economic element. And to this day it seems to me that it had a more realistic understanding of public affairs than anything that I could see for years afterwards in the English press. It was indeed almost a generation later that men like Lincoln Steffens began to appreciate what *Die Arbeiter Zeitung* was saying in 1892, that behind the "bosses" and the corruption of our politics were the economic interests that did the bribing because it was cheaper to hire politicians than to enter politics directly, and thus take time out from lucrative business enterprise.

As soon as I learned to read English, I began to borrow books from the Aguilar Free Library, which was located on the top floor of the Educational Alliance (formerly the Hebrew Institute) building. Unless I am mistaken my first book was called *A Child's History of the*

Civil War. The only other books that I remember of that period were Abbott's biographical histories of Hannibal, Alexander the Great, Pyrrhus, and Cortez. Alexander the Great had been a familiar figure to me through the reading of Josephus, and Hannibal through the Yiddish translation of Flaubert's *Salammbô*. But it was the book on Cortez that stirred me most and my remembering its contents helped me considerably on a later occasion.

My brother Sam had acquired a small collection of paper-bound books — a series called "The Seaside Library." On the covers of those books was an appealing picture of a lady sitting on a cliff by the open sea and reading a book. In my brother's collection were a number of volumes by Dumas and Victor Hugo. As I was already familiar with the first part of *Monte Cristo* which I had read in Yiddish, I devoured the whole of it in English, even though there were many passages and incidents of aristocratic life which I did not understand, or saw only as through a thick mist. Later I read several sequels to *The Count of Monte Cristo,* of which *The Son of Monte Cristo* contained many stirring adventures of the Italian War of Liberation. The final scene of the latter, in which Monte Cristo is left alone after burying his only son, impressed me at the time, and still does, as one of the most profound symbolic expressions of the fundamental tragedy of life, which for all its high adventures and treasured attainments leaves the human soul in the end alone to face stark nothingness. I was similarly moved by Hugo's *Toilers of the Sea,* in which extraordinary Herculean labors in the conquest of nature leave the hero alone on the rock with nothing to live for.

Other books of Victor Hugo which I read then were *Les Misérables,* and *The Hunchback of Notre Dame.* Not only did the adventures of Jean Valjean fascinate me, but I was led to a strong and enduring indignation against the injustices of our system of imprisonment, and to realize that the suicide of Javert was a symbolic expression of the bankruptcy of mere legalism. To this day, while I recognize the cheap clap-trap of Hugo's melodramatic prose narratives, I feel that the touches of human sympathy and resentment at injustice make *Les Misérables* worthy of occupying a place among the world's classics.

Later I read with great delight Dumas' *Three Musketeers* series, but was much more intrigued by the series of novels of the French Revolution — *Joseph Balsamo* and the rest.

My inability to find suitable companions (that is, boys of my own age with similar interests), and my physical ineptitude and lack of skill in ordinary boys' games, compelled me to go on solo walking tours, to explore the city of my new home. In those days there were not many skyscrapers in New York. The tallest structures on the East Side were the Pulitzer Building with its golden dome, the Cooper Union Institute and the towers of the Brooklyn Bridge. Farther south the spire of Trinity Church stood out and indicated the position of Wall Street.

My very first walk was to Battery Park, which I reached by following the Second Avenue Elevated. I loved to look at the bay and watch the ships come and go. My walks to the northern part of the city seldom took me beyond Tompkins Park or Union Square. Although, at one time, my father took us to Central Park and showed us the menagerie, the distance was a little too much to walk to the park and then back home. However, I explored a considerable part of lower Manhattan. Thus I observed the building of the Third Avenue cable-car system and saw the introduction in New York of street cars which were not drawn by horses. Only in Brooklyn had there been trolley cars, and so its baseball team was called the "Trolley Dodgers."

My exploration of New York made me acquainted with the vicinity of Brooklyn Bridge where the *World* and the *Sun* had their offices and which served as a center from which newsboys would spread over the city. After school was over in June, 1893, I decided to supplement the family income by selling newspapers in the afternoon. For some reason or other, my father and brothers were not very enthusiastic about the plan, nor did I start with adequate knowledge and capital. Moreover, I was limited by the fact that I could not work on Saturday. Still, I managed to increase my earnings to between thirty and forty cents per day, which my mother found very helpful.

In the summer of 1893 my parents finally determined on what they thought was a good investment for the money that they had saved during all the years of hard work and frugal living. My mother's instinct for trading had its last flair when she invested the proceeds that the sale of the brick house in Minsk had brought her in cutlery. She then sold it at a reasonable profit to father's employer, Mr. Riemer, and with the proceeds my parents bought the equity of a house in Brownsville which had two stores and several apartments. But the fates were against her and my father. The vendor omitted to tell my father that in addition to the first, there was also a second mortgage on the property; and the lawyer who was engaged by my brother Sam because of his prominence in the labor movement, was rather slow in discovering the fact. I did not understand how the matter was finally adjusted, but very soon after the purchase was completed, the panic of 1893 reached its height, and put a crimp in the development of Brownsville, which left the property valueless, for the tenants were poor and could not pay rent. My father and my brother Sam were soon hit, like many others, by the panic. Their employer ceased manufacturing, and after weeks of unsuccessful search for work my father and mother decided that it would be cheaper to live in an apartment in our own house in Brownsville than to pay rent in Manhattan.

Brownsville WAS at that time a Jewish boom town, whose bloom had been nipped in the bud. It had a number of newly built houses, as well as a scattering of houses belonging to old settlers. Everywhere there were vacant fields and in the direction of Canarsie, meadows, woods, brooks and marshes. Almost all of the natives, old and young, played baseball and so did the Jewish boys of my age.

At the time we moved into our house on Rockaway Avenue my father had some hope of finding work in Brooklyn or in New York, but this turned out to be illusory. He once tried his hand as a glazier, but on his first job he got into some difficulty with the owner of the house where he was to put in a window pane and the latter called him a "sheeny" and threatened to beat him up. My father came home terribly depressed, and though it was Friday night and mother tried to provide the usual Sabbath cheer, father broke down after saying *kiddush* and wept bitterly. After that he was more or less reconciled to the fact of unemployment. Nor was my brother Sam much more successful, though for several weeks during the winter he did find some work. We lived on the little rent that we were occasionally able to collect from some of the tenants, one of the stores being almost always vacant. Despite my mother's wonderful management we often arrived at the state of not having any money or food in the house. I would then walk to New York over the Brooklyn Bridge and ask my brother Tom, who had not lost his position as clerk in Kaufman's Shoe Store, for money to buy bread.

When I applied for admission to the Brownsville Public School I was asked in what grade I had been in New York, and when I told them the truth, that I had just been promoted into the grammar department, they told me that the Brooklyn schools were more advanced and that I would have to enter the last primary grade. This seemed to me an intolerable humiliation, and so I walked a considerable distance to a Brooklyn school on Chauncey Street and applied for admission to its grammar department. When the assistant principal asked me in what class I had been in New York I told her that I had been in the seventh grade, thinking that I would then be placed in the eighth and so avoid losing a grade. She, however, wanted to make sure of my qualifications and asked me what I knew in arithmetic. I told her that I could do fractions and so to my great elation she put me into the seventh grade. My elation, however, subsided when I entered the classroom. A grammar lesson was in progress, and each pupil in turn was called upon to parse certain words in sentences which were on the blackboard.

I had never before known anything of English grammar and such expressions as "third person" and "neuter gender" were so much Greek to me. But as I was almost the last one to be called on, I managed to obtain the drift of it from the constant repetition, so that when I was called upon I got by on the strength of some judicious guessing and perhaps a little prompting on the part of the boy who sat next to me. But that afternoon when I arrived home, I read through the major part of the grammar book and I had no difficulty the rest of the term.

For the first half-year I was the only Jew in the school; however I got along fairly well with my schoolmates. Two of them, Mosher and Meyer, invited me to their homes and presented me to their mothers as the brightest boy in the class. But on the way to school I had difficulties. Beyond Dean Street I passed a number of houses inhabited by Germans who delighted to set their young children on me, yelling "sheeny," and running after me as if they were going to attack me from the rear. When I turned around they would retreat, but as soon as I resumed my walk they would return to their annoying pastime. One day I became so irritated that I ran after one of the youngsters and slapped his face. At once, his older brother came out of the house and gave me a good thrashing for hitting someone below my size. But the total result was satisfactory, for the youngsters thereafter left me alone.

I encountered another annoyance: a young fellow of my size

who whenever he saw me began to abuse me and acted as if he were going to attack me, but he desisted when he saw that I was going to defend myself. Some time later he joined a group of our Jewish boys in a baseball game. I recognized him though he did not recognize me. I said nothing about the matter, but when he next met me and began to abuse me as a Jew and pretended that he was going to attack me, I went for him; I told him that I knew who he was and that he had better look out for himself. He slunk off abashed. I did not, however, get off entirely free from a serious beating. One winter day as I was coming home from school a group of boys, every one much older and bigger than myself, saw me and some one shouted, "There goes the 'sheeny'." They rushed me and pummelled me mercilessly until one of them with a little more humanity than the others called out, "That's enough! Let up on him!" My nose was bleeding and I had several marks on my face for a week or so thereafter. But I think that most of the boys were ashamed of the result and I do not recall that I was ever attacked again.

The first class to which I was admitted was in the care of a substitute teacher for some time. When a regular teacher, Mrs. Phinney, assumed control she began the day's work by asking all the boys to recite with her the Lord's Prayer. Naturally, I was not moved to protest. But when she scolded a boy and said to him, "Don't walk like a 'sheeny'," I was naturally depressed. It was bad enough that the boys called us that. It was not long, however, before Mrs. Phinney and I became very good friends. Once she asked the class, after a geography lesson on Mexico, to write a composition on that country as if we were reporters for a newspaper. I took her at her word and wrote in the first person singular, describing my impression of the country as I imagined myself travelling from the low coastal plain of Vera Cruz to the heights of Mexico City. I then went on to give some account of that city, which I remembered from the book on Cortez, and I concluded with an account of my travel on horseback from the capital city to Acapulco on the Pacific.

When Mrs. Phinney finished reading my composition she jumped out of her seat and went to the assistant principal with it. (I think that the name of the latter was Miss Jones.) They came in together and told me to stand up and turn my back to them. Perhaps they thought that I could not overhear what they were saying to each other, if I remained in this position. I was sure, however, that they said nothing evil behind my back. After that I was first in everything, and everything that I did was faultless in my teacher's eyes. I was awarded the term prize, a book on the voyages of Captain Cook.

The day before Christmas all the pupils brought presents to our teacher. As I did not have any money to buy something I took a large piece of paper and decorated it in some way and brought it to her. After she graciously thanked all the boys, she held up my gift and said, "There is one who has taken a lot of trouble and labor to express his kindly feeling and good wishes to me. I appreciate it very highly."

At the end of the term I was naturally advanced to the next grade. The teacher of this grade was Mrs. Swansea, a widow who had a young son named Burke. She was a kindly old lady, but I learned practically nothing at all in her class. It was a repetition of familiar ground.

As there was no public library in Brownsville my intellectual food was restricted to *Die Arbeiter Zeitung* and the few paper books in my brother Sam's collection. But the lack of reading matter was fully balanced by the opportunity to play with the Jewish boys of the neighborhood, far more than I had done in New York or even in Minsk. It was in Brownsville that I was introduced to the various forms of boy's baseball. Sometimes we played with only two forming a side or even with three of us playing what was known as "one o'cat" (that is, one at bat, one catching and one pitching and fielding). I played for a considerable time in the fall of 1893, and I began again early in the spring of 1894 — the first year of my life in which I had anything like a proper share of exercise and outdoor existence.

In those days the Brooklyn baseball club of the National League played in Eastern Parkway, not far from Rockaway Avenue, where we lived. I went almost every afternoon to watch part of the game through the various cracks in the fence. Once my brother Sam took me to a neighboring house from which the field was visible. At one time when there was a tie game between Brooklyn and New York and the gateman had left his post after the eighth inning several of us actually went in, and I was thrilled to see my hero, Jouett Meekin, pitch and hold the Brooklyn team down. I also saw the new sensational first baseman, Jack Doyle, play for New York. I regarded myself as a New Yorker and rooted for my home team, so that the boys called me "Giant." That year the New York team, after a bad start, rose to second place and would have beaten the pennant-winning Baltimores if the season had been longer. They certainly beat them four straight for the Temple Cup after the regular season was over, largely through the great pitching of Rusie and Meekin. After 1894 the career of the New York Giants was for years far from glorious, but I have never been able to get over my early emotional loyalty to that team, though the number of their games that I have actually witnessed probably does not exceed a dozen. But I read a good deal about the game, saw many amateur teams, and used to enjoy the close matching of wits called "inside baseball" in the days before the fast ball made home runs plentiful and made fine strategy pointless.

Early in July the position of my parents in Brownsville became untenable. To add to our difficulties mother became seriously ill as a result of giving birth to a baby daughter who died during labor. Her labor pains began earlier than was expected. I remember her cries of agony. She sent me for a doctor, but it was some time before I found a doctor to attend her. He was an old gentleman with a fine understanding of actual conditions. He attended mother for hours, and quietly accepted the one dollar which was all that we had left in the house after paying for the necessary drugs at the apothecary's. The doctor — I am sorry that I never thought of asking for his name — continued to come every day until my mother was out of immediate danger, and I think that my father managed to get together a few more dollars in order to pay him. For several weeks we had to have a practical nurse to help mother in her fight for life, and after that father attended her himself. My mother remained an invalid for a long time thereafter. This, however, did not prevent her from embarking a few months later in a new business, the operation of a soda water fountain on Staunton Street.

Naturally it was out of the question for my parents to be able to pay the taxes or the interest on either mortgage. To save the holder of the second mortgage the expense of foreclosure, my mother arranged to sell him our equity for about sixty dollars. On the basis of this pitiful remnant of a life's savings that had been regarded as a considerable fortune in Minsk, the family moved back to New York in July of 1894. My father found work as a tailor, and his wages, supplemented by my earnings as a vendor of newspapers, soon brought in just enough to keep us alive.

CHAPTER SEVEN

I DISCOVER ENGLISH LITERATURE
AND OTHER THINGS

By SEPTEMBER, 1894, the economic position of my parents was somewhat improved. My father had obtained fairly steady work and the pressure on me to leave school and go to work in his "shop" as a "basting puller" was thus eased. My father told me that he would let me go to school another year if I were able to skip a class, as I had done when we had moved to Brownsville. I was so anxious to accomplish this feat, that I thought I might as well try to jump two classes, the fifth and fourth. Thus I applied for admission to the third grade in Public School 75 on Norfolk Street. Miss Boyle, the Principal's Assistant, gave me a problem in arithmetic and I solved it very quickly, employing a method with which she was unfamiliar. Moreover, when she said that my answer was wrong, I readily proved to her that my method and result were correct. She looked at me and said, "I am not going to put you in the third grade; I shall give you a trial in the second, and I hope you will make good." I was overjoyed, for it opened the hitherto undreamed-of possibility of my going to college.

The work of the new class was unfamiliar to me and I had considerable difficulty, especially in spelling, nor was our sharply satirical teacher, Mr. Ryan, patient with me. But my fear that I might be put back proved groundless; I caught up very soon and rose to be near the head of the class. The problems in arithmetic and grammar interested me exceedingly and Mr. Ryan was really an excellent teacher. He first made military history — a large part of our school history — really intelligible to me. I also enjoyed being with classmates of my own age, background and general range of interests. They fully accepted me and several became my close friends, especially Charles Horowitz, known to his intimates as Sammie. His mother was

82

an intelligent and cultivated woman who worked hard to support her two boys. They lived in a two-room apartment, and when I visited Sammie in the evening she seemed to enjoy the conversations we held. Though he went to work and I went to college after graduation from public school, we kept up our friendship for many years, until he met a premature death when he was hit by an automobile.

One day a tall, distinguished-looking young man, somewhat older than the rest of us, was brought into our classroom with the explanation that he was a foreign student who would be able to go along with the class once he mastered the English language. Mr. Ryan asked Ben Ridgik and myself to assist the newcomer, and we gladly did that. This brought me frequently to his home. The young man was Julius Greenstone, who was already a distinguished Talmudic scholar, and his subsequent career amply conformed to his early promise.

A classmate who evoked a strange admiration from me was named Brown — an unusual name for a Jew in those days. He had a remarkably impassive face and a flow of satirical phrases that made him unapproachable, though his one intimate companion, Benjamin Helprin, was a good friend of mine. Yet, whenever I was doubtful of whether a certain course of conduct was proper or not, I asked myself, would Brown do it?

At the end of the first term, about a dozen of us were promoted to the graduating class which was preparing for college. The other graduating class was supposed to prepare for a commercial career. In those days the public schools had a peculiar arrangement: promotions were generally made at the end of January and June, but graduation from school took place only on the latter date. When we were promoted to the class of Mr. Adams, who was preparing students for the college entrance examinations, half of the term's work had already been completed. Mr. Adams told us that he was going on with his regular schedule, and could not give us any special attention, and that we should do our best to catch up with the class. Should we, however, make the grade, we would be eligible to take the entrance examinations to the City College. Only then did I realize how fortunate I was to have been admitted to the second grade in September. If I had spent a year in the third and second, it would have required another year before I could have taken the examinations.

The work in the new class did not prove very difficult. And in most of the written examinations I came out either first or second, to the great surprise of Mr. Adams, who did not like the idea that we, who had not received his training, should excel those who had had that advantage. I must confess that I was not very agreeable. I was inattentive to his rather long monologues and often preferred to read some good book while he was eloquently rehashing his experience with the Red River Expedition during the Civil War. Once, in the midst of one of his orations, he caught me reading Emerson's essay on "Self-Reliance." He chased me around the room with his stick until he became somewhat winded. Thereupon he demoted me to the foot of the class, which made me much more comfortable. There I could read more freely and without his frequent interruptions, which I considered as irrelevancies.

Towards the end of the term we went up to the City College to take our entrance examinations. I thought I did fairly well in arithmetic, history, geography and drawing, but during the grammar examination I got into a nervous stew. I wrote, not on both sides of the paper, but on what I supposed to be the wrong side of the paper. When I discovered my mistake, I hurriedly began to rewrite the whole thing. Naturally I could not finish and I was certain that I had failed. During the two weeks or so before the results of the examinations were announced, I was downcast and stayed awake at night, forming all sorts of plans as to how I might continue my education. I thought of taking the Regents' examinations to qualify for some professional school. I was of the opinion that his work as a tailor had suppressed my brother Sam's finer abilities and I was determined to struggle against a similar fate. On the afternoon when Mr. Adams was to inform us of the results of the examination, I came to school in a resigned mood. To my utter amazement Mr. Adams announced that "the highest mark was attained by Morris Cohen, who is thus entitled to the Adams gold medal." He asked me to come up and be congratulated. I looked sheepish; I could hardly believe that this was true. Even when I went home I could not realize that I had actually passed. My mother at that time was bed-ridden, and when I told her that I had passed the examination and was thus admitted to college, a flood of tears came into her eyes. She was not at all interested in the fact that I had received the gold medal. It was only later that I appreciated her discriminating wisdom. The medal made little subsequent difference, except that occasionally we were able to borrow a few dollars on it. However, my admittance to college did make a tremendous difference. When one of my aunts remonstrated with my mother, "You cannot afford to send your boy to college," she replied, "If need be I'll go out as a washerwoman and scrub floors so that my Morris can have a college education." For people who had all their lives been scrupulously careful not to incur any expense which could possibly be avoided, this was a lavish luxury. But by a rare good fortune it proved the best investment that my parents ever made.

The academic year of 1894-95 marked not only the completion of my school career and entrance into college, but also my arrival at what may be called mature manhood. It was one of great intellectual as well as physical awakening. Through books like Hilliard's *Sixth Reader* I became acquainted with great masterpieces of English and American literature and became interested not only in classic stories and novels, but in essays, histories, and lyric, as well as narrative, poetry. In the grammar book which we used, Gould Brown's, there was a large number of quotations from the classics and they stimulated my interest in the great poets. I cannot say that I then appreciated the real beauties of Shelley or Keats — that came later; but I read the narrative poems of Scott and Byron, and many of the shorter lyrics of Wordsworth and others in Palgrave's *Golden Treasury*. Among the essays were many of Macaulay's and Carlyle's, some of Addison's and Emerson's. I am sure that at that time I did not understand fully the mood which binds together Emerson's disparate, atomic sentences. But at the end of the year I was thrilled to read Plato's shorter dialogues and the first two books of the *Republic*. The years since have convinced me that they can be appreciated by, and serve as proper food for, ordinarily intelligent young people of fifteen. Perhaps they gave me an undue taste for Socratic questioning, but on the whole I think it was unfortunate that my reading of Plato was interrupted and not resumed until five years later.

The book, however, which exercised the most practical influence on me at the time was Franklin's autobiography. The notion of keeping a check on yourself through an account of your thinking in a diary appealed to my critical bent and to my introspective mood. I soon developed the habit of jotting down the day's reflections on scraps of paper — I did not think I could afford to buy a diary or notebook for the purpose. Franklin's diary was an acknowledged model in some of my earliest jottings. On October 26, 1897, for example, I wrote:

The reason that few become great writers by study and imitation of the classics, is because every man has a certain character and can express himself naturally only in that style. To perfect that style, he must study one like it, and we can seldom find a writer of the same spirit as we are. Franklin, for example, struck upon the right plan in imitating the Spectator, but any one of an impassioned nature would do well to study Byron or Shelley, in order to improve his style. Thus, for an unimpassioned nature Swift's or Defoe's seem to be well adapted. The right mixture of different elements, Macaulay, Irving and Swift, might produce something more universal.

In those days after I was promoted to Mr. Adams' class I heard about a literary society to which some of the members of the commercial and college preparatory classes belonged. The fact that my marks on examinations were the highest in the class gave me some standing, and so I asked some one to propose my admission. An investigating committee, of which the chairman was Isador M. Levy (who was not in my class), interviewed me and told me that though they heard that I was a good student, I would not fit in with the plan of the club. This report aroused indignation at the next meeting of the society and the president, B. Helprin, insisted on a re-hearing. Exercising his right as an *ex officio* member of the committee, he was present at the re-hearing and accordingly I was admitted. The Young Men's Benevolent Society allowed us to meet on Sunday nights in the basement of its building on Attorney Street.

At that time there was a large number of such literary clubs on the East Side, generally named after some well-known poet or writer such as Longfellow, Tennyson, Emerson, Irving and the like. The program of the meetings usually bore the following pattern: first, a recitation of a poem or oratorical selection; second, a debate on a topic assigned by the Executive Committee; third, a reading of the club journal in which the literary efforts of the members were contained; fourth, a criticism of the entire proceedings by an official critic. If a schoolteacher or another older person was present, he naturally performed that function; otherwise some outstanding member of the club took over this function. In the Bryant Literary Society,

Charles Cohen, later famous as Charles A. Cowen of the Zionist movement, generally acted in that capacity.

The tenure of the officers lasted three months, and immediately after my admission campaigning for the next election began. The boys were initiated in the minutiae of parliamentary procedure as described in *Cushing's Manual,* and at times the amount of noise was deafening, even though the president had the right to fine members for not behaving properly.

At the second meeting which I attended I was assigned to be one of the participants in a debate. The question involved was "Whether the Whipping Post Should Be Introduced in the State of Delaware?" I have forgotten to which side I had been assigned. All I remember is that I read some articles in the *North American Review* and other periodicals, and prepared so thoroughly that when I began to speak I soon became dizzy and I had to sit down without finishing my argument. Charles Cohen, the critic, who, I later found out, was the one who instigated the opposition to my admission, was handsomely kind in referring to this incident. This encouraged me and at the very next meeting when one of the debaters was absent I volunteered to take his place and won the decision of the judges. The question was whether General Hull was justified in surrendering Fort Dearborn to the British in the War of 1812, and though I made no special preparation, my knowledge of the history of the case carried the day. Several months later, at the festive annual meeting, I was chosen by the club as one of their star debaters, on the question of the consolidation of Brooklyn and Old New York.

Charles Cohen and I became very close friends for a time, and I used to go to his home, where I enjoyed talking to his Americanized but piously learned father and to his sisters, especially the youngest one, whom I thought very handsome. As far as I recall she was the only girl of my age to whom I spoke in those days and for a long time afterwards.

When I became a member of the Executive Committee, I proposed that we equip ourselves with a library. The moneys to be expended came from the accumulated funds of the Society resulting from the receipt of fines and dues. Charles Cohen and I spent a good deal of time together discussing the various books which we planned to buy if we could get them cheap enough. After we were graduated from Public School 75, he obtained a position as an office boy in a firm headed by Isaac Fromme, and later he became a protégé of Richard Walling. I kept on, in vain, answering advertisements in the "Help Wanted" ads of *The New York World.*

IN SEPTEMBER, 1895, I entered the college which was to nurture and sustain me through the major part of my life. City College then, as in later years, offered a frugal though nourishing intellectual diet. Since the College was free, attendance brought no social prestige. Since admission was not limited by race, class, creed, or social status, it had to be limited by rigorous scholastic standards. Social life, sports, social polish, and the other superficial attractions of American college life were neglected. The consequence was that those to whom these extracurricular goals mattered found their way to other more congenial colleges and universities. Those who chose City College did so only because its courses seemed to offer a key to a wider intellectual world. It was thus the student body rather than the faculty that created the intellectual tone of the College.

In its earlier years the College student body was a fair cross section of the population of New York City. This meant that New Yorkers of many races and creeds could learn to understand each other in the formative years of college life. Close friendships that developed between Irish Catholic and Jewish boys at the College helped to make New York a civilized place to live in as these boys acceded to positions of civic leadership in the community.

In my undergraduate years, and even more in later decades, an increasing proportion of the students was Jewish, many of them foreign-born, and very many of the others children of foreign-born parents. Many of us, therefore, were familiar with what are today provincially called "un-American" ideas. Certainly, a large part of the student body of the College has always been peculiarly open-minded and critical towards the accepted commonplaces of the complacent. These

89

students came prepared to weigh and consider new, as well as old, ideas, and their intellectual eagerness was encouraged rather than restrained by home conditions.

It was hard for a teacher who was not a master of his subject to survive this sort of intellectual climate, but many did. In this, worthy pedagogues and scholastic drill masters were protected by a tradition of military discipline which had been fixed upon the college by its first two presidents, both West Pointers — Dr. Horace Webster and General Alexander S. Webb. Rigid discipline and pursuit of marks were more important to most of the teaching staff than love of learning. But what the professors lacked in love of learning, the student body made up. There was no need to preach to us the importance and value of scholarship, or to instill in our hearts a love of learning. That was why we were there. There was nothing else that we could hope to get out of the College. The intellectual companionship of my fellow students thus came to mean a great deal to me.

Because the College made no effort to impose a single pattern of social behavior upon its graduates, its militarism was not tainted by totalitarianism. Many of its graduates have become rabbis, others have become Christian ministers, communist leaders, financiers, and distinguished statesmen and jurists. The College thus, despite the mediocrity of its teaching staff in those days, embodied what has always seemed to me the essence of liberal education as opposed to dogmatic indoctrination. I do not know of any charge that has been brought against our Jewish boys of the City College that could not have been brought against me personally, at the comparable age, and yet the College was willing to ignore or forgive my defects in the social graces, as well as the unorthodoxy of many of my views. That the College tolerated me became, to me, a symbol of liberalism in education. It gave me a sound education in mathematics, languages, and the natural sciences and thus opened the gates to a wider intellectual world than I had dreamed of.

The five-year course in those days combined what is now considered high school and college work; science, mathematics, languages and history made up the substance of the curriculum.

In my first, or as it was then called subfreshman, year at City College I studied geometry and algebra with Reynolds, Timme, Veiller and Galston, French with Augé, English with Turner and Perrin, anatomy with Meighan, botany with Sickles, electricity and magnetism with Doremus, and drawing with O'Brien. The best teacher I had this year was Meighan, my anatomy teacher, who helped me to realize what I had never before considered particularly important, namely that I had a body and would, in all probability, never have another one. I cannot say that I immediately grasped all the implications of this fact, but they came to me forcibly enough in later years. My English teacher, Perrin, under whom I studied for three years, was a soft-spoken gentleman, whose reading of Matthew Arnold's "Sohrab and Rustum" left an impression that has not faded these many years.

In the course of my subfreshman year and during the following summer, I made up for the lack of any history course in my curriculum by reading various books on history, including Mommsen, Gibbon, and Green's *History of the English People*. Soon after my entrance into college my father found that he could not make a living on the wages that he was receiving and he conceived the idea of setting up a cigar and soda water stand in the pool room that my brother Sam had opened. I was his assistant, outside of college hours. When I was not making sales or cleaning up I would read Gibbon's *Decline and Fall of the Roman Empire* and this continued for a little over a year. I believe that Gibbon made a more enduring impression on my thinking than any of the books I read in my courses. Other books that I devoured during the academic year 1895-96 were Milman's *Notes on Roman History*, Freeman's *Ten Great Religions* and the volumes of the "University Extension Series," which I found at the Astor Library. I also did some reading in Plato, but it was only four years later that I really came to grips with Plato's thinking.

During my second, or freshman year, I continued my study of mathematics with Parmly, of French with Fabregou, and of English with Perrin. I also began the study of German with Kost, and took courses in descriptive geometry with Sigel and Thomas, in zoology with Stratford, and in history with Meighan and Morse. Again, Meighan was the best teacher I had. Of all the textbooks I read at City College Meyer's *General History* probably influenced me the most. Meyer brought a fine liberal spirit and gave us a gist of world affairs. Some of his details I later learned to have been mythical, but the substance of his book nourished the understanding.

After a summer spent at my father's newspaper stand on Houston Street, I returned to college in September, 1897, for a sophomore year marked with courses in mathematics with Legras, logic with Galston, French with Fabregou, German with Ilgen, and history with Johnston, who particularly impressed me with his competence. The course in French literature particularly stands out in my memory. Professor Fabregou somehow managed to combine the enthusiasm of youth with the courteous dignity of an older generation, in his role of host at an intellectual banquet. The stirring poetry of Racine and Corneille, the incisive human irony of Molière, the artful prose of Voltaire, and the grandeur of the poetry of Victor Hugo came to us through a mind freshly appreciative of the great things of life, which is the condition of vital teaching. Another class that I have not forgotten was the class in logic. It was my first course in philosophy. Though it did not make very much of an impression at the time (except for the fact that I won the Ward Medal in Logic) it stirred up doubts and questions that later acquired an urgency of their own. At the time, I remember, I was led to read Mill's *Logic*. A few months earlier I had heard Edward King give a talk on John Stuart Mill and the Radical Club, which made a great impression on me, because it showed how general ideas on logic and reason tied in with issues of social reform in which I was coming to be deeply immersed. I found Mill's *Logic* quite unpersuasive, and went on to read some of the philosophical writings of Carus, Watson, Comte, Spencer, and Palmer. In between my college classes and my outside reading I managed to earn a little money by tutoring.

My junior year at City College, 1898-99, was, for me, college at its best. Perhaps I had better teachers in that year than I had had in earlier years. Perhaps it was just that I was more mature and more at home in English literature, after six years' residence in this country. At any rate my ego was gratified by the golden compliments paid me by my German teacher, Werner, and by the fact that at the close of my mathematics course with Mason I was awarded the Belden Medal in Mathematics. The course I had with Mott in English made a deep impression. Though he was inclined to be abstract, he taught us to enjoy the quest for the precise meaning that a poet puts into his lines and to be satisfied with nothing short of that in our reading. Other courses I took included economics with Galston, American history with Johnston, and mechanics and acoustics with Compton. The year's one disappointment was my failure to win the editorship of *The College Review*.

City College had no library to speak of, in those days, but I began to frequent the library of Columbia University, and there I found ample opportunity to return to the interest in ancient thought which my grandfather had nurtured in my boyhood days. I read voraciously in Hebrew history and the higher criticism of the Bible, in anthropology, prehistory, and the history of Egypt and Assyrian Babylonia. My philosophical reading was directed particularly to the pre-Socratics, and I read the guide books and translations with avidity. Plato's *Parmenides* and Aristotle's *Metaphysics* were tough fare for a philosophical babe, but I tackled them resolutely, along with Bernheim, Pomeroy, Barth's *Die Philosophie der Geschichte als Soziologie*, and Hegel's *Encyklopädie*.

My last year at the College, 1899-1900, did not make a deep impression on my intellectual development. I ploughed through my courses: pedagogy with Duggan, Spanish with Baralt and Fuentes, chemistry with Doremus and Friedburg, astronomy with Compton, geology with Stratford, aesthetics with Woolf, and psychology with McNulty. My intellectual interests were, by the time I had reached my senior year, pretty thoroughly tied to my work at the Educational Alliance, under the leadership of Thomas Davidson, and to the other extracurricular activities, socialist and philosophical, that were in the air for the men and women of my age.

CHAPTER NINE

BEYOND COLLEGE WALLS

T HE LIFE OF THE EAST SIDE in the days of my adolescence was characterized by a feverish intensity of intellectual life and a peculiar restlessness. We had no patience with the prevailing evils and corruptions of the day. Our eagerness to help usher in a better social order was well-nigh desperate and our anxiety about our own achievements and shortcomings in this endeavor was almost morbid. In all this we reflected not only the traditional current of European Jewish life, with its emphasis upon intellectual values, but also the impact of the New World on eyes that could see its problems and potentialities with the fresh vision generally ascribed to foreign visitors or to the "man from Mars."

The eastern Jewish immigrants to this country in the 1890's had, for the most part, been subjected to a highly rigorous training along pietistic lines. Ten hours or more of study day after day took up the childhood of every self-respecting eastern Jewish boy. Fortunate were those who were permitted to continue this routine as students of the Talmud, as teachers or as rabbis for the rest of their lives. Those not so fortunate were expected to devote the same long hours and endless energies to the mastering of some trade or business. But even those who were not permitted to devote their adult years primarily to learning were expected to devote a considerable portion of their time to reading, prayer, and argument, carried on in a sacred language and dealing largely with a totally foreign environment.

The migration to the New World broke the old patterns. The old limitations on the proper subjects of intellectual inquiry and discussion were removed, but the intellectual passion, the tradition of study, the high value which the family circle put upon learning and

94

skill continued. Parents continued to grind their own lives to the bone in order to make it possible for their children to achieve some intellectual distinction or skill that might be considered a New World substitute for the Talmudic learning which represented the highest achievement in the old environment. So it was that many of the first generation and many more of the second, despite the difficulties of a new environment and a strange language, brought to the tasks which the New World presented a force that was more than the force of any single individual. It was as if a great dam had broken and the force of water accumulated over many years had been let loose. This mighty force permeated every nook and corner of human endeavor.

Opinions may differ as to the worth of many of the enterprises to which this force was directed. The second generation had its boxers, gamblers and shyster lawyers, as well as great judges, teachers and scientists. Doctors, movie magnates, writers, merchants, philanthropists, communists or defenders of corporate wealth all showed an intensity that must have seemed a bit outlandish to the more comfortable and easy-going segments of the American population. Perhaps something of the same intensity characterized earlier American generations disciplined under the hard patterns of Puritan, Quaker or Mormon protests against the life of ease and comfort.

This intensity of life, this striving for perfection in diverse fields, surrounded me and the men and women of my generation at the turn of the century, in City College and in the various clubs, circles and societies that dotted our intellectual horizons.

The habit of organizing groups of kindred spirits about some teacher or moral leader, for the purpose of solving the world's problems, goes very far back in the Hebraic tradition. The spirit that infused our various groups and societies was expressed with particular clarity in a letter of Thomas Davidson's:

There is nothing that the world of to-day needs so much as a new order of social relations, a new feeling between man and man. We may talk and teach as long as we like, but until we have a new society with ideal relations and aims we have accomplished very little. All great world movements begin with a little knot of people, who, in their individual lives, and in their relations to each other, realize the ideal that is to be. To live truth is better than to utter it. Isaiah would have prophesied in vain, had he not gathered round him a little band of disciples who lived according to his ideal. . . Again, what would the teachings of Jesus have amounted to had he not collected a body of disciples, who made it their life-aim to put his teachings into practice. . . .

You will perhaps think I am laying out a mighty task for you, a task far above your powers and aspirations; but it is not so. Every great change in individual and social conditions — and we are on the verge of such a change — begins small, among simple earnest people, face to face with the facts of life. Ask yourselves seriously, "Why should not the coming change begin with us?" And you will find that there is no reason why the new world, the world of righteousness, kindliness and enlightenment for which we are all longing and toiling, may not date from us as well as from any-body. A little knot of earnest Jews has turned the world upside down before now. Why may not the same thing — nay a far better thing — happen in your day and among you? Have you forgotten the old promise made to Abraham: "In thy seed shall all the nations of the earth be blessed"?

This was the spirit in which, even before Davidson came among us, we organized in our literary, socialist, and philosophical clubs and circles. After the demise of the Bryant Literary Society, in the summer of 1896, I became involved for a year or so in another literary society beginning in the spring of 1897. This we called the Young Men's Literary Society. Among its members were Louis Lande, Rosen, Dave Klein, Friedman, Leo Jacobs, Schiff, Ben Ridgik, Shlivek, and Rosen-blatt, our leader and critic. Mr. Isaac Spectorsky, the Superintendent of the Educational Alliance, was also interested in the Comte Synthetic Circle, an organization led by Edward King. He proposed that our Young Men's Literary Society should join the latter organization. The move was not popular, but I was the only one who had the courage (or lack of chivalry) to voice an objection, and my objection prevailed. This was, of course, before I met Mary Ryshpan and her two sisters, Bertha and Sarah, who were members of the Comte Synthetic Circle and who, along with Leonora O'Reilly, an ardent Irish Republican and a founder of the Women's Trade Union League, were its most active sponsors.

The public meetings of our Young Men's Literary Society, and my activities as editor of its journal were not marked by enthusiasm for Mark Hanna and the Republican Party, which had just succeeded in electing McKinley President. The Bryan campaign in the summer and autumn of 1896 had brought me face to face with the issues of American politics. I had been interested in the socialist movement, perhaps because the Jewish Socialist weekly, *Die Arbeiter Zeitung*, was the most intelligent newspaper that I could find. Bryan, though not a socialist, appeared to me as a great liberating force, especially after McKinley became President in the spring of 1897. During the winter of 1896-97, I helped to run a young workingmen's class on Market Street as part of my work in Daniel de Leon's Socialist Labor Party. During the election campaign of 1897, when Henry George was running for Mayor of New York, I was active in the campaign of Daniel de Leon, who was running for assemblyman in the district in which I lived. Our hopes that he might become the first Socialist representative in the New York State Legislature were not realized. On election night, I met Eugene Schoen and we decided to organize a Marx Circle. Louis Roth, Willie Hirsch, Harry Simmons, Abe Kovar, Frank Silverman, Simon Frucht, Sidney Bernstein, Jimmie Alman, Abramson (our first "editor"), and a few other congenial friends met at the Henry Street Settlement and various other meeting places to read and argue about Marx's *Das Kapital*, *Merrie England* and other socialist classics.

Though I had opposed joining with the Comte Synthetic Circle, I soon found myself irresistibly drawn to it. This society was organized around the personality of Edward King, whose lecture on Mill had so impressed me. I attended a good many of its meetings during the year 1898, and it was there that I came to know one whose aspirations and hopes were so close to mine that we soon became companions for life.

Mary Ryshpan was in the forefront of the struggle of those who, growing to young womanhood amidst the intellectual currents of the immigrant East Side, helped to break the Jewish tradition that had excluded women from full participation in the highest intellectual pursuits. Throughout her life she was an ardent admirer of George Eliot, whom she took as her model of womanly courage. Completely selfless in her relations with others for whom she sought to make real the opportunities of the New World, she was a teacher, guide and protector to a host of relatives and friends. In those days it was not usual for Jewish girls to go to college, and she saw to it that her advantage in this respect did not remain a personal one but was shared with all for whom she could help to open the gates of a wider and richer intellectual world.

This indestructible urge which she and I and so many of our mutual friends had, to possess for ourselves the fruits of the Age of Reason, dominated all our activities. Even in the field of social reform our socialism was, above all, not a seeking for better food or drink or clothing or even homes for ourselves and our less fortunate fellows. It was a protest against economic conditions which denied to so many of us, and to our less fortunate brothers and sisters, access to the riches of the spirit. Those who toiled twelve hours a day, month after month, from childhood to old age, were deprived of all the things that made human life worth living. And so our socialist activity, though often cast in Marx's materialistic terms, was directed primarily to the conquest and democratization of the things of the spirit.

The world that we faced on the East Side at the turn of the century presented a series of heartbreaking dilemmas. To the extent that we made the world of science and enlightenment a part of ourselves, we were inevitably torn from the traditions of narrow Orthodoxy. For some two thousand years our people had clung to their faith under the pressure of continual persecution. But now, for us at least, the walls of the ghetto had been removed. We learned that all non-Jews were not mere soulless heathens. We found that the Jews had not been the only conservators of wisdom and civilization. And having been immersed in the literature of science we called upon the old religion to justify itself on the basis of modern science and culture. But the old generation was not in a position to say how this could be done. With all respect for our old Orthodoxy, it would not be honest to deny that it harbored a great deal of superstition — indeed, who is free from superstition? But because this superstition was regarded as an integral part of Judaism, because no distinction was drawn between ritual and religious convictions and feelings, the very word "religion" came to be discredited by many liberal people — who, whatever might be said about their errors, at least attempted to think for themselves.

What ensued was a struggle between the old and new ideals, resulting in a conflict between the older and younger generations fraught with heart-rending consequences. Homes ceased to be places of peace and in the ensuing discord much of the proverbial strength of the Jewish family was lost. As the home ceased to be the center of interests, the unity of life, nurtured by pride in the achievements of one's forebears and by parental pride in the achievements of children, was broken. There was scarcely a Jewish home on the East Side that was free from this friction between parents and children. This explosive tension made it possible for the same family to produce saints and sinners, philosophers and gunmen.

We might, if we could, mask our unorthodox ideas, and use the word "God," with Spinoza, to mean what scientists call the system of nature, or, by proper verbal camouflage, otherwise conceal our departures from the old, pious outlook upon the universe. Every impulse of filial piety, of gratitude to the parents who had made it possible for us to enjoy the fruits of the world of science, drove us to this hypocrisy. But to the extent that we succumbed, we could not preserve the integrity of the intellect and the spirit. And this meant that young men and women were forced to play the hypocrite at the very dawn of their moral sense. No wonder that the development of religious sentiment was stunted among us and that cynicism or pessimism came so often to displace the natural idealism of youth.

However we resolved this dilemma, and whatever concessions we made to the old ritual, the loss of the religious faiths which had sustained our parents through so many generations of suffering left a void in our lives which we tried with every fiber of our beings to fill in one way or another. All our organizations and circles were attempts to fill this void. None of these attempts amounted to very much in the long run until the advent among us of a wandering Scottish philosopher who had been the spiritual inspiration, in England, of the Fellowship of the New Life and its more activist offshoot, the Fabian Society, as well as one of the founders of the Aristotelian Society, and who was destined to give to many of us on the East Side the same kind of inspiration that he had given to men and women like Havelock Ellis, Sidney and Beatrice Webb, and Edward Carpenter.

BOOK THREE

THE EDUCATION OF THE WAGE EARNER
(1898-1900)

CHAPTER TEN

MY FIRST MEETING WITH DAVIDSON

ONE DAY IN THE FALL of 1898, a member of the Marx Circle reported that a certain Professor Davidson was giving a course of lectures at the Educational Alliance in which he was defending the principle of individualism. I remarked that that was an old story. But Frank Silverman of our Marx Circle and several others insisted that there was something new in Davidson's point of view. Such an approach implied a challenge to socialism and so, confident of the failure of the individualistic philosophy from the days of Martin Luther to those of Herbert Spencer, some of us thought it would be a good idea to go to heckle the professor. Accordingly, I went to hear him speak on "The Educational Problem Which the Nineteenth Century Hands on to the Twentieth." I was not favorably impressed with his gospel of salvation by education, which to me meant preaching. I was convinced that no substantial improvement of our human lot was possible without a radical change in our economic setup. It was apparent to me that the lecturer did not have any program of social action and was unsympathetic to any solution or procedure except that of ethical exhortation as a way of removing social evils. Completely convinced of my own premises, I took advantage of the question period following the lecture to heckle the speaker, which I continued to do in later lectures, on all possible and many impossible occasions. To my surprise Davidson did not resent my views or my manners but responded to my attacks in the friendliest way.

At the conclusion of this first lecture, a young man — the ill-fated Julius Fein — arose and stated that it was quite proper for the lecturer to solve all problems through the means of education, but how were people, such as he, who had to work every day, to obtain this education? Thereupon Davidson offered to come down and conduct a class one evening every week.

Such a class was arranged, and it began early in January, 1899, meeting every Saturday night. I was not interested. But I kept hearing, especially from Leonard Cohen, whom I had met through my friend and classmate Joseph Kahn, that this class was an unusually large and enthusiastic one, and that Davidson was constantly attacking socialism. I thought, therefore, that I ought to come around and try to upset some of his arguments. On my first appearance in the class, John L. Elliot of the Ethical Culture Society substituted for Davidson, as the latter was ill. Elliot spoke of the inadequacy of nature to support a population such as that of India, and his words convinced me all the more that the class was in need of a sound Marxian interpretation of the relation between man and nature.

Later, when Davidson had recovered and was able to conduct the class in his informal way of question and comment, I came and participated in the discussions. I found him to be very interesting because of the multitude of topics and personalities that he referred to. Some of his erudition opened up new fields to me, such as the higher criticism of the Bible. I remember my amazement when I heard him refer to "my friend, William James." I could not have been more impressed if I had heard him refer to Kant or Napoleon. William James, whose *Will to Believe* I had read in part, was to me one of the Olympians, and it appeared almost unbelievable that an actual mortal should be on terms of familiarity with him.

After one of the meetings, Davidson came over to me and said, putting his hand in a friendly way on my shoulder, "You have a fine mind. You ought to cultivate it." I was startled. It was years since anyone had paid me such a compliment. I asked, "What makes you think so?" And he said, "I am an old schoolmaster and I have never met anyone whose eyes are as far apart as yours who did not have a good mind." The remark pleased me more than I realized at that time. I told him that I was going to college and was trying my best to learn what the world was all about. Thereupon he invited me to visit him at his rooms on Stuyvesant Square. I decided to do so, but through shyness or other reasons I delayed my visit. One day as I was crossing Stuyvesant Square on my way homeward from college, Davidson met me and greeted me most cordially. He picked up the book I was carrying, Mill's *Political Economy*, and commented interestingly on the fine personality of Mill and on the limitations of political economy generally and of Mill's in particular. Walking thus together we went up to his rooms on Stuyvesant Square, where he was living with Sydney Clarke, and continued the conversation, which I enjoyed immensely. Davidson inquired with such genuine solicitude about my circumstances that I was greatly touched, and I came to the next meeting of the class with the ardor of a young swain going to see his inamorata.

When Davidson informed the class that he was leaving for his summer home in the Adirondacks, I felt as if I had lost something. At the end of the meeting he invited the members of the class to visit him in his place in the Adirondacks, Glenmore, where he was going to finish his *History of Education* and to conduct his summer school. The fare to and from the Adirondacks was prohibitive as far as I was concerned, and I did not dare to think of accepting his invitation.

I decided, however, to make Davidson my confidant in regard to the specific worries which were troubling me and thus there began a correspondence between us which, though it lasted only through the months of May and June, 1899, caused a transformation in my life plans. I was then very much perplexed about my future. My income from private lessons was small and my father's wages were not sufficient to justify me in accepting his support, while my mother's health was getting progressively worse. The Socialist movement was going on the rocks, because of De Leon's bitter determination to have no one in the Socialist Labor Party who was not his "yes-man." Furthermore, my excessively introspective life developed within me a consciousness of personal failure, especially in regard to strength of will.

There were few bright spots or joyous occasions in my life. I was therefore glad to start a general correspondence with Davidson and was almost intoxicated with joy at the warmth of his replies. To me, they were the most marvellous letters I had ever read. It has been one of the regrets of my life that the correspondence was destroyed through the stupidity of someone in whose custody they were temporarily placed. But some extracts from the letters to me, omitting the personal touches, were copied by my wife for Knight's *Memorials of Thomas Davidson*.

My father was somewhat puzzled by the way in which I became engrossed whenever I would receive Davidson's weekly letter, and to satisfy his natural curiosity he had one of his employers, Mr. Blitz, read one of the letters to him. At first I resented the entire episode, but I was glad when I realized that it had increased the respect in which my father was held by his co-workers in the "shop," and how my mother was pleased when Mr. Blitz invited my father to bring me to the "shop" so that he might talk with me.

In his last letter Davidson invited me to be his summer guest at Glenmore. He overcame my scruples and pride by offering maintenance in return for certain services to his school. So on the first of July, after my school examinations were over, my mother tied up a few of my belongings in a sheet and I met a Mr. William Warren, a neighbor of Davidson's, who was to take me to Glenmore. Our train left Grand Central Station in the evening and for the first time in my life I saw a sleeping car. The Negro porter who made up my upper berth had the name Wagner on his uniform and I found out only later that it was the name of the company which operated the sleeping cars for the New York Central. The porter awakened us a few minutes past four and told me to go into the smoking room. I put on my clothes and I found several men dressing in the smoking room. I was ashamed to make my toilet in their presence and I, therefore, went into the dressing room at the other end of the car and was embarrassed to see a woman coming toward the cubicle just as I was leaving.

Mr. Warren was met on arrival at the station by a coach and four. He took the reins and we sped along the twenty miles from Westport to Glenmore. On the way we stopped just long enough to build a fire and make some tea to go with the sandwiches Mr. Warren had provided. Upon our return to the coach I climbed in rather clumsily and my shoes touched some bags. Mr. Warren's annoyance was definitely audible.

When we arrived at Glenmore, the eight o'clock breakfast bell rang. Davidson greeted Mr. Warren while I sat in the carriage, not knowing what to do next. But it was not long before he cordially invited me to step out and greeted me most affectionately. The breakfast of oatmeal and cream, bacon and eggs and coffee was a novel one to me.

But even more novel was the kind of company. So far as I recollect, there were only a small number of ladies. I recall Mrs. Ruutz-Rees, Miss Kent, Mrs. Neumann, and a Mrs. Kilpatrick with her two children Kenneth and Marjorie. Before the meal and after, Davidson read a passage from Saussaye's *History of Religion*. Davidson's conversation was most fascinating. I recall his referring to the fact that Faust's streaks of sentimentalism always came before his most vile acts. I recall too his quoting the line from Hay's Song of Kilvani ("The Law of Death"): *"The living are few, the dead are many."*

CHAPTER ELEVEN

THE SUMMER OF 1899 AT GLENMORE

J ULY AND AUGUST at Glenmore gave me my first taste of what a traveler in the desert of life feels when he first comes to a green oasis. It was in every way joyful and inspiring. The sheer physical comforts were beyond my expectations. After a few days in the house which was located near the dining and lecture hall, I moved to a tent on the hill adjacent to the one on which Davidson's house was located. Wood-chopping and mountain-climbing with occasional bathing in the near-by Gulf Brook constituted a routine of which I had never before had any idea. The result was that when I returned to the city in September, hardly anyone who knew me refrained from remarking how well I looked. But it was the intellectual and emotional stimulus which I received from Davidson that was important. The tie between us grew as the summer advanced and our relation became like that of an affectionate father and son. He insisted on my studying Latin, which I did quite unwillingly, but I found great joy in reading Hume's *Treatise on Human Nature,* after which I began Kant's *Critique of Pure Reason.* Although Davidson was, as the historian Höffding described him in a letter to me, one of the most beautiful figures in modern philosophy, he did not have a well-disciplined philosophic mind, as evidenced by the failure of his books to impress a scholarly world.

Davidson had little patience with purely abstract speculation. He felt so passionately what he believed to be the truth that he had no patience with what seemed to be erroneous. Hence I got little help from him in the study of Kant and Hume. The excessive terms of praise with which he spoke of my philosophic equipment naturally aroused my enthusiasm, but did not enrich my philosophic understanding. His general conversation was full of recondite and interesting information which opened up new vistas for me. Early in August he allowed me to give a lecture on "Common Sense, Science and Philosophy." It was the fulfillment of an ardent, youthful ambition, and his words of praise after its delivery lifted me to the seventh heaven.

Thomas Davidson was a man of contagious enthusiasm. His love of Scottish song and poetry, of fireplace conversation and the rugged scenery of the Adirondacks woke echoes in my heart that come down through the years. But the enthusiasm of Davidson that influenced me most was the dream of an Encyclopedia of Philosophy that should do for the culture of the twentieth century what the Brothers of Sincerity did for the tenth, and Diderot and d'Alembert did for the eighteenth. This dream has dominated my whole intellectual life. All my reading somehow or other gets fitted into that scheme. And though I was never to realize that youthful ambition, it has given form to all of my fragmentary efforts at the statement of a philosophical position adequate to the understanding of the problems of modern civilization.

Apart from Davidson's own influence, Glenmore brought me the stimulating companionship of Wilmon Sheldon, who had just received his doctorate at Harvard and gave some lectures for Davidson. Especially stimulating was William T. Harris, who took a kindly interest in me, and whose lectures I found full of meat. In Davidson's library there was a set of the *Journal of Speculative Philosophy*, and I read some of the articles in it with great avidity. In addition, I discovered Tennyson as a poet. I had read a few of his selections in the classroom at college, but in the quiet of Glenmore I was able to read his longer poems with sufficient attention to appreciate their scope. I have never felt that Tennyson belonged to the first line of the world's great poets and many of his sentiments offended me, but I have always felt that only blindness or insensitivity can explain the persistent attempt to deny the obvious fact that there is great poetry in his work.

CHAPTER TWELVE

A BREADWINNERS' COLLEGE

URING THIS SUMMER Dr. David Blaustein, the Superintendent of the Educational Alliance, came to spend a week with Davidson at Glenmore. The three of us planned the expansion of Davidson's class into a school in which people who worked during the daytime could pursue cultural studies in the evening. Davidson was to continue his class on Saturday evenings; Dr. Blaustein was to give a course on the evolution of religion; Dr. Joshua Frank was to lecture on natural science; Dr. David Muzzey was to teach a class in the Greek language and literature, and I was to give thirty lectures on the history of civilization. To give the work a distinctive character, it was planned that we should have the use of a separate building on East Fifth Street, in which the Educational Alliance conducted children's classes during the day.

Davidson's Adirondack neighbor, Felix Adler, was of the opinion that our resources were too inadequate for the magnitude of our enterprise. But Davidson, who boasted of Norse Viking blood and ever craved the life of the free lance, with his characteristic courage and optimism was certain that if we started at all the work would naturally grow. That Davidson should have asked me, then still an undergraduate and only four years out of public school, to give a course of thirty lectures on the history of civilization was characteristic. As a youth in Aberdeen, in his early twenties, he had gathered around him a group of young men and had become their natural intellectual leader as they met in his rooms on Sunday evenings for a simple Scottish Sunday supper. His ability to grasp the highest possibilities in those with whom he came in contact, and to arouse their creative energy by expecting heroic accomplishments was demonstrated by the distinguished careers of these boyhood disciples — among them Sir George King, the botanist who did so much for the utilization of quinine and the conquest of malaria in India, George Croom Robertson, the editor of Britain's leading philosophical journal, *Mind*, Professor McKendrick, the great physiologist of Glasgow, and John MacDonnel, who became the leader of the Society for Comparative Legislation. Davidson's use of the heroic method was based on his psychological postulate that every individual tries to live up to what is expected of him, from which he drew the conclusion that heroic achievements take place only when the apparently impossible is expected of one.

The beginnings of our school were certainly modest. Dr. Frank's class in general science never was started and Dr. Blaustein, after two or three lectures, found that his work as Superintendent of the Educational Alliance did not permit him to continue with his small class. Dr. Muzzey's class had barely more than half a dozen students, and the only classes that really functioned were Davidson's own class on Saturday evenings, with an attendance of about 150, and my own class in history, which started with about thirty-five members. A number of younger people in Davidson's group wanted to prepare for college, and I organized a special class in elementary mathematics, which later on was divided into two sections.

The split in the Socialist Labor Party which occurred in the summer of 1899 caused a rift within our Marx Circle. This, coupled with the difficulty of obtaining a meeting room, compelled us to discontinue our sessions. My friends, Eugene Schoen, William Hirsch, Louis Roth, Simon Frucht and Abe Kovar, joined the Davidson class at my suggestion.

After some weeks a number of my friends at City College, who, like me, were taking the pedagogic course and were thus unable to have any class in general philosophy, asked me to induce Davidson to lead them in the study of philosophy. Davidson consented, and the class was given on Sunday mornings. We began with the pre-Socratic philosophers and reached some of the Platonic *Dialogues*, when Davidson left for Glenmore in May, 1900.

In connection with this course, I read Zeller, Gomperz, Burnet, Tannery, and Fairbanks. The special task assigned to me was to write an essay on Xenophanes. To accomplish this, I compiled a large package of notes — so large that I never had the time and courage to shape them into essay form. I had a similar experience with my second assignment, Plato's *Parmenides*. But as I was attending college and spending more than twenty-five hours a week on the preparation of my lectures on history, and was tutoring private students, Davidson forgave my lapse in this respect.

With all this work, the winter of 1899-1900 was a hard one. I was in a rundown condition, not only from too much indoor life, but because I carried my various philosophic problems to bed with me, and it was hours before I could fall asleep. The great tragedy of the year, however, for me was the deterioration of Davidson's health. At the beginning of the year he underwent an operation for the removal of a cancerous growth and later in the year he suffered considerable pain. The last time that Davidson came to my house he was in great distress, but my mother tactfully directed the conversation to topics that brought out his unquenchable hopefulness. In reply to my father's question as to what I should do after graduation from college, Davidson suggested that he would adopt me legally as his son and send me to Germany for my doctorate in philosophy.

After his departure a situation arose which brought an element of strain between us. The Educational Alliance reported that Professor Davidson was fighting socialism, and the Yiddish socialist papers, the *Abendblatt* and the *Forward* took up the challenge. Those of us who had been in the Marx Circle felt that it was up to us to declare ourselves as socialists, and we revived that group. Eugene Schoen, who was the secretary of the Circle, reported our decision to Davidson. Davidson thought that his whole class had turned Marxist, and became highly incensed. At the same time, a letter which he wrote to me was misdirected and, as I did not get my weekly communication from him, I assumed that he did not wish to see me and that, under the circumstances, I should not write to him. Thus, each of us felt that the other was angry. Finally, the whole situation was straightened out. When I received an appointment to teach in Dr. David Davidson's Collegiate Institute, Thomas Davidson (upon whose recommendation I had been appointed) wrote to me a very tender and affectionate letter. Also, at the same time, I received a letter from the mother of Arthur Amson, saying that I had taken the place of Amson in Davidson's affection. (Amson was a gifted boy whom Davidson had adopted and to whom he had become intensely devoted.

He sent him to Germany to study. Amson died after a short illness and Davidson grieved for him all his life.) At the end of June I was back in my tent at Glenmore.

Meanwhile a group was formed — S. P. Frank, Herman Friedel, Louis Michaelson, Leo Jacobs, Louis Hussakoff and Louis Dublin — who called themselves Rodfe Zedek (Seekers after Righteousness). They adopted in its entirety Davidson's religious philosophy, which I could not accept without reservations. Thereupon, Davidson appointed them as a managing committee.

CHAPTER THIRTEEN

THE DEATH OF DAVIDSON

EARLY IN SEPTEMBER, Davidson's condition became so grave that he had to be taken to the hospital to be operated on again. His physician, Dr. Abbe, was in Europe and the journey to New York was too far. Thereupon Davidson was taken to Montreal. A few days later I returned to New York and received employment for a week as a substitute teacher. On the Friday of that week I came to our rooms in Madison Street and I heard the sad news that Davidson had died. Leonard Cohen saw Mr. Warren and arrangements were made to have three members of the Davidson class go to the funeral at Glenmore.

In the few days' interval between my departure and my return to the Adirondacks, the fall had set in rather rapidly. The leaves were falling; the colors were beautiful in the clear, crisp, and decidedly cold air. Felix Adler delivered the funeral oration and the body of the man who had meant so much in my life was buried on the lonely hill in back of the house in which he had lived. A few neighbors, as well as a small number of remaining guests in Glenmore, were the only ones present. I sat on a stone some distance away while Dr. Adler was speaking, and the sadness of Davidson's entire life gripped me. I felt then that the work which he had started with the boys and girls of the East Side of New York would live and grow; its roots were planted deep in the ground of human needs, and it would draw strength from the light of heaven. But my spirit echoed in an anguished manner the concluding words: "The stars will continue their course over this neglected spot, but he who was the life of this place will be no more." "No more, no more" reverberated in my mind. How little does the life of man count against the cosmic background. Here was a man who lived on a grand scale, communing daily with the great spirits of humanity, in many ages and lands, a man who had led a tempestuous life struggling for freedom to express his own ideals, and yet, in the end, he is as nothing, a figure writ in the sands of the sea, which a wave washes away, leaving no trace.

CHAPTER FOURTEEN

THE HERITAGE OF DAVIDSON

A FEW WEEKS AFTER Davidson's death, we who had been his disciples gathered at a memorial meeting and sought to appraise the heritage which we had from him. We all knew that our lives would be richer and nobler by reason of Davidson's influence. To me was assigned the difficult task of expressing our understanding of that heritage. I doubt that I could improve today upon some of the words that I used on this occasion when the fresh sense of grief made so clear the vision of what we had lost by Davidson's death and what we had gained by his life. And so I quote from the language that I used on that occasion:

Those who knew Thomas Davidson will understand that it is utterly impossible to give anything like an adequate summary of the life or character of Thomas Davidson. The life of a truly great man cannot be ticketed or labelled. There is no formula or abstract characterization into which you can cramp a large personality like that of Thomas Davidson. Even if you have said all that *can* be said about him, you cannot help feeling that the man himself was a great deal more than all that.

Nevertheless, there are certain traits of his character which are especially significant for those of us who are trying to continue his work.

To my mind the most fundamental characteristic of Thomas Davidson was that he lived philosophically on a truly large scale. He lived for the really great things of life, and stood far above the petty issues and the petty rewards for which the multitude is always struggling. He refused to be dragged into any of the petty muddles of the day but constantly strove to be on the great streams of reality. He refused to accept our popular current half-hearted ideas, but persisted in testing everything by his own reason and tracking his thoughts to their home in ultimate reality. None but the very highest enjoyments and motives had any existence for him. Above all, he judged all actions by their most far-reaching consequences, by their eternal results. He lived for eternity and that is why the effects of his life cannot easily die.

The life of Thomas Davidson was essentially a heroic life. Though, as I knew him, one of the most sympathetic souls that ever trod this globe, he had absolutely no sympathy with anything unheroic. He had a generous faith in human nature, believing that there are heroes and heroines, now more than ever before, to be found in every street and on every corner, and that it is only our own blindness that prevents us from appealing to the heroic in them. It was just because he led this large life and expected it of everyone else that it was more than a liberal education in itself to have been intimately acquainted with him; and we cannot do better than attempt to continue his work, judging ourselves by the standards by which he would have judged us, and thus stimulating ourselves to ever greater hopes and tasks.

The life of Thomas Davidson was essentially an earnest life. It cannot be exactly said that he taught us to be earnest; for according to his own testimony, we were terribly in earnest when he first came amongst us. But he did impress us with the tremendous importance of grappling with the great problems concerning the issues of life and to be fearless and bold in the pursuit of the very highest truth.

There is a popular tendency, nowadays, especially among "practical" people, to look down upon all attempts to grapple with the deep problems of existence. Some try to ease their consciences by declaring all such problems insoluble and calling upon us to devote our attention to the more "practical" problems of the East or West Side. But Thomas Davidson showed in clear and unmistakable terms that it is only sheer sloth and cowardice that can urge us to declare certain problems insoluble before we have exerted all our efforts to solve them. And he also showed how absolutely futile must be any attempt to solve our problems as "East-Siders" without taking into consideration our problems as men and women. Now as ever the commandment holds true:

"Seek ye the kingdom of God and his righteousness and all the rest shall be added unto you."

Thomas Davidson insisted as I have known no one else to insist, on the sacredness of truth. He put it paradoxically when he used to say, "Truth does not need the cloak of sacredness. It is sacred itself."

He taught that the highest reverence is due to human reason; the highest duty to search for the truth with unbiased mind; and the highest courage to follow the truth always and everywhere regardless of where it may lead us.

But with all his deep erudition he did not overestimate the value of learning. He was interested in knowledge only as a motive to right living. He insisted on our becoming acquainted with every branch of human knowledge, science, philosophy, art and literature, but only in so far as they help us to lead rational lives.

He also realized that mere knowledge alone will not enable us to solve the profound problems of life, that sympathy is an essential part of a right attitude to the riddles of the universe. You must tune up your heart to catch the music of the spheres. But above all he realized that we do not truly know until our so-called knowledge is tested in real life, that life cannot be learned merely in the study without experience in the arena of life itself, that wisdom is not to be obtained from text books but must be coined out of human experience in the flame of life. He recognized that the solution to the problems of existence depends on a combination of scientific insight, apostolic sympathy and enthusiasm, with practical activity; and he both lived up to his idea himself and demanded it of everyone else.

This is what led him to the idea of establishing a Breadwinners' College. In his letters to the class he pointed out the great defect in the ordinary college and university education, viz., "that it stops with knowing and does not go on to loving and doing. It therefore, really never is appropriated, for knowing that does not pass into act and habit, is never ours, but remains an external thing, a mere useless accomplishment, to be vain about." "If everyone of you," he wrote to us "would translate his or her knowledge into love and work, [then] we should have an Educational Institute, a Breadwinners' College, — call it anything you like — such as the world has never [yet] seen," an institution which will teach men and women to become public-spirited, generously cultured, pure and high-minded, an institution which will help more than anything else to banish ignorance and moral poverty.

Our colleges teach science and cultivate scholarship, but they do not create any large ideal or enthusiasm in the student's soul. They leave that to the church. The church does aim to build up a high ideal which has little influence on the course of actual life, because it is based on a super-natural view of the world, which is no longer tenable.

There is, therefore, an urgent need for an institution which will combine the advantages of both college and church without their weaknesses. Such an institution Thomas Davidson wanted us to form, and such an institution will be formed if we are true to ourselves.

We who had been his students were resolved to carry out the last cherished wish of our beloved teacher, by making a reality of our half-started Breadwinners' College. Here would be an institution that would make no distinction of race or creed, would be open to rich and poor alike, and would be founded upon the principles that Thomas Davidson had sought to perpetuate. Organizing ourselves as the Thomas Davidson Society, we gave our best efforts to the task we had inherited. The Educational Alliance building was our campus.

We had no financial angels and so our teaching had to be on a completely volunteer basis, which helped to establish a unique personal relationship between teacher and student.

We adopted a consistent policy of not duplicating work which could be done as well by other institutions. For that reason we always recommended those in need of elementary instruction to attend the public evening schools. However, during the seven months of the year in which these were closed, very successful classes were carried on in English grammar, composition, United States history, geography and arithmetic. Soon this department was reorganized into two grades, each preparing students for our academic or high schools.

Later we organized our academic department into a regular evening high school. The aim of this course was to afford young working people, especially those who had just left school, the opportunity for a good systematic course of study which would provide the proper mental discipline and lay the foundations of a liberal education. The course was primarily a culture course intended to make the pupils broadminded, willing and able to take an intelligent and active interest in the various important questions of life. For this reason, history, literature, civics and economics were emphasized although science, mathematics and language training were not neglected.

Our elementary and academic departments were preparatory and incidental to the main work that was the nucleus of our Breadwinners' College. This consisted of a series of classes in philosophy, cultural history, literature, and social science. Our class in philosophy was helped by three good friends of Thomas Davidson's, Professor Charles M. Bakewell, Professor Josiah Royce, and Dr. William T. Harris, United States Commissioner of Education. Our course in the origins of modern thought began with a year's study of the Hebrew prophets in relation to the contemporary scene, and went on in the second year to a study of the contributions of Greek thought and civilization, and, in subsequent years, treated Roman and medieval elements in modern civilization. Reading and study of great poems from the sociologic or ethical point of view occupied alternate sessions of these courses in the history of civilization. I persuaded Mr. Percival Chubb, the Associate Leader of the Ethical Culture Society, to come every other Saturday to read Tennyson's "In Memoriam" with us. For the alternate Saturdays I outlined a program of papers to be delivered by the members of the class on the development of the Hebrew contribution to civilization, following, in part, Davidson's outline of lectures on the origins of modern thought.

In connection with this course, we invited Rabbis Kaufman Kohler and Joseph Schulman to address us. Their reports about the character of our meetings helped us to establish a good reputation with the directors of the Educational Alliance. Few of these directors, however, took an active interest, and their neglect to express any appreciation of Mr. Chubb's generous services made a rather unpleasant impression. The members of the class, however, presented to Mr. Chubb a beautiful desk in token of their appreciation.

The main burden of running our Breadwinners' College was on our own young shoulders. The difficulties that we had to contend with seemed insurmountable. When we began, we had no adequate rooms, no textbooks or stationery, no desks, and none of the appliances of classrooms. None of us had financial means to remedy any of these lacks. When, after a year or two, we had progressed enough to attract public criticism, we were criticized for alienating Jewish young people from Judaism, for alienating young socialists from socialism, and for making young people work too hard after their daily tasks were over. We were criticized for duplicating the work of the colleges; but we were satisfied in our own minds that more important than the higher education of the colleges, which attempted to train scholars rather than personalities or even citizens, was education directed, in the Davidsonian key, to appreciation of the values and problems of humane living. So, too, we were criticized, as our work expanded, for duplicating the social work of the settlement movement; but again, we felt that what we were doing, in expecting heroic devotion and sacrifice from every member of our school, was far more important than giving material things or amusements to people in need. Indeed, to many of us, it seemed that the social worker's attitude of expecting little and giving much led inevitably to the taint of condescension and necessarily failed to call forth the highest potentialities of those whom the social workers sought to help. Our objectives were on a more demanding plane.

Though we charged no fees for our classes, it was clearly understood that whatever was acquired in these classes was to be held in trust and transmitted to others. We had undertaken to pay others for what Thomas Davidson had done for us. We expected those who came after us to react in the same way. As the years passed, the most active members, teachers and club leaders of our school and society were those who had attended our classes.

When some of the friends of Thomas Davidson heard of us in those years, they expressed surprise that the death of Davidson had not put an end to our work. But the truth was that our real labors began with the death of Davidson. So long as he lived, there was a stream of people coming and leaving our classes who had nothing but a momentary interest in his remarkable personality. When Thomas Davidson died, the nucleus of those who had a permanent interest in his work alone remained. With a few new recruits, we were soon giving courses in which the attendance had risen from about two hundred to about six hundred.

Others will measure our success or failure in crystallizing Davidson's hopes for a Breadwinners' College. The work at the Educational Alliance which we carried on could not be permanently maintained. Like many other worthy enterprises of the human spirit it died in the First World War. Joe Kahn and I gave the last course of lectures in 1917 at Stuyvesant House. The death of our school was not dishonorable. Most of the objectives of our work had been taken over by the evening session of City College, and by various extension courses, workers' schools and other institutes of adult education which are today so important a feature in the intellectual development of America.

But whatever our success or failure in transmitting Davidson's ideals to other generations, we, ourselves, had been influenced in a way that we never want to or can forget. The annual gatherings of Davidson's old disciples are still occasions for measuring ourselves by the highest standards and resolutions of our youth. To me, as a youth of nineteen, Davidson had been a father, a guide into fields where he thought my highest possibilities lay, and an inspirer of efforts which became my life's passion. To all of us Davidson had brought standards more subtle yet more lasting than those of worldly success. And as we have seen one after another of our number testify to the impermanence of man's life and the fruits of his work, we have come to prize ever more highly something that Davidson embodied in his own life and kindled in the lives of so many others. None who were touched by his spirit can ever forget his heroic devotion to the pursuit and expression of truth as he saw it "in scorn of consequences" or his magnificent disdain for worldly goods whenever he might serve the spiritual needs of those with whom he came into contact. None of us can ever forget the teacher who showed us that there are values of character which remain when all else decays and that theirs is the enduring victory.

BOOK FOUR

THE VALLEY OF HUMILIATION
(1900-1912)

CHAPTER FIFTEEN

MY FIRST YEAR AS A TEACHER

AFTER MY RETURN to New York City I tried to find employment as a substitute teacher, but I was dispirited and did little until Rabbi David Davidson opened a private school. He employed me to teach the common school subjects to the upper class, which at first consisted of only four boys and later of five or six.

In after years, Rabbi Davidson spoke in rather kind terms of my teaching, but I am quite sure that I could have done much better if my mind had not been engrossed in the Thomas Davidson Society classes.

The death of Davidson left the group known as Rodfe Zedek in control of the Thomas Davidson School. One of the organizers of this group, Louis Michaelson, had succeeded me as president of our embryo school in the summer of 1900. But early in 1901, Louis Michaelson began work with Nissim Behar and I was re-elected president of the school. My conduct of the meetings did not please some of the members, who considered it dictatorial. In the spring of that year, the regular elections occurred and Louis Hussakoff was elected. Some of the members felt very badly about this display of what they regarded as ingratitude for the work that I had done but I felt confident that I could continue to direct the work along the lines that Davidson would have wished.

I spent the summer of 1901 as tutor, or guide — we now call it counsellor — in Rabbi Davidson's summer school at Coolbaugh, Pennsylvania. The boys came from rather wealthy homes and their interests were decidedly worldly as compared with the eager idealism of my companions in New York. I read old copies of the *Monist* and the *Open Court*. Eugene Schoen sent me a copy of Locke's *Essay* which I found rather dull. The book which made a great impression on me during that summer was Edgar Saltus' *Anatomy of Negation*. Its light-hearted and ill-informed knowledge of skepticism offended me and I criticized almost every page of it. Finally, I realized that Saltus expressed a mood and that moods cannot be refuted. Such reflections, together with miscellaneous readings in the literature of mysticism, cured me of a certain strident and over-confident rationalism. I realized the obvious truth that things cannot be proved except to those who are willing to accept your premises. This taught me the lesson of intellectual liberalism, of listening to, or at least reading, authors with whom I disagreed. With the intent of understanding what they had to say from their point of view, I read the sermons of St. Bernard with great interest. And though I do not adhere to the various classical forms of mysticism, I have never since taken stock in the too-facile refutations of it. This opened my mind to writers like Emerson whom I could not previously follow with sympathy because I could not see that they proved anything.

During this summer I carried on an active correspondence with several members of the Davidson Society (as it became known by that time), especially with my class in Roman history, which continued its weekly sessions during the summer along the paths that I had outlined for it. I corresponded, as well, with Mrs. Ruutz-Rees, who remained my staunch friend throughout her life.

During that period, the two most active members of our philosophy class, Joseph Kahn, who later gave courses on Kant at New York University, and Edward Endelman, were at Glenmore. The relation between the Jewish boys and girls of the East Side of New York and the older habitués of Glenmore had an element of strain, as was to be expected from a consideration of the differences of background, habits and outlook. But William T. Harris was a saint. He took our boys under his protection and helped them with their philosophic studies. Bakewell planned to publish some essays written by the students of Davidson, and Joseph Kahn undertook to collect them. I sent him the draft of my lecture on "Common Sense, Science and Philosophy." I never knew what became of it. In later years I feared that it would fall into the hands of someone who would publish it. It was definitely a juvenile performance.

THE ACADEMIC YEAR 1901-2 opened under unfavorable auspices. I expected a teaching appointment in the New York Public School System and I resigned from my position with Rabbi David Davidson. Weeks passed and no appointment came. My attempts to find employment as a substitute teacher were unsuccessful and when I did find a vacancy I could not control my classes. Finally, in October I was appointed to teach in a public school on Seventieth Street and First Avenue, which was at that time a predominantly Czech neighborhood. Many of the boys were decidedly underfed and lethargic, the victims of unfavorable home life. Indeed, one of them was later killed defending his mother from a brutal attack by his drunken father. Others were naturally stupid, but worst of all was the fact that I could not summon the necessary amount of attention to do the best I could with the material thus thrust upon me in the middle of the term. It was far from a pleasant occupation and as the year passed, the daily fatigue of teaching became ever greater. In that spring I was frightened by an attack of palpitations of the heart. I had to continue my work and by a careful husbanding of my strength, I soon recovered my usual rhythm.

The one sustaining outlet for my intellectual aspirations in this year was afforded by my role as secretary and discussion leader of the Thomas Davidson philosophy class. We wrote essays and discussed the nature of common sense, imagination, reason, and immortality, as developed in the third book of Aristotle's *De Anima*. We then took up the problems presented by Aristotle's *Ethics* and *Politics*. We also enjoyed a lecture by Professor Royce on the conception of the infinite, and engaged in a series of discussions on Thomas Davidson's theory of man and the world and William T. Harris's critique of Davidson's teachings.

A visit with William T. Harris in the summer of 1902 at Glen-more, in the company of Mary Ryshpan, Augusta Salik, and other loyal Davidsonians, helped to lay the basis for an expansion of the work of our Thomas Davidson School. And a summer session at Columbia, where I took courses in general philosophy, genetic psychology, and education, helped to equip me, I thought, for my role as principal of the Davidson School and for the task of setting up in it a high school department.

In November of 1902, the dreary task of teaching public school children who did not want to learn that in which I had no particular interest, terminated when I received an appointment at the City College and began to teach more mature young men algebra and geom-etry. The manner of my appointment was quite accidental. Two vacancies occurred in the Department of Mathematics, and Professor Sim, the Director of the Townsend Harris Hall High School, the preparatory school of the College, asked my friend Louis Dublin if he knew someone competent to fill a vacancy. Louis came to my house, roused me from my bed, and within twenty minutes I was on my way to an interview with Professor Sim. I told him that I had won the Belden Medal in Mathematics as a student, and he gave me directions as to how to fill out the application form. With my usual carelessness, I did not follow his directions in all respects, and he was kind enough to return it to me for amendment. Within a few weeks I was notified that I had been appointed and was told to report at once. I bade good-bye to my principal, Heydenis, and began my work at the City College.

This was highly unsatisfactory, for I was occupied not only with my work at the Davidson Society, but with my graduate studies as well. I was attending classes at Columbia University, under Professors Woodbridge in philosophy, Felix Adler in ethics, Strong in psychology, Giddings in sociology and Seager in economics. I did not prepare my lessons adequately and my impatience and irritability did not make for the best order in my classroom. Moreover, I naturally followed the harsh methods of teaching which I had experienced as a student.

The next year I had a heavier teaching program at the College. Classes were larger, and all of my students lower C's — that is, students who had just graduated from the elementary schools and entered the high school department of the College, which had expanded, since my undergraduate days, to a three-year course. I was still carrying on graduate studies in philosophy at Columbia under Professors Woodbridge and Sheldon. My health took a decided turn for the worse. I had never gone to a doctor, but Simon Hirsdansky persuaded me to visit his brother, Dr. Max Hirsdansky. The latter gave me little help and less encouragement. I realized that I was working too hard, especially at the Thomas Davidson School, in which I stayed almost every night. I acted as principal and taught classes when our volunteer teachers did not show up, which — except in the case of Mary Ryshpan, who gave the advanced English courses, and Simon Hirsdansky, who gave the elementary English course — happened quite often. Besides acting as principal and general substitute, I was giving a course in English history in the first-year high school class and courses in philosophy and the Book of Job in our so-called "culture class." During the Christmas week I enjoyed a rest at Grandview through the kindness of Miss Lillian Wald, Head-Worker of the Nurses' Settlement on Henry Street. This helped me considerably, but twice during the next term I became ill with high fever. It was obvious that this could not continue much longer. By this time Mary Ryshpan and I had decided to get married, and I realized that I could not support a family unless I was promoted from my tutorship to the grade of instructorship. At that time the possession of a doctor's degree was required for an instructorship. I applied for a fellowship in philosophy at Columbia University, but despite the high opinion which Professors Woodbridge and Adler had formed of my equipment for philosophic studies, some one else was appointed.

A paper of mine on "Aristotle's Theory of the State" made a very favorable impression on Professor Felix Adler and as he knew something of my work at the Davidson Society, he conceived the idea that I might be helpful to him at the Ethical Culture Society. Thereupon he invited me to attend his meetings with his co-leaders. During the academic year 1903-04 these meetings were devoted to comparative studies of the great ritual ceremonies in the different religions and I remember preparing papers on "The Confessional" (with special reference to the Buddhist Patimokha) and on "The Funeral Oration" as prescribed by Hebrew law and custom. At the end of the spring of

1904, when Professor Adler realized my desperate condition, he considered offering me one of the fellowships of the Ethical Society. He had some hesitation in the matter, because of certain doubts as to whether my physical appearance and careless dress would not always be a handicap, but my dear old friend Mrs. Ruutz-Rees persuaded him that I had enough character and stamina, and I was finally awarded a fellowship of $750. Under the circumstances, Harvard seemed a natural place for me to go for my doctor's degree. I would not have to publish my thesis, and I would not be distracted by what was going on at the Davidson Society. My good friend and prospective brother-in-law, Simon Hirsdansky, had been elected principal teacher of the Society, and this gave me a feeling of assurance that the ideals we shared would still help to guide the work that Davidson had begun, and to which I felt that my life was dedicated.

CHAPTER SEVENTEEN

PHILOSOPHY AT HARVARD

THE TWO YEARS that I spent at the Harvard Graduate School from September, 1904, to June, 1906, gave me the opportunity to lay the foundations for my future career as a teacher of philosophy, but they were not happy years. Nervous strain and poor health cut down my effectiveness so that it has long been a mystery to me how I managed to emerge from my two years at Cambridge with the respect and friendship of such teachers as William James, Josiah Royce, Ralph Barton Perry, Hugo Münsterberg, and George Herbert Palmer.

I plunged into my graduate studies with great avidity in September, 1904, taking on courses and seminars, in ethics, logic, metaphysics (with James and Royce), Kant, Descartes, Leibnitz and Spinoza, the Hebrew religion, the science of religion, and the history of religions.

Besides working on a thesis on "The Nature of Goodness," I managed to find time to serve as a sort of ambassador of the Thomas Davidson Society and the Ethical Culture Society, which was financing my first year of graduate work. With Frank Parsons I helped to organize, and did some lecturing at, what was known as the Breadwinners' College, in Boston. I also managed to organize a series of meetings at Cambridge under the auspices of the Ethical Culture Society. I recall that the crowning triumph of my efforts along the latter line was getting President Eliot to address our circle.

Despite these importations that I brought with me into Cambridge from the spiritual ferment of the East Side, the dominant impression that Cambridge made on me was one of peaceful charm and quiet. My bare little room at Divinity Hall, the wealth of the philosophical library, and the stimulation of James, Royce, and other teachers and fellow students gave me a chance to think philosophically without the tension that had dominated the four years since graduation when I had to sandwich reading between long daytime teaching hours and long evening hours teaching and managing at the Thomas Davidson School. I remember particularly the long walks and peripatetic philosophic discussions with my close friend, Leo Mayer. Later Leo Mayer introduced me to a cousin of his, Arthur S. Meyer. A lifelong friendship which sustained me in many dark hours dates from that introduction.

After three months at Harvard I felt that I was really coming to grips with the thoughts of Kant. I had put in more consecutive intellectual labor than ever before on a single problem, but I felt my time had been well spent. The greatest teacher I had at Harvard was Josiah Royce, who had a marvelous capacity for concentrating all his learning and logical acumen on the point at issue. But the best friend I found on the Harvard faculty was William James. No one could have come into contact with William James without being stirred by his gloriously fresh vision and amazingly daring honesty of expression. I could not, however, share his psychologic approach to philosophy. His psychologic explanations of necessary truth did not seem to me to bear on their logical nature. James never seemed to me to go beyond Mill, who was killed for me by Hegel and Russell. Our intellectual disagreements were often violent. But as a human being James was not only a never-failing source of warm inspiration but a trusted counsellor in all my difficulties of health and finance and in my lowest days of depression.

Apart from its intellectual opportunities Harvard helped me to learn how to get along with people of radically different backgrounds. Davidson and the company of his associates at Glenmore had helped me to appreciate the importance of getting behind the superficial differences of manner that are always to be found between men and women brought up under different environments and to appreciate the importance of getting to the human mind underneath the externals, with its powers and values that are so much more important than manners and forms of speech. But the men and women of other backgrounds that I had come to know through Davidson were mostly of an older generation, and in my own generation all my close friends, like Eugene Schoen, Abe Kovar, Simon Hirsdansky, and my bride-to-be Mary Ryshpan, had been boys and girls who had shared my own cultural heritage and environment. At Harvard, far from all my old friends, keenly aware anew of the great void that Davidson's death had left in my life, I came to appreciate ever more clearly how important a part of education it is to get to know well people with whom at the beginning we have no sympathy, people who do not immediately strike responsive chords in our hearts. Only so, I came to realize, does one achieve spiritual growth.

Notwithstanding a few spells of depression and poor health, I finished my first year's thesis, came through my examinations with flying colors, and won an appointment as assistant in the Philosophy Department, working under Professors Royce and Münsterberg, at a salary of $250 for the following year.

I went back to Cambridge in the fall of 1905 fresh from a walking tour through the Berkshires and the Connecticut Valley, following a summer vacation at Glenmore — which had rapidly degenerated after Davidson's death from a summer school to a private summer camp with just enough lectures to maintain its memories. In Cambridge I shared a room at 1707 Cambridge Street with Felix Frankfurter, and we spent many evenings together talking law and philosophy. I soon developed a profound interest in the theoretical side of jurisprudence, which was to prove one of the guiding threads of my future philosophical development.

A few weeks after my return to Cambridge I began to suffer from a breakdown of my health. Nervous indigestion accompanied by palpitations of the heart left me completely exhausted and dispirited. Finding that most food seemed to disagree with me, I began to reduce my diet, and since I was naturally underweight it was not long before I was in a serious condition, which reflected itself in a loss of ambition and zest for life. I found myself weary of what seemed the ceaseless struggles and prizeless victories of life. There was, withal, no sense of resentment. As I looked out on life and saw so many people ceaselessly struggling to achieve the unattainable, knowing that to cease struggling is to cease to be, I came to feel that all other sentiments need to be subordinated to that of compassion. Realizing that there was nothing unique about my own wretchedness I was at least saved from the depths of self-pity. I felt that the world had treated me as well as I deserved, if not very much better. I was prepared to surrender any claim to happiness. Unhappiness had lost its sting and without that sting I lacked the energy to take proper steps to build up my physique through diet, relaxation, and exercise. I recognized that my mental and spiritual depression was connected with my poor health, but felt that I had made heroic efforts for five and a half years to improve my health and that my almost total failure to accomplish any lasting results proved that my disposition was itself the cause of my illness.

In December I found myself sick and unable to carry on, notwithstanding the patient and loving care that my roommate Felix Frankfurter lavished on me. I was forced to go to Lakewood for a rest. I seemed to improve but upon my return to Cambridge, I soon found myself again at low ebb. Notwithstanding the poverty which had been one of the elements of strain under which I labored — at times I found myself completely penniless and my debts kept mounting — I was induced in February of 1906 to undertake a rest cure at Glen Springs in Watkins Glen. A course of bath and massage treatments, relaxation, and nourishing diet brought flesh back to my bones and peace to my heart. After a month or so the doctor permitted me to begin work on my thesis, on "Kant's Doctrine as to the Relation between Duty and Happiness." In April I was back in harness at Cambridge, working hard to complete the thesis on which depended my doctor's degree, with its promise of a teaching career and marriage to the girl I loved.

A few weeks later it was finished. On June 13, 1906, Mary Ryshpan and I were married and eagerly planning our honeymoon trip to Glenmore in the Adirondacks and then to England and Scotland, to the haunts of our beloved teacher Thomas Davidson, to the glens and mountains of his youth that he had brought into our springtime. There we hoped to gather materials from old friends and neighbors for a book I planned to write on Davidson's life.

Later, Professor Bakewell, Davidson's literary executor, found another writer, Professor Robert Calhoun, for the task, and I turned over to him the beginnings of my biography. It was not the last book that I have planned but not finished.

CHAPTER EIGHTEEN

A STRUGGLE FOR PROMOTION

A FTER RECEIVING my doctorate in philosophy at Harvard in 1906, I returned to teaching at City College bearing recommendations from William James, Josiah Royce, George Herbert Palmer, Ralph Barton Perry, Felix Adler, and William T. Harris that President John H. Finley characterized as the finest he ever read in his life. But my application for a transfer from the Department of Mathematics to that of philosophy was ignored. At Columbia, thanks to Felix Adler, I was honored with an appointment as Lecturer in Philosophy, but the position was without compensation and my efforts to win a better post were unsuccessful, as were all my efforts to find a teaching position in philosophy at other universities.

Marriage had brought a fresh wind into my life that swept away the melancholia that had developed during the last year at Harvard. But my health was still frail and twice during the academic year 1906-7, I was incapacitated by illness. Well do I remember the special clarity that ideas seemed to have in hours after the passing of fever. And vivid in my memory are the dark night views of those years when, leaving our room at 493 West 135th Street, I would go out into the dark still night and find as much cleansing of my troubled spirit as in the afternoons when I reclined on the rocks in the little park across the way to regain my breath after the hectic hours of teaching.

These years were bitter years to me, and my life was marked by a deep sense that I had proved a failure. By June, 1907, all my previous plans in life seemed defeated. Work in the Socialist Party had become impossible, and my nervous breakdown showed me the impossibility of my developing the educational work of the Davidson

Society. But what was even more disheartening was that a career as a teacher of philosophy seemed definitely defeated on all sides. I had to teach twenty hours a week of elementary mathematics and felt lucky when I got through the day's work alive and a tolerable human companion to my sweet and devoted wife. To this sense of failure was added the bitterness that went with my inability to get promotion. The poverty of my early years as a teacher impressed itself upon the lives of my wife and my children. We could not afford to give any of the children a whole orange when they wanted it. "When papa is full professor" came to be the children's preface to almost all expressions of worldly hope.

My disappointment at what I considered my failure as a teacher and my bitterness at my inability to secure either promotion or recognition were brought to focus on an occasion when I overheard two friends speaking of people they knew who seemed to have promising careers before them as teachers. My name was not mentioned.

The fact is that my teaching bore many resemblances to the instructional methods of a drill sergeant. Not only had my childhood experiences with education been filled with whippings and the fear of whippings, but my student days at City College itself had been dominated by the harsh standards approved by the first two presidents of the College, both West Point graduates. Pursuit of marks and avoidance of "demerits," rather than the genuine pursuit of knowledge, were the all-important concern of many students and too often the chief concern of the teacher. When I first began to teach I inherited this rigorous system. I used to teach at the Davidson School at night and treated the students as my children — as Davidson had treated me — but when I came to College I was a petty drillmaster. I have never been able to understand the warmth of feeling which some of my students of those days showed me years later. It took me a long time before I could rid myself of my drill-sergeant attitude. I have always been grateful to Harry Overstreet, who came to the College without a trace of that attitude. Under his influence I found my teaching methods gradually become less harsh.

There was little personal or intellectual satisfaction in the years that I spent in the teaching of mathematics. The best judges of a teacher are his students. I remember one student who said, "Cohen does not know any mathematics." He was not far wrong. Not only was my knowledge of mathematics limited, but my mind and heart were not in my teaching. The center of my intellectual interest lay elsewhere — particularly with the Breadwinners' College of the Davidson Society — and my college teaching was a mere incident in my daily routine. I had expected a transfer to the Department of Philosophy on my return from Harvard, and it was only in the latter years that I became reconciled to the teaching of mathematics and put my heart into it. With all my shortcomings, John R. Sim, the head of the department, was a kind father to me, and the recollection of his kindness leaves a sweet fragrance in the memory of a painful period.

The heavy schedule of classes and the frailties of my own health left me little time or energy to devote to professional writing. Possibilities of advancement, of recognition, and of leisure seemed blocked on all sides. In the winter of 1909-10 at the urging of my friend Sam Rosensohn, I studied law at night at New York University Law School. Sam Rosensohn was then, and remained all his life, one of my most devoted friends, and he felt keenly the economic difficulties that Mary and I faced in those years. He was sure that after receiving my law degree I would be earning at least $3,000 a year, more than twice the salary I was then earning as a mathematics instructor. If I ever entertained any idea of becoming a lawyer I soon gave it up, but the feel of cases and legal method that I gained in this way helped me overcome the fear that keeps so many philosophers from trespassing on the premises of the law.

After the N.Y.U. Law School experience, I returned to teaching for the Thomas Davidson Society at nominal pay. This proved very disappointing. As a volunteer I had been respected, but as soon as I began to be paid people looked upon me with different eyes. This was a deep humiliation to me.

Unable to find opportunities for the teaching of philosophy, I turned to the only modes for philosophical discussion that were open to me, the philosophical journals and the annual meetings of the American Philosophical Association, to which I had been duly elected after receiving my doctorate. These gatherings, with their democratic give-and-take of philosophical argument, were adventures to which I looked forward each year. I have never outgrown the feeling that such meetings are of great importance not only in imparting zest to the life of reason but also in demonstrating the possibility of mutual respect and co-operation among adherents of doctrines more divergent than any for which opposing armies have battled.

Beginning with the meeting of the Association in December, 1908, at Johns Hopkins University, where I read a paper on "Kant's Doctrine of the *Summum Bonum*," I made a point, for several years, of submitting a paper at each meeting of the Association, and was fortunate enough to have each of these papers accepted. In December, 1909, when the Association met at Yale University, I read a paper on "Concepts of Philosophy," and in December of 1910 at Princeton I read a paper on "The Present Situation in the Philosophy of Mathematics." These and other papers read in later years were generally published in the philosophical journals, along with book reviews of various works of philosophy and science. This writing brought no income. The free books that I got for reviewing helped to build my library but did not pay for carfare to Association meetings. Still, in the long run, this unpaid writing brought me more returns, even material returns, than anything that I ever wrote for cash.

In 1910 Overstreet was appointed head of the Philosophy Department. It was through him that I won the chance to teach philosophy. He recognized my philosophical ability, though he had some doubts as to my merits in other respects. One day he told me that he and President Finley had agreed that John Pickett Turner was to get the appointment to a current vacancy and that I was to be tried out for a second position and appointed if I made good. I wrote an answer to Overstreet in which I asked whether he himself had been taken on trial. At the same time I wrote a sharp letter to President Finley saying that if he had no confidence in my ability after my splendid record at Harvard and after I had taught at the College so many years I did not care to be tried out and wished to withdraw my application. Finley replied that he was sorry — reiterating that my letters of recommendation were the finest he had ever read in his life. At about that time, in December, 1911, I went up to Harvard to a meeting of the American Philosophical Association to read a paper on "Mechanism and Causality in Physics," part of a projected statement of my general philosophical position, which appeared twenty years later under the title *Reason and Nature*. Overstreet was so impressed that he decided that he wanted me on his staff.

When Overstreet got my letter he was very unhappy but didn't know what to do, being concerned about Finley's reactions. When I returned from Harvard after reading my paper he came to me and said he had decided to recommend me and Turner for two positions. Whereupon I told him, somewhat ungraciously: Nothing doing. I was appointed to teach mathematics and I would teach mathematics and have nothing to do with his Department of Philosophy. He asked me what I wanted. Nothing, I replied, but if he wanted me he would have to meet my terms. "What are your terms?" he asked.

I wanted to be a professor and I wanted to be senior to Turner, and if President Finley would not agree I would continue to teach mathematics. Overstreet undertook to consult with Finley and reported that Finley was very much displeased, feeling that I was throwing down the gauntlet. But Overstreet courageously insisted that the College had sent for him and must meet his needs and that he needed me. Towards the end of the academic year, President Finley finally agreed to my terms, and my transfer to the Philosophy Department as an Assistant Professor was approved. Ironically it was J. P. Turner who eight years later recommended me to full professorship. It happened that Overstreet was away on sabbatical leave during the academic year 1920-21. I had been invited to serve as head of the department but declined, preferring teaching to administrative duties. Turner became acting head of the department and as such made the recommendation which finally, in January, 1921, brought me my full professorship.

The post of Assistant Professor of Philosophy at City College in 1912 promised little in the way of relief from the financial burdens that we faced with our three infants. But it was always possible to borrow money from faithful friends — all of whom, I believe, were finally repaid — and the position came to me as the fulfillment of a cherished youthful ambition. I have always treasured the letters of congratulation that came to me in the summer of 1912 from old friends and old teachers who knew something of the heartaches that had gone into the struggle for the privilege of teaching the subject I most wanted to teach to the boys of the college that had been my second mother.

BOOK FIVE

MY CAREER AS A TEACHER OF PHILOSOPHY

MY APPOINTMENT AS an Assistant Professor of Philosophy in July, 1912, marked, for me, the end of a long valley of humiliation. I had labored for six years with the Leah of mathematics, yearning for the Rachel of philosophy that I thought I had won with my Harvard doctorate in 1906.

When the news of my appointment came, I was engaged in writing an article on the teaching of philosophy for Monroe's *Cyclopedia of Education*. (I know much less about the teaching of philosophy after thirty years of teaching than I did then.) I spent a good many weeks on this, though the cash remuneration was only $40. Indeed I became so absorbed that I stayed behind when my wife and our three youngsters, Felix, aged five, Leonora Davidson, aged three, and little Victor William, just a year old, made the long trip to the Adirondacks to celebrate my promotion with a brief and lonesome summer vacation in the vicinity of our beloved Glenmore.

My reading and writing on the teaching of philosophy had been given a special urgency by my appointment, and I asked myself with some concern to what purpose I should direct my energies. Until fairly recently the teaching of philosophy in American colleges had been viewed as a branch of Christian apologetics and teachers of philosophy had long been selected on the basis of piety and pastoral experience rather than on professional training and competence. Indeed, even in recent years I have had letters from highly respected ministers who, upon being appointed to teach philosophy, ask me to recommend a good book on the subject. But clearly I had not been appointed to teach philosophy at City College on the basis of my piety. What, then, should the role of a philosophy teacher be in a liberal civilization? Why should a great city, in which many races and creeds sought to live and work together in peace, employ a philosopher as a teacher of its sons?

When it was first proposed to found a Free Academy in New York, at the end of the Mexican War, a violent protest was raised by the wealthier classes, who objected to the unprecedented use of public money for that purpose. The objections were snowed under in a popular referendum, but the *New York Sun* continued for at least ninety years to echo the old protests against the institution of the College of the City of New York as a thinly disguised method of robbing the rich to pay for the education of the poor. The steady growth of the College, despite the opposition of certain groups of taxpayers, indicates that the service it has rendered has endeared it to the hearts of the citizens of New York.

The fact is that higher education in the past had always been the possession of the privileged classes, to be used as an ornament and a source of power. The idea of adapting higher education to the needs of the great multitude who have to go to work relatively early in life has not yet become an integral part of our national system of education. The struggle to achieve this result is still going on; in most other lands it has hardly begun. New York is still unique in the history of civilization with respect to generosity in matters of education. That such generosity might help to save liberal civilization from the dark forces that threaten it had long been an article of the faith I lived by. This made teaching at City College a challenge. Here was the front line of the struggle to liberalize education in a democracy. To make available to the poorest member of society the highest experiences of the human mind had been the driving objective of my early socialist dreams. Now, at last, I was privileged to play a significant role in that process.

That role I did not find an easy one. When I started to teach philosophy in City College I found myself devoid of the gift of verbal fluency, and so I naturally resorted to the use of the Socratic method: teaching by means of searching and provoking questions. The head of the department, who was not similarly handicapped — in fact he was exceptionally gifted as a lecturer — at first demurred.

"What do you do to make your students into fine fellows?" he asked.

To which I replied, "I'm not a fine fellow myself, at least not so much better than my students that I can venture to impose my own standard on them."

And this I meant not by way of irony or false modesty but in all sincerity. As a son of immigrant parents I shared with my students their background, their interests, and their limitations. My students were, on the whole, relatively emancipated in social matters and politics as well as in religion. They did not share the Orthodoxy of their parents. And breaking away from it left them ready and eager to adopt all sorts of substitutes. Though many of their parents were highly learned, as was not uncommon among Russian Jews, my students had gone to American public schools, and the learning of their parents, being permeated so deeply with the Talmudic tradition, was in the main foreign to them. City College offered a rich variety of courses in languages, literature, and science, but the curriculum allowed few courses in philosophy itself. I therefore saw no adequate opportunity for teaching philosophy along traditional lines. Instead I had to give courses primarily in related subjects, hoping to bring philosophic insight to my students through courses on the nature of civilization, the philosophy of law, and the topics covered by Santayana in the last four volumes of his *Life of Reason*.

Even when I essayed, in later years, to give more technical courses in philosophy, as in metaphysics and advanced logic, what gave life to the give-and-take of classroom discussions was the fact that these courses afforded an opportunity to press a thorough-going analysis of living ideas beyond the points where polite conversation generally stops. In later years when I faced more placid Western students who were less interested in bringing to light their own first principles, I came to realize more clearly how much student attitudes at the City College had contributed to the form of my teaching and of my thought.

Never having discovered for myself any royal road up the rocky and dangerous steep of philosophy, I did not conceive it to be part of my function as a teacher to show my students such a road. The only help I could offer them was to convince them that they must climb for themselves or else sink in the mire of conventional error. All I could do to make the climbing easier was to relieve them of needless customary baggage. This exposed me to the charge of being merely critical, negative, or destructive. I have always been ready to plead guilty to that charge.

It seemed to me that one must clear the ground of useless rubbish before one can begin to build. I once said to a student who reproached me for my destructive criticism, "You have heard the story of how Hercules cleaned the Augean stables. He took all the dirt and manure out and left them clean. You ask me, 'What did he leave in their stead?' I answer, 'Isn't it enough to have cleaned the stables?' "

Knocking logical errors and comfortable illusions out of young people's heads is not a pleasant occupation. It is much pleasanter to preach one's own convictions. But how could I hope, in a few weeks of contact with my students, to build up a coherent world-view that should endure throughout their subsequent lives? And even if I had had the time, respect for the individual personality of the student before me would still have kept me from trying to impose my own world-view on those whose temperament, tastes, and experiences were different from mine. Davidson had long ago cured me of the natural urge which so many men and women never outgrow to remake God and the universe in our own images. Davidson himself had made it a rule of his life to quarrel with all those who agreed with him, and his favorite pupils were those who most radically differed from him. Why should I assume that my own convictions represented the summits of wisdom in philosophy or anything else? It seemed to me a more important service in the cause of liberal civilization to develop a spirit of genuine regard for the weight of evidence and a power to discriminate between responsible and irresponsible sources of information, to inculcate the habit of admitting ignorance when we do not know, and to nourish the critical spirit of inquiry which is inseparable from the love of truth that makes men free. The critical and scientific spirit can be trained in philosophy as it is trained in the special sciences.

That, at any rate, has been my dominant idea so far as I have had any ideas as to the teaching of philosophy. I did not make the mistake of thinking that because this was the thing I could best teach, it was the only important thing in life. Civilized life demands a division of labor. It would be enough if I could lead pupils out of the Egypt of Bondage into the Desert of Freedom and leave them there.

I had faith that they would enter the Promised Land without me. Though I am liberally skeptical I have a firm faith that if you remove certain obstructions the free mind will thrive by its own energy on the natural food which it can gather from its own experience.

Judging by the unprecedented attendance and the eager response I received from my students, I seemed to have aroused genuine interest in philosophy not as a body of doctrine but as a liberation from superstitions, new as well as old. By challenging the opinions current among young people at the time — such as the uncritical acceptance of psychoanalysis, economic and other forms of materialist determinism, the complacent cult of progress, and other myths which parade as modern "science" — I think I succeeded in bringing to some of my students the realization that the problems of philosophy are matters of such vital importance that they have to be faced most seriously in every realm under penalty of otherwise falling into grievous and devastating error.

This experience strengthened my conviction that the main function of teaching philosophy should be the opening of the human mind to new possibilities, rather than the inculcation of any new set of doctrines. To me, this did not mean the old-fashioned liberation of the mind from all traditional beliefs, but rather the supplying of students with new points of view that would enrich their outlook and thus help them to attain intellectual independence. This in practice meant attempting to teach future scientists, lawyers, economists, and citizens to think philosophically about the problems of science, law, economics, and citizenship.

As a teacher I could claim to belong to the class of Garman and Howison, who trained thinkers rather than made disciples. Teaching undergraduates who were preparing to enter diverse fields of activity, I sought to cultivate their powers of critical reflection so that they would become more intelligent members of the community rather than technical philosophers. Knowing from experience the difficulty of finding positions in the teaching of philosophy, I never encouraged any of my students to become professional philosophers, although many have already had distinguished careers as teachers of philosophy — Ernest Nagel, Herbert Schneider, Sidney Hook, and Paul Weiss — and others have given promise of similarly distinguished philosophical careers — among them Joseph Ratner, Philip Wiener, Daniel Bronstein, Leo Abraham, Morton White, and Milton Munitz.

As a teacher in City College, I was under pressure to teach regular and often large classes, rather than distinctive individuals. There was little opportunity for instructor and student to get together for more intimate conversation. If a teacher is also sensitive, as I have always been, to the danger of imposing his own personal attitude and views on his pupils and prefers to encourage them to struggle alone and arrive at their own conclusions, he too readily accepts this limitation of impersonal classroom companionship even in the pursuit of the intensely personal truths of philosophy. This, at any rate, partly explains to my own mind why I never became intimately acquainted with more than a very few of my fifteen thousand or so students.

Whatever my failings as a teacher, I tried to tell my students what I thought they ought to hear, rather than what I thought they would like to hear. The process of demolishing youthful illusions would have hurt sensitive students keenly even if I had been more circumspect than I knew how to be in salving tender feelings. Actually I found the method of treatment by shock the most effective way of leading students to appreciate the nature and dimensions of ignorance. Though I had deep respect for the personality of the individual student, I lacked, except on rare occasions of good health, the courtesy of Socrates. One of my students, when I asked for criticisms of a course that had just come to an end, commented, "Justice Holmes said he envied the youth who sit at your feet. It is evident that he never took a course with you." I know that many of my students have felt that way. The cynic acid that I used for the purpose of dissolving hazy confusions must have left scars on a good many sensitive youngsters. I suppose my reputation as a hard and exacting taskmaster was well-deserved. This made the expressions of student esteem and affection that came to me in the later years of my career at City College especially moving. Particularly do I cherish the memory of the dinner that my students tendered me in 1927, on the twenty-fifth anniversary of my joining the teaching staff of the College. It was a great and unique event in my life and proved to be a profound religious experience to me and to many others. I could not but be deeply stirred by the generous words of Justice Holmes, Felix Frankfurter, Bertrand Russell, Frederick Woodbridge, John Dewey, Judah Magnes, Nathan Margold and other revered teachers, dear friends, and gallant comrades in the adventures of the spirit. It was good to know that those who had been loyal friends in times of obscurity and frustration could feel that their confidence in me had not been misplaced.

The dinner was arranged at a time when my position at the College had become quite difficult with the accession to its presidency of a man who had no sympathy for what I was trying to do as a teacher. I had found myself, on occasion, in a minority of one at faculty meetings, and I recalled grimly the remark of my teacher of comparative religion at Harvard, George Foote Moore, that the only academic freedom worth bothering about is freedom from committee meetings. The distractions of teaching had forced me to put off from year to year and from decade to decade the completion of the books that were close to my heart. Poor health seemed to make the completion of these works a vain hope. Perhaps it was an appreciation of these difficulties that led old students like Max Grossman, Nathan Margold, Herman Gray, Isidor Lazarus, Dave Rosenstein, Jack Schapiro, Henry Auerbach, Al Eolis, Dan Krane, and their confederates, foremost among them my devoted wife, to arrange this ceremony. Certainly it confirmed my faith in human nature and in the effort to teach the truth, at a time when such faith needed strengthening.

The dinner was held in October, during Succoth, the Jewish harvest feast. At the dais sat my mother and father, who were just preparing to celebrate their sixtieth wedding anniversary. They did not follow all the dialectic of Bertrand Russell or all the learning of Woodbridge and Dewey — though Dewey spoke with feeling and penetration of the spiritual presence of the scholars, rabbis, and learned men of Russia and the Orient whose thinking was a living part of my thinking. Nor did they fully appreciate all the gallantry and wit of the toastmaster, Felix Frankfurter. But on this Succoth two brave hearts gathered the fruits of parental faith.

CHAPTER TWENTY

LAST YEARS AT CITY COLLEGE

T EACHING HAD ALWAYS seemed to me so much more divine an occupation than college administration that I could never understand why in American universities it is considered a promotion when a teacher becomes a college dean or president. I had stuck to that conviction when in the academic year 1920-21 I declined the position of acting head of the Philosophy Department, feeling that it would distract me from giving my best efforts to my teaching. But much against my will I found myself being drawn more and more, in the later years of my career at City College, into administrative issues which had little to do with the teaching of philosophy.

In part these administrative issues involved the responsibilities of teaching and the defense of academic freedom, especially freedom of research. As one of the founding members of the American Association of University Professors, as Chairman of its City College section and as a member of the College's first committee "to report on ways and means to stimulate constructive scholarship among members of the staff," I was naturally subject to call whenever the right of teachers to freedom of thought or speech was attacked. This responsibility might at times infringe considerably upon my own opportunities for thought or research. But such service was a small price to pay for one's own freedom — even when it involved long and arduous efforts in fields not my own as was the case when Bertrand Russell was kept from occupying my chair after my retirement from the College by the maneuvers of a cowardly mayor and an ignorant judge.

During the twenties and thirties, however, student problems were a more fertile source of distraction than the problems of repressed professors. I had had unusual opportunities to study the cultural backgrounds not only of the majority of the students of the College, but of their parents here and abroad. Most of my colleagues on the faculty came from very different backgrounds. I had also enjoyed an unusual opportunity of exploring student thinking on the problems of civic responsibility and justice, as their teacher in the College course in legal philosophy. When problems of student life came before our faculty for consideration, the responsibility for developing basic issues and essential facts often fell upon me. It was a responsibility I could not refuse. Some of my colleagues were disappointed that in our faculty meetings I did not berate the bad manners of our younger generation in accordance with the ancient custom of older generations. (When I did berate student bad manners it was only to the students themselves.) But I remembered very vividly my own bad manners as a student. And what was more important, I could not feel that the defects of our boys in point of manners were as important as their extraordinary attachment to the values of the spirit. Humanity in the years following the First World War was passing through a period of disappointed hopes and blasé cynicism. It was becoming more and more difficult to preserve the spiritual aims of our college teaching in such an atmosphere. The obvious crudeness of youth, whose fine idealism had not been tempered by hard and cold realities, struck some of my colleagues as the chief evil which the colleges of the country needed to correct. I could not share this view. More important than the effort to improve student manners seemed to me the effort to keep the youth of the land from losing faith in the spiritual ideals acquired through generations at a fearful cost. Chief among those ideals was the maintenance of a free and fertile field for the competition of ideas in the search for truth. This, to me, seemed an essential part of science, of philosophy, of liberalism, and of democracy, academic or political. The lines between classroom responsibilities and loyalty to the ideals of our College were sometimes hard to draw.

The old rigid disciplinary tradition which City College had inherited from its first two West Pointer presidents had been somewhat relaxed under the leadership of Presidents Finley and Mezes, but such vestiges of it as compulsory military drill, compulsory chapel, and alumni and faculty censorship of student publications, irritated high-spirited students. At City College, as at many other American colleges in the mid-twenties, students were beginning to concern themselves with wider issues of citizenship and democracy. As the editor of the college paper, *The Campus,* my son Felix became a spokesman for a student generation that wanted to bring more democracy into the life of the college. Some of his editorial writing on the subject of student conscription aroused national attention — particularly an editorial published on Armistice Day, 1925, which consisted simply of quotations from the military drill manual, without comment. Though he was scrupulous to avoid involving me in any of his activities, I made no effort to conceal my hearty agreement with the students' position on this issue, and when the voice of the students was temporarily suppressed I myself wrote and circulated among my fellow faculty members a brief in support of the student plea that the compulsory military training course should be replaced by an optional course. It seemed to me that conscription had thrown a pall over European civilization and brought in its train many hideous manifestations of nationalism and intolerance. I felt that peacetime conscription in the seedbeds of American democracy was likely to bring similar developments in its train and could not be justified by any of the traditional arguments with respect to its hygienic, disciplinary, or even its military value. Only sixteen other professors agreed with me when the matter came to a vote of the faculty, and we were snowed under — for a few months.

In this situation, President Mezes, handicapped by poor health which kept him out of touch with the ramifications of student activities, and relying upon poor advice, pursued a course that, however well intentioned, only put him and the College in an unfortunate light. First he denied that the *Campus* editorials represented the views of the students; a student referendum promptly gave overwhelming support to the *Campus* position. Then he ordered *The Campus* to cease discussion of the subject; a blank column in the next issue, edged in mourning bands, brought more discussion inside and outside the college than any words the column could have carried; the order of censorship was soon revoked. Then he attempted to dismiss the matter with the phrase, "boys will be boys"; whereupon a poll of the students' parents was taken, which again showed overwhelming opposition to compulsory drill. He finally attempted to veto the students' selection of the *Campus* editor to represent them at an intercollegiate convention on the World Court held at Princeton; but the student convention declined to honor his veto.

After two months of such incidents President Mezes on January 11 very magnanimously asked me to serve on a faculty committee to inquire into the subject of compulsory drill. At the end of the spring term we recommended that students who preferred to take physical training should be permitted to do so. The majority of the faculty accepted our recommendation, reversing its earlier stand. So, in the fall of 1926, military training ceased to be compulsory. The campaign of the students had been successful.

At this juncture President Mezes, whose health had been failing, took a sabbatical year's leave, from which he never returned. It was with genuine regret that I saw him leave the College. His advent to the presidency in 1914 had marked a new and happier era in my life. As a former philosophy teacher himself, he appreciated the spiritual values of our educational work at the College, which, though intangible, are among the things of enduring worth that make everything else worth while. I had always regarded him as the most liberal and tolerant of City College's presidents, and he had shown me many kindnesses and deep respect. From the outset we had exchanged notes and articles and views on the universe in general and the problems of education in particular. Whatever our disagreements, we had always accepted them as differences stemming from a common devotion to the College and to the cause of liberal education.

I did not find these qualities of intellectual and spiritual leadership in President Mezes' heir apparent. The first man to whom I expressed this view was Dr. Robinson himself. In the spring of 1926, when his imminent election to the presidency had become the common talk at the College, I thought it my duty to tell him before telling it to anyone else that I thought a man of an altogether different and more scholarly type was needed for the office; that while he could undoubtedly look after the administrative side of things — for which he had a natural bent — we needed a leader who could inspire and maintain the enthusiasm for scholarly achievements which is the real life of the College. In the years that followed he did nothing to give me any ground for changing my views. When he was elected president I gave serious thought to the question whether I should resign from the College or stay in it and do the best I could under the circumstances. I took a year off in 1927-28, mainly to improve my health, and partly also to think the matter over. Finally, the enthusiastic and affectionate expressions of students and former students persuaded me to continue my teaching at the College. As I have never been gifted in the art of diplomatic dissimulation, and have also consistently upheld the principle of respect for the constituted authorities of our democratic institutions, I made it a rule not to speak at all about my college president except to intimate friends. Yet my reluctance to discuss the merits or demerits of Dr. Robinson was not shared by the student body. Class after class was graduated from City College after 1926 without any real respect for the president of their college, and feeling that he had no respect for its students. From this followed a series of incidents that made the pursuit of philosophic studies at the College increasingly difficult for me.

The first of these incidents developed when a handful of members of the College chapter of the scholastic honorary society, Phi Beta Kappa, undertook in the fall of 1926, to punish my son Felix, the leader of the anti-conscription campaign, by excluding him from membership, though he had been graduated *magna cum laude* and had received five or six academic prizes. The rest of the membership was highly aroused by this departure from the usual standards of admission, but could not block the action since it took only five blackballs to prevent an award of membership. Thereupon another handful of members blackballed all the other candidates for admission, and admissions to Phi Beta Kappa were at a standstill while committees of inquiry and committees for the revision of the bylaws worked for a solution of the impasse. Both sides sought my assistance in ironing out the difficulty, but for two years all my efforts at peacemaking were failures. When I tried to withdraw my son's name from candidacy I was rebuked by the chapter. My suggestion to him, made at the urging of an old friend, that he withdraw his own candidacy was equally unsuccessful; he felt that since he had not presented his name it was not for him to withdraw it. Being away at Harvard during the whole period of the battling, absorbed in graduate studies in philosophy, he had no opportunity to discuss his case with members of the chapter and therefore refused to take any action on it.

In vain I protested that according to the Jewish law a father ceases to be responsible for the sins of his son when the latter attains the age of thirteen. Equally vain was my protestation that I had never given any encouragement to the little group that insisted on blackballing all applicants in order to secure a change in the by-laws. On the other hand, I would not denounce those who took this course since apparently they conscientiously felt this to be the only way of preventing an injustice. My attempts to stick to philosophy were completely fruitless, and my efforts as a peacemaker were completely unsuccessful.

Eventually, a special committee brought in a report vindicating the integrity of the former *Campus* editor, and another committee devised a more democratic rule for voting on admissions. In November, 1928, this struggle was terminated, and in Phi Beta Kappa I was the brother of my oldest son.

The echoes of this controversy had hardly died when a great economic depression began to shut the doors of opportunity to the graduates of our College. The cruel uncertainty that faced young men who had obtained a degree and did not know where to turn to earn a living shook old-time boyish complacency to its roots. Undergraduates began to wonder what was the trouble with a world that with all its vast resources of nature and science could not give jobs to men equipped and anxious to serve their fellow men. The wonder was sometimes mixed with hopelessness; other more irrepressible spirits found hope in new forms of old superstition.

The controversy over compulsory drill had been carried on by all concerned on a high level of courtesy, so that at one time the *New York World* ran an editorial commending the College, its administration, and its students for the fine example of freedom and courtesy which had been set in a difficult situation. Later student campaigns, however, particularly when the Communist Party came to dominate various youth groups, did not always limit themselves to the traditional American methods of editorial-writing and voting. Student disturbances stimulated by a handful of idealistic but fanatical students and aggravated by the repressive measures of a president who did not scruple to use an umbrella as a weapon against picketing, made the atmosphere of the College more and more unacademic. Censorship, picketing, demonstrations, interferences with College programs, suspensions of students, of papers, and of clubs, expulsions, and mass demonstrations against expulsions developed in cycles. The gap between faculty and students widened and efforts at mutual understanding based on mutual respect seemed quite utopian. Faculty meetings came to be taken up increasingly with problems of discipline rather than of teaching.

I urged that we free ourselves of this concern with discipline by giving adequate powers to the joint student-faculty discipline committee and this was done. But while this helped to bring an end to serious student disorders, it brought no relief to me, for the committee, as revised, consisted of three faculty members, three students, and an impartial chairman agreed to by both sides. The students insisted that I had to be the impartial chairman. I demurred, as did the faculty members, but the students would accept no substitute and no compromise. Once we had yielded, the students, year after year, made the same demand and neither I nor my fellow faculty members on the committee offered further resistance. Even some of the teachers who had been most critical of my influence on the student body came to feel, judging by results, that student judgment had turned out, in this case, to be sounder than faculty fears. The result of all this was that I found an increasing amount of my time taken up at the College with the quite unphilosophical concerns that arise to plague any impartial chairman and particularly the impartial chairman of a faculty-student discipline committee at City College in the 1930's.

The attacks on my attitude towards student difficulties did not always come from the administration side. I recall one occasion when two students were accused of violating some order of the College authorities. As chairman of the discipline committee I received a letter from the student council of the Twenty-third Street Building protesting against any proceeding that might lead to any punishment. Such letters, of course, are not unusual. Almost every day I receive letters asking me to protest against the indictment or conviction of some one who, the writer assures me, is entirely innocent, and every time I receive such a letter I think of what I would do if the writer assured me that a certain accused person was guilty, that there was danger of his being freed, and that I should write to the judge or perhaps to the jury to be sure to convict. That the machinery of justice sometimes goes wrong I have no doubt. But I also often have doubts about how well informed my correspondents are on the facts of the case. Accordingly I wrote to the protesting students that if any of them were witnesses and could testify that the accused had not done what they were charged with, my committee would gladly hear them. But if they knew nothing of the actual case, they had no more right to urge that those accused should be freed than that they should be found guilty. For this I was denounced as a reactionary.

Having become thus involved in at least some of the undergraduate troubles of these years, I was promptly blamed in many quarters for all student uprisings. Prominent alumni pointed to the large number of avowed Communists who had been my pupils — among them Bertram Wolfe, Jay Lovestone, Simon Gerson, and Joseph Starobin. (They did not list all the judges, rabbis and Christian ministers who had also been my students, nor did they note the violent diatribes that the Communist magazines directed against me.) They blamed me for the troubles in Phi Beta Kappa where resolutions were being regularly adopted in criticism of the College administration's repressive tactics in student affairs, much to the displeasure of the chapter's Old Guard. Above all, they blamed me for the movement for the removal of Dr. Robinson from the presidency of the College which was gaining ground year by year among thoughtful alumni.

Throughout my years at the College I had been somewhat of a recluse and forced by my physical frailties to be even aloof from those who would naturally be my friends. Under the circumstances I could not complain because some of my colleagues knew so little about me as to conceive me as a Machiavellian super-politician with a large following planning all sorts of intrigues.

Whatever the consequences for my own peace of mind, I could not refuse to stand up at faculty meetings for the things I believed in. One of these was faculty democracy, and particularly the vesting in all the members of each department of a share in the responsibility for running it. Another was the importance of encouraging research, on the part of students capable of it. To lay open to undergraduates the adventure of independent investigation and original writing — and thus to help train future leaders in science and scholarship — called for a more flexible form of faculty guidance than the old classroom and examination routine permitted. And if such research was not to be prematurely narrowing, there was need to see that the student brought to his task a comprehensive knowledge of the general field.

This meant that teachers looking at a world that is not as neatly departmentalized as a college curriculum would have to meet together for the give-and-take of seminar discussion with the students whose research they were guiding. Such at least was the idea behind what came to be known as the "honors work" program. In the long run the faculty and the Board of Trustees supported each of these reforms.

If the efforts put forth in these campaigns brought any lasting results, they were still a very small return on the generous investment by New York City in the education of an immigrant boy. The teaching that I managed to do in the intervals between committee meetings continued to give zest to life. But as the years passed I felt that the give-and-take of classroom questioning was losing the eloquent acidity which had once given it sparkle. Declining physical energy combined with the growing size of classes and the distraction of extracurricular interests had brought changes in my teaching methods that were not improvements, from my point of view. I was questioning less and lecturing more, and, while I suppose the quality of my lecturing — especially in the course on the philosophy of civilization — improved somewhat from the standpoint of the boys, I was getting less and less stimulus out of the teaching process. Worse yet, I feared that lecturing would unconsciously beget an easy omniscience and satisfaction with apparent or rhetorical truths. No man, no matter how critical, can stand up before a class and refrain from saying more than he knows. I found myself longing for more of the keen destructive criticism which one's professional colleagues are usually ready and most willing to accord to any new views. Perhaps it would be easier away from New York to come up against young philosophers who had not had their thinking influenced by any of my courses. It occurred to me that there might be quite a large association formed of those who were not pupils of mine, and that it would contain some very distinguished names.

A visit to Harvard in the spring of 1934 turned out to be a stimulating plunge into quiet water. I wondered whether I would have had a more intellectually active and productive life as a teacher there and whether I had still enough energy to start a new and free school of philosophic studies. The old Davidsonian dream of a society of scholars building a philosophy for a new age glowed again. I began to look forward to opportunities to work with maturer minds and to wrestle with more advanced problems than one could take up with beginning students. Had my physical strength been greater, I should have continued to turn a deaf ear to other universities offering easier hours, or greater opportunities for quiet and research. But in the summer of 1934 my health took a decided turn for the worse and by the summer of 1937 I felt that the time and strength that remained to me for work would not suffice for the things I wanted most to do if I continued longer at the College.

On the one hand, I wanted to finish at least ten long-planned books that had weighed on my conscience for many years.

Ever since 1917 I had planned a treatise on law and justice, of which only fragments had been published in 1934 in a collection of essays, *Law and the Social Order*. The work of integrating my views on our basic legal institutions remained to be done. Perhaps a series of graduate seminars would help me to reduce my thoughts to order.

Then there was a long-planned volume on metaphysics that cried for utterance, to which, again, seminar contact with graduate students might contribute.

For years I had been planning a preface or prolegomena to logic which would deal with the central philosophical question which so many modern logicians seemed to be ignoring, that of the relation of logic to physical and moral realities.

There was an unfinished volume on "Roads to Philosophy," on which I had done a good deal of work in the summer of 1937, in preparation for my last regular lecture course at City College. It had been planned as a text or guide book designed to reveal philosophy to students, or other newcomers to the subject, as simply stubborn thinking about problems in all fields of life's endeavor — thinking which refuses to accept as final the common limitations at which creatures of habit stop thinking. It would deal with natural curiosity or wonder about the nature of the world, things, life, knowledge, art, religion, and morality as roads leading to a common concern with perennial problems.

Then there was a fifteen-year-old desire to get out a reasoned statement of the liberal outlook that would help to rescue the word "liberal" from its association with *laissez-faire* economics, superficial politics, or mushy-minded sentimentality, and instead show liberalism as simply scientific method stubbornly at work on human problems.

I was tempted to go through the addresses and papers on Jewish problems that I had written during the past twenty years and whip them into a coherent volume.

Beside all these there remained the old dream of a work on the philosophy of history, and the unfinished book I had been promising to publishers since 1920 on the history of science, and the half-written book I had been promising for at least ten years on the development of American thought. And in the last few years, particularly in the last months of companionship with my mother in 1935 and 1936 when, after my father's death, she shared our home, I had developed a burning desire to tell the story of the generation which cut its roots in the old home, crossed the ocean into a strange land, and brought up its children to make their contributions to a free world. This would be the epitaph I should write upon the graves of those who had struggled heroically to open the gates of opportunity to me and to my children.

With all these unwritten volumes pressing for expression and so little strength for the task at hand, the teaching of undergraduates was coming to be felt as a distraction and no longer as a medium for the development of my thought. In days of debility and pain I could not escape the reflection that so much of my intellectual program would never be achieved. One might seek for consolation in the thought that the number of books we leave behind will make no difference when we are no more. But there was always the answer that my whole life had been geared for formulating certain important ideas; it was not pleasant to think that they would die with me. If these moody reflections vanished in sunshine on days of tranquillity, there was still the sense of transiency: If I do not do something now I shall have less to look back upon to buoy me up when the twilight comes in which I shall not be able to stand up.

The longing to have more time for thinking and writing might not by itself have sufficed to break the ties that bound me to the College. I was accustomed to postponing the writing of my books. But the Conference on Jewish Relations, which I had helped to start in 1933, was demanding an increasing share of my thought and energy. I had been profoundly disturbed by the rising tide of anti-semitism in the United States, which seemed to me to be part of a general decline of liberalism. The bitterness of the Roosevelt opposition during

Members of the Department of Philosophy, C. C. N. Y., 1938

Seated, from left: Professors Marsh, Cohen, and Overstreet; *standing, from left:* Messrs. Peatman, Bronstein, Edel, Wiener, Smith, Hertzman, Krikorian and Aronson.

the 1936 campaign, a bitterness which gave birth to every manner of excess, had clearly revealed in America the germs of that unreason which had swept so much of Europe. The pursuit not only of philosophy but of all free learning was being crushed throughout the world by the military spirit which brooks no freedom of thought. The universities were falling before the Nazi onslaught; it had been officially proclaimed that the science of von Humboldt and Planck was dead. In Spain the progress of the rebels of General Franco was being followed by the closing of schools. In our own land elements sympathetic with Franco, Hitler and Mussolini were arrayed against the progress of democratic education. All that was precious in American liberal civilization seemed at stake. The situation was critical, though not hopeless — the temper of the American people, unable to sustain hatred over long periods of time and inclined to cherish the right to vote and other democratic rights even when their exercise seems to bring little gain, made the defense of American liberalism far from utopian. Teaching philosophy to youngsters would make a difference fifty years later. But issues were being joined from which I could not stand aloof, for those who were fighting on my side seemed so often to lack the facts and the understanding which an organization like the Conference on Jewish Relations could supply.

The decision to retire from the active service of the College in January, 1938, was not an easy step for me to take. It involved a wrench in the roots of my being. I doubt whether there is anyone in whose life the City College has meant more than it has meant to me. My connection with the College dated back to my boyhood days in 1895, when I entered its halls as a student straight from the elementary public schools and realized even then that without its existence as a free institution the benefits of a college education and of all that is based on it would have been denied me. Since 1902 my life work as a teacher had been centered at the City College, and I was tied to it not only in my devotion to the ideal of a free, higher education for all who are prepared to receive it, but also by the bonds of personal affection for my students and colleagues. The responsiveness and the enthusiastic appreciation which my students had accorded me, despite my painfully conscious limitations as a teacher, had been one of the great supports of my life. The generous attitude of my colleagues had helped me to carry on when poor health and other circumstances tempted me to quit teaching and devote myself exclusively to philosophic study and writing. I felt that my department head, Harry Overstreet, had been particularly greathearted in his patience with my frailties of temper, and I could never forget my gratitude for his action in effecting my transfer to his department and thus ending a period of frustration and painful humiliation to me. It would be hard to part from fellow teachers whose help I had so often sought in trying to pick up threads of scholarship in many fields beyond my competence, or to whom I would so naturally turn in order to try out what seemed to be a new idea. Hours of talk with Paul Klapper, J. Salwyn Shapiro, Carlton Brownson, Abraham Goldforb, Morton Gottschall, Nelson Mead, Paul Saurel, Leigh Hunt, and many other old colleagues crowded the horizons of friendship. But it seemed to me that these ties of friendship, loyalty and gratitude had to give way before the demands of a world outside the College where the need for voices of reason, even a rather quiet voice, was becoming increasingly poignant and manifest.

The student council adopted a resolution against my resignation and the student paper blazed an editorial headline, "We Won't Let Him." But on February 1, 1938, a crisp, sunny day, I woke up in the morning to my first day as a retired professor.

BOOK SIX

THE DEVELOPMENT OF MY PHILOSOPHY

CHAPTER TWENTY-ONE

ROADS TO PHILOSOPHY

IF PHILOSOPHY IS VIEWED broadly as the love of wisdom, I may say that such a love was awakened in me between my seventh and tenth year by my grandfather, who, though he never learned to write and had only a moderate knowledge of Hebrew, had become master of an extraordinary amount of knowledge and wisdom. Walks and talks with him in the little town of Neshwies first stimulated my imagination about the world at large and its history. They gave a special zest to reflections on law and ethics which form the substance of Orthodox Hebrew education. His talks to me about Maimonides and the Book of Cusari stimulated an interest in the philosophy of religion that has never waned.

I took to philosophy as a poet takes to poetry. Ever since those childhood days, to philosophize has always seemed to me as natural and desirable in itself as to sing, to dance or to communicate with those we love — and as little in need of ulterior justification.

Philosophy, after all, is one way to aspire to the beautiful in life. I have long been rather skeptical as to how far philosophy can help the world solve its great problems — apart from doing the basic and difficult job of getting the world to realize that it has great problems. Indeed, I believe the philosopher may often do the world great harm by attempting to remedy its ills even if only for the reason that they often demand a technical knowledge which the philosopher does not possess. Too many philosophers have failed to recognize the importance of the division of labor — that the business of the philosopher is well done if he succeeds in raising genuine doubts, and that it is the business of others to resolve those doubts. It seems to me that the real importance of philosophy lies in its very independence from the petty actualities of daily life. I remember a student's once asking me, "What is the use of metaphysics?" And I replied, "Thank God metaphysics has no use." By "use" people mean bread, butter, shelter and such trivial, even if necessary, things. And I say that it is degrading to human nature to put such things as bread and butter as the final aim of life. It is the appreciation of beauty and truth, the striving for knowledge, which makes life worth living. Philosophy satisfies the desire to learn; it satisfies the eternal search for truth. Of course, it has its moral values also. It liberates the mind from prejudices. Every one of us is born into a certain class of beliefs which are considered absolute truths. Philosophy enables us to analyze and compare these "absolute" truths and find their relative values.

When, in 1895, I entered the College of the City of New York I found solid courses in mathematics, physics, chemistry, biology and economics but, apart from an elementary course in logic, no courses in philosophy. It was only in later years when I tried to teach mathematics that reflection on the underlying principles of mathematics and scientific method made me see that science no less than law, ethics, history, and religion, involves unrecognized assumptions that philosophy can clarify.

Though my parents had begun to refer to me as "the philosopher" — meaning theorist or Stoic — in 1893, I did not become interested in technical philosophy until 1897.

The specific occasion that led me to enter technical philosophy was my interest in socialism, which seemed to me to offer the only scientific analysis of the economic evils and political corruption of our age as well as of the main course of human history.

The defeat of Socialist and liberal candidates in the national election of 1896 and the city and state elections of 1897 led a group of us who had been active in the Socialist Labor Party to undertake a co-operative study of socialist fundamentals. We hoped that we might thus prepare ourselves for more active and intellectual propaganda. Calling ourselves the Students' League, or Marx Circle, we began to read the socialist classics.

I have never ceased to be grateful for the illumination which I found in studying Marx's *Das Kapital*. It not only helped me to recognize the poverty of most non-economic interpretations of history, but also prepared me to see that the recurrent breakdowns of capitalist economy are not unforeseeable accidents but a consequence of the private ownership of the machinery of production, whereby the processes of industry are directed for the profit of individual capitalists rather than for the satisfaction of our common needs. It helped me to see that the old optimistic but essentially anarchistic notion that the good of all will best be promoted by "rugged individualism," by each pursuing his own selfish economic gain, is a cruel superstition which men possessed of both reason and a decent amount of human sympathy cannot long maintain in the face of the hideous miseries that flourish in the shadow of man's mighty productive powers. On the other hand I was troubled by the exaggerated materialism that pervaded Marx's thinking. This was evidenced in his concentration on the production of commodities and his ignoring of the immaterial services of scientists, inventors, doctors and other non-proletarian groups. It was even more evident in the Marxist boast, which I could not swallow, that Marx never spoke of justice. Without an appeal to hatred for the injustice of the prevailing economic order, would we not be dumb and ineffective exponents of the socialist message?

In the course of our reading, the references in Marx and Engels to Hegel's dialectic method gripped me. My courses in logic and economics at college under Clarence Galston, later a distinguished Federal judge but then a budding instructor just out of City College himself, had led me to John Stuart Mill, whose individualism I found unsatisfying. I felt that the fundamental issue between individualism and socialism was inextricably bound up with the difference between the introspective method of Mill and the historical method of Marx and Engels. Not having any competent guide to philosophy, I naïvely turned to Hegel himself and tried to get enlightenment from an English translation of the third part of his *Logic*. This, of course, was too tough a diet for a philosophic babe, yet I could not abandon my quest. I had a vague conviction that there was something radically wrong with Mill's doctrine of induction and his attempt to build up an economy out of individual preferences and a world out of independent things, facts, or "states of mind." After all, somehow or other things are intimately connected in the same universe.

My search for enlightenment led me to the Neo-Hegelians. The books which offered me most food for reflection were Watson's *Comte, Mill and Spencer*, and Dewey's *Psychology*. They confirmed my aversion for the positivists who thought that natural science could dispose of the problems of reality. Yet I could not accept the large claims of the Hegelian and Neo-Hegelian philosophies. I had a strong repugnance to a certain vague supernatural element in Hegelianism that is incompatible with the spirt of the natural sciences, which have always seemed to me man's supreme achievement in the way of solid knowledge. The intellectual world was thus divided for me into two camps, individualism or atomism on the one hand and absolutism on the other. I could not be at peace in either. I therefore fell into a slough of philosophic despond from which desultory reading and agonized efforts at original thought could not extricate me.

Zest for the philosophic venture was rekindled by Thomas Davidson in the spring of 1899. He aroused in me the great dream of a group of congenial spirits co-operating to create a philosophic world view adequate to the needs of the approaching twentieth century. My heart was thus set on the systematic and comprehensive aspects of philosophy and I was led to read generally along diverse lines. With the poverty of time and energy at my disposal then and for many years after, the spreading of my interests filled my intellectual life with many enterprises that fell just short of completion. Davidson himself, at that time, held to an extreme individualism and subjectivism which neither gratitude nor personal admiration could induce me to accept. He introduced me, however, to Hume and Kant and helped me to read and understand Plato, Aristotle and the Pre-Socratics. He even insisted that I study Latin and Greek, which I did, on my own, with some help from another favorite pupil of Davidson's, Mary Ryshpan.

Davidson was intent on diverting us from our concern with issues of social reform, for which he thought we lacked knowledge and understanding, and leading us to the more fundamental problems of mind and matter. In this he was at least temporarily successful. I remember how he persuaded me of the truth of Aristotle's comment that young men are more fit to cope with the problems of mathematics and physics than with the larger and more complex problems of ethics and politics. Accordingly, though I never abandoned the interest in history which had been nourished in infancy by my grandfather, my Rabbi Nehemiah, and my reading of Josephus, and which had later been fed by

the Marxist writings on the interpretation of history, my intellectual
life began to center more and more upon the problem of the nature
of knowledge.

When, at Davidson's urging, I read Hume I was left with a profound admiration for the clarity and honesty of Hume's skepticism but
irritated by what seemed to me the flat contradictions in his fundamental position. If, as Hume argues, our minds know only their own
impressions, then we cannot, as Hume also assumes, know that we
have a mind which receives impressions or that there is an external
world from which impressions are received.

At Davidson's further suggestion I turned to Kant to find an
answer to the problem that Hume presented. But my reading of Kant
was interrupted, to be resumed years later in my graduate studies at
Harvard, for upon Davidson's death in 1900 I assumed the burden of
continuing the practical educational work which he had begun. For
a number of years I thus conducted classes in cultural history, in which
I tried to apply the evolutionary philosophy to the history of industry
of the family, of religion and of Greek and Hebrew literature. It was
only the reading in later years of some of Professor Boas's anthropological writings that opened my eyes to the inadequacy of all formulas of universal evolution, whether Hegelian or Spencerian.

A study of Aristotle which I had begun under Davidson and
continued in a two-year seminar with Professor Woodbridge in the
Graduate School of Columbia University in 1902-4, made it clear
that neither historical nor psychological explanations of beliefs can
serve as substitutes for the discriminating inquiry into their truth. At
the same time, Felix Adler, with his insistence on the inescapability of
moral issues in every field of life, helped me to see that history alone,
while it may extend our vistas, will not solve our contemporary ethical
problems.

It was the study of Russell's *Principles of Mathematics* which I
began soon after I was appointed to teach mathematics at the City
College in 1902, that finally liberated me from the feeling of helpless
philosophic bewilderment and enabled me to undertake an independent journey. Russell came closer to being my philosophical god
than any one before or since. When I first met him, thirteen years
later, he was already turning from his concern with eternal truths to

the fleeting issues of the day. But I prided myself on remaining faithful to his original teaching even when my philosophical god departed somewhat from the way.

Russell's demonstration that pure mathematics or logic cannot be identified with either psychologic or physical events but constitutes a part of the real world as well as of the world of thought, seemed to me to offer a well-grounded and fruitful starting point for philosophy. Here was a standpoint that explained the fruitfulness of mathematical method in building up scientific knowledge.

This renewed faith in logic showed me how to avoid both Mill's extreme individualism, which denies real connections, and the absolutism of Hegel and Marx, in which there is no room for real individuality. In mathematics there are no pre-eminent numbers. One is as real as two or three, but not more so. Circles are not more real than squares, equality is not more real than inequality, variables are not more real than constants. Accepting the ultimate validity of logic and mathematics thus made it possible for me to see that unity and plurality, similarity and difference, dependence and independence, form and matter, change and permanence, are equally real. It also showed me that no one of these conceptions can exist or have meaning without the other, just as the opposite blades of a scissors or the north and south poles of a magnet cannot function except in pairs, united in opposition. When any one of these conceptions, unity or plurality, independence or dependence, is blown up to include the entire universe and so swallow up its opposite it ceases to have any meaning. This standpoint freed me from subservience to false absolutisms, in law, in politics, and in metaphysics, as well as in religion. The idea that the nature of things depends upon the equilibrium of opposing forces, and that therefore the way to get at the nature of things is to reason from opposing considerations, came to be a permanent part of my philosophical outlook, reinforced by suggestions that came to me from Professor Felix Adler, from Professor Josiah Royce, and from Marshall's *Principles of Economics*. The idea that opposite viewpoints could each embody elements of truth was strengthened by Wilmon Sheldon, whom I had met at Glenmore in 1899 and under whom I studied at Columbia in 1903-4. I was much impressed by the insight of Sheldon's observation that philosophers were generally right in what they affirmed of their own vision and generally wrong in what they denied of the vision of others.

The realization that Euclidean and non-Euclidean geometries, individualistic and socialistic viewpoints, and monistic and pluralistic philosophies could exist side by side and each reveal some aspect of a common truth gave me a new insight into the nature of liberal civilization, which owes its strength, as do science and philosophy, to the encouragement and tolerance of different outlooks upon a common reality. My long-standing interest in history came to center more and more upon the problem: What are the conditions of a liberal civilization? And in the effort to deal with this problem I found a fruitful point of departure in the intimate connection between scientific method and liberal civilization. Science, it seemed to me, is not, as it is popularly conceived, a new set of dogmas taught by a newer and better set of priests called scientists. It is rather a method which is based on a critical attitude to all plausible and self-evident propositions. It seeks not to reject them, but to find out what evidence there is to support them rather than their possible alternatives. This open eye for possible alternatives, each to receive the same logical treatment before we can determine which is the best grounded, is the essence of liberalism in art, morals, and politics. The liberal views life as an adventure in which we must take risks in new situations, but in which there is no guaranty that the new will always be the good or the true. Like science, liberalism insists on a critical examination of the content of all our beliefs, principles, or initial hypotheses and on subjecting them to a continuous process of verification so that they will be progressively better founded in experience and reason.

The fanatic clings to certain beliefs and in their defense is ready to shut the gates of mercy on mankind, precisely because he cannot see any alternative to them except utter chaos or iniquity. Rational reflection, however, makes us see other possibilities and opens our minds to the thought that some of the moral or physical principles that seem to us self-evident may be only sanctified taboos or inherited conventions.

Rational reflection thus enables us to frame policies of action and ethical judgment fit for wider outlooks than those of immediate physical stimulus and organic impulse. In enabling us to anticipate the future and adjust ourselves to it in advance, it lifts us above the necessity of living from hand to mouth in the mere immediacy of the moment. It thus enlarges our being and gives us strength to contemplate new physical and moral possibilities without that dizzy bewilderment which comes to creatures of mere routine when they face the unfamiliar.

As I wrestled with technical questions of philosophy in my youthful days I was buoyed up by the thought that I could some day return to the problems of social reform better equipped to deal with their basic elements. But the priests of the temple of philosophy seemed to me too much preoccupied with ritual or technique. It seemed to me that our philosophers had little to offer to the student of civilization in the way of genuinely sustaining intellectual food. The technical issues that absorbed the attention of writers in *The Journal of Philosophy* did not offer the synoptic vision which I needed to pull together my various intellectual interests and to bring adequate perspective into my view of life. It was therefore with much sympathy that I first heard William James declare that the essence of philosophy is vision and not technique, that where there is no vision the people perish.

Pride in ritual and technique has always been deadly to intellectual achievement. One who has learned a sacred or scientifically revered language can often obscure the emptiness of his own thought by simply exhibiting his command of proper terminology. This has always seemed to me to explain the poverty of much modern writing in psychology and sociology. This was the theme of my first philosophical essay to find its way into print, a paper called "The Conception of Philosophy in Recent Discussion," which I read in December, 1909, at the meeting of the American Philosophical Association at Yale University, and which was published a few months later in *The Journal of Philosophy*, of which my teacher, Professor Woodbridge, was an editor. This essay was essentially a protest against the then prevailing tendency to restrict the subject matter of philosophy to more or less technical problems of the nature of knowledge and to avoid the larger task of viewing critically all phases of human life. It was an appeal to professional philosophers to recognize the ancient need of a more or less integrated view of the general panorama of life and existence. If, as I thought, philosophy could be considered as a reflective view of the world, then why assume that where two philosophies differ one must be wrong? Two pictures of the same object taken from different points can both be true, in spite of radical differences. Philosophy, then, might be something more than an exact science. It might be, in some sense, an art form, a way of life and vision. And as such it might have as close affiliations with law, literature and economics as with physics, chemistry or other exact sciences.

Twenty years later I would put forth a similar plea in my presidential address delivered before the American Philosophical Association in December, 1929. But in this latter address I was careful to add the observation that without laborious and thoroughgoing technique neither art nor science nor philosophy can prosper or live worthily, and that while philosophy is primarily a vision and all great philosophers have something in common with poets and prophets, serious philosophy must go beyond poetic image or prophecy and, like science, concern itself with the rigorous search for demonstrable truth. The seed which ripens into vision may be a divine gift, but the labor of cultivating it so that it may bear nourishing fruit is the indispensable function of arduous scientific technique. How does philosophy as the love of wisdom differ from the love of opinion, if not by its unswerving determination to seek the truth by clear and demonstrative evidence? Without rigorous logic and technical development philosophical vision is a dark night in which all cows are black.

But delivering a presidential address before the American Philosophical Association was no part of the landscape for me in 1909, when philosophy itself was something to engage in by stealth outside of long hours teaching mathematics and studying law.

CHAPTER TWENTY-TWO

A STRAY DOG AMONG THE PHILOSOPHERS

HAVING EXAMINED the claims to exclusive truth put forward by various philosophies and judging them all to be unsupported by the evidence, I resigned myself to a position of skepticism towards all philosophical systems and system-builders. In the pride of youth I came to refer to myself as philosophically a stray dog unchained to any metaphysical kennel. It seemed to me better to brave the muddy realities of the unprotected out-of-doors, the uncertain food, the attacks from the watchdogs of comfortable homes, and above all the chilling rains and winds of factual experience. For the roving way led through bracing airs over green hills to broad sunny plains and sparkling rivers flowing to distant seas. I have never become completely at home in even the greatest of academic philosophies. I can never forget that there is a world outside of their boundaries, and their guards look askance at me because I never completely get rid of the out-of-door mud.

I suppose it was this unabashed skepticism towards inflated claims that led Justice Holmes to epitomize our common viewpoint in one of his earliest letters to me, written May 27, 1917:

. . . I think we are at one in not believing that man can swallow the universe. I at least go on very comfortably without the belief that I am in on the ground floor with God or that the cosmos, whether it wears a beard or not, needs me in order to know itself. I suppose it needs me as it needs any grain of sand, because I am here. And the whole, if there is a whole, would be I know not how much other, if an atom were subtracted from it, but I do not believe that a shudder would go through the sky if our whole ant heap were kerosened. But then it might — in short my only belief is that I know nothing about it. Truth may be cosmically ultimate for all I know. I merely surmise that our last word probably is not *the*

MORRIS R. COHEN

"A Stray Dog among the Philosophers"

last word, any more than that of horses or dogs. It is our last word none-
theless. And I don't see why we shouldn't do our job in the station in
which we were born without waiting for an angel to assure us that it is
the jobbest job in jobdom. But we are all like the old Knights who
wouldn't be satisfied with your admission that their girl was a very nice
girl, but would knock your head off if you didn't admit that she was the
best ever — bar the Virgin Mary, perhaps.

Though I could not swallow the universe, I could, I thought,
take bites out of it. And so, at least until the onset of the years of
post-rheumatic wisdom, I devoted most of my philosophic explora-
tions to rather specific problems in the fields of my special interests,
notably in jurisprudence and scientific method.

JURISPRUDENCE

Reflection on law was a major part of the Talmudic studies of my
childhood. The Hebraic God is primarily a law-giver, and the great
cultural hero of the Hebrew tradition after whom I was named (Morris being the current Anglicization of the Hebrew Moishe or Moses)
has always been regarded as primarily a law teacher. Thus I could not
help viewing the law, from the first, as a pattern of life, rather than
as a set of rules to be memorized, obeyed, or watched out for.

When I came to America and saw the effects of legal rules and
judicial decisions on the daily life of those nearest to me, my thinking
inevitably recurred to the meaning of law in the lives of men and
women. At first I used to think that the havoc-working opinions of
our courts in labor cases were simply the product of a lack of sympathetic understanding of the actual conditions under which most men
and women work and live. But when I came to study the history of
human thought I found that the road of relief for the oppressed and
the needy was also barred by an old philosophy whose limitations had
often been demonstrated in the purely intellectual realm. American
thought, it seemed to me, was suffering from a belated adherence to
the eighteenth-century philosophy of natural rights, which was being
invoked to smash all progressive legislation in economic fields. As the
teaching of philosophy became my daily occupation, I found that legal
material gave new and pointed significance to old issues in logic,
ethics, and metaphysics. The craving for absolute moral distinctions
and the confused effort to apply them to practical life — the source of

so much of our spiritual grandeur and misery — appear nowhere more clearly than in the history of the law. Law, philosophy, and social justice thus became merged in an absorbing theme of reflection.

Though as a philosopher I could recognize the limitations of philosophy in the realm of practical politics, as a citizen I felt the obligation of informing myself on political questions at issue. When, therefore, after some years of immersion in the simpler and more definite problems of non-Euclidean geometry and mathematical logic I turned to the study of political issues, I naturally brought with me the critical attitude to axioms which is so essential to modern mathematics. In that light I could not help feeling that a great deal of contemporary political discussion rested on very tenuous ground. The shoddy reasons which conservative bigwigs were resorting to in their denunciation of the Progressive movement during New York state electoral campaign of 1910 and the national campaign of 1912 made me, at least for the time, an enthusiastic defender of the Progressive cause. In 1912, when I ceased to teach mathematics and found more time for the study of social problems, the Progressive campaign was at its height. The argument over the recall of judges was in full force, and I undertook to analyze the arguments of those who were defending the courts from popular criticism. I prepared a short piece, "The Recall of Political Axioms." The piece was never published, but writing it and getting criticisms on it from friends like Felix Frankfurter and Sam Rosensohn helped me to block out the outlines of a legal philosophy.

It seemed to me that the hypocrisy of the current legal orthodoxy centered in the axiom that judges do not make law. This appeared to be not only untrue but hypocritical in so far as those who proclaimed this axiom in defending judges against popular clamor also, in unguarded moments, paid homage to the contributions of various judges to the development of the law.

Axiomatic among the conservative lawyers of the period was the doctrine that the judge is simply a legal automaton or phonograph playing the records of precedent and entirely uninfluenced by any economic or social theory or prejudice which he might have when off the bench. I had been reading judicial decisions, especially in labor cases, with some care, at least since the year at Harvard in 1905-6 when I roomed with Felix Frankfurter. I knew how different the reality was from the arbitrary and often unenlightened conceptions that judges entertained of the various aspects of industrial employment. I could not, therefore, help seeing that the social and economic beliefs of judges remained potent even where they were unconsciously held and that a man's philosophy is not necessarily true just because he has never examined it.

The attempt of the legal conservatives to bolster their position with the slogan that we live under a government of laws and not of men seemed to me to ignore the human aspect of the judicial process and of the role of lawyers themselves in influencing the course of judicial decisions.

The critique of these traditional legal views is today perhaps a matter of common currency. Indeed I have felt that those who in recent years have proclaimed the importance of judges in molding the law, the large role of judicial philosophies and prejudices, and the human failings of judges, have often overstated and exaggerated valid points. But in 1912 these ideas were very far from the beaten track of philosophers, lawyers, judges, and even law teachers. A plea to philosophers to consider "Jurisprudence as a Philosophical Discipline," which I presented at the meeting of the American Philosophical Association in December, 1912, left the waters of academic philosophy unrippled.

Yet I was convinced that the union of legal thinking and philosophy offered great promise for the clarification of contemporary political issues as well as for the reviving of academic philosophy. This conviction grew in discussions and arguments, in Childs' Restaurant and other places of free discussion, with Sam Rosensohn, Alvin Johnson, Emory Buckner, and other friends, in which we pushed back from the issues of the day to the underlying philosophic presuppositions and attitudes that these issues embodied. Roscoe Pound helped me to discover that though the stage of American legal philosophy was nearly empty, vigorous thinking and writing in Germany, France and Italy had much to offer towards an understanding of the underlying issues of the American scene. For by and large, the "standpat" philosophy of our own legal conservatives followed ideas developed by Savigny and other Continental opponents of law reform a century ago. The criticisms which had been directed against these musty champions of European conservatism over many decades offered a good deal of light on the weaknesses of American legal thought. In particular the concern over the creative functions of the judge developed by Hermann Kantorowicz and other exponents of *Freie Rechtsfindung,* and the concern with the relations of law to economics and other social sciences developed by French, Austrian, and Italian jurists seemed to me to have much to offer to students of American jurisprudence.

With some encouragement from my new department head, Professor Overstreet, I decided to try to bring together representatives of legal and philosophic thought. Such a match, I hoped, might make philosophers a little more conscious of the way in which philosophy, and especially legal philosophy, contributes, for better or worse, to the life of civilization. It might also make law teachers, at least (I had no hope of reaching lawyers and judges) more aware of the unspoken assumptions of their teaching, which only philosophizing could bring to light. So was born the Conference on Legal and Social Philosophy. John Dewey was chairman, and I was secretary.

Our first two-day meeting was held in 1913, at City College on April 25 and at Columbia University on April 26. The subject was "Law in Relation to Social Ends." Our reporter, Professor W. E. Hocking, observed, however, that no time was lost drumming upon the truism that law ought to have some relation to social ends: instead the speakers attacked the central problem of determining what social welfare is, how changes in ideals of welfare bring about changes in conceptions of justice, and how law could be adjusted to these changes. Roscoe Pound, a teacher then and not yet a dean, opened the conference with a discourse on "The Philosophy of Law in America." Felix Adler and James H. Tufts discussed the criteria of social welfare, the anthropologist Alexander Goldenweiser expounded "The Ethnological Approach to Law," and Dean William Draper Lewis, the genial chairman of the resolutions committee of the Progressive Party and later Director of the American Law Institute, spoke on "The Social Sciences as the Basis of Legal Education." Other papers on the borderland between law and ethics were read by Professors Isaac Husik, W. W. Willoughby, H. R. Marshall, G. W. Kirchwey, and Simon N. Patten.

I had done a good deal of further reading and writing on what I called the "phonograph theory" of the judicial process, and read a paper on "The Process of Judicial Legislation," which, published a year later in *The American Law Review,* created more of a stir than anything I had ever written. Much of the stir was quite unfavorable but this did not make it ungratifying. The deans of some of our largest law schools wrote me that while the contention that judges do have a share in making the law was unanswerable, it was still advisable to keep up the fiction of the phonograph theory to prevent the law from becoming more fluid than it already is. But these protests did not disturb my abiding conviction that to recognize the truth and to adjust one's self to it is, in the end, the only civilized course in a democracy.

The little group that attended our 1913 conference decided that the experiment was worth repeating on a larger scale. And so, on the motion of Felix Adler, a committee was set up to organize a second conference in the spring of 1914.

Our second conference was held in Chicago, on April 10 and 11, 1914, in conjunction with the Western Philosophical Association. Chicago was then a center of sociologic thought and philosophic pragmatism, and some of the country's leading philosophers and teachers participated, among them Professors John Dewey, Roscoe Pound, Warner Fite, John Wigmore, Albert Kocourek, Frank Sharp, Albion Small, Henry M. Bates, W. F. Dodd, James P. Hall, and Jesse S. Reeves. Some of the papers, such as Ernst Freund's "Legislation and Administrative Discretion" and Roscoe Pound's "Rule and Discretion in the Administration of Justice" made a lasting impact upon American legal thinking.

My own paper at this conference was an outgrowth of my reading in European legal philosophy, which led me to appreciate that the idea of "natural law" is not an outworn superstition based on false history, but rather a perennial effort to appeal from the idolatrous woi ship of the work of men's hands to a higher ideal of righteousness. My defense of the concern with social justice embodied in the doctrine of "natural law," published two years later in the *Philosophical Review* under the title "Jus Naturale Redivivum," became one of the blocks for the building of my first philosophical treatise, *Reason and Nature*.

Heart trouble that became severe on Thanksgiving Day of 1914 and led me to take a leave of absence in the spring term prevented me from participating in our third conference, held in December, 1914. Various other complications arose to prevent a well-attended meeting, although Professors Freund, Overstreet, Mead, and Dodd read stimulating papers.

The last formal meeting of our conference was held on November 26 and 27, 1915, at Columbia University. A number of new recruits were enlisted on our roster of speakers, among them Louis D. Brandeis — who was nominated to the Supreme Court two months later — Felix Frankfurter, and Arthur Lovejoy. Harold Laski wandered down from McGill University at Montreal to escape the cold weather, he said. At our first meeting we became friends for life.

In an effort to bring our thinking into closer contact with Continental developments in the borderland between law and social science, I had prepared an analysis of recent literature on legal philosophy in French, German, and Italian. I also presented a paper, " 'Real' and 'Ideal' Forces in Civil Law," which was an attempted appraisal of opposing materialistic and idealistic views of law. Subsequently the paper was published in the *International Journal of Ethics,* though not before its editor, Professor Tufts, had warned me that it is easier for a reader to drop a magazine than it is for a listener to sneak out of a lecture room. The moral was that I should use more guile in appealing to the reader's interest and less of the bristling technical vocabulary of professional philosophers or professional lawyers.

Meanwhile, I had bearded the lawyers in their den by reading a paper before the New York State Bar Association in Buffalo on January 22, 1915, on "Legal Theories and Social Science." The title was intended to be provocative, inasmuch as lawyers and judges like to think that law is scientific and has nothing to do with social "theory." The fact, of course, is that law is full of untested theories which fall far below even the very modest scientific standards of economics or anthropology. My appeal to the bar was in the mood of Emerson's words, "Why should we grope among the dry bones of the past, or put the living generation into masquerade out of its faded wardrobe? The sun shines to-day also. There is more wool and flax in the fields. There are new lands, new men, new thoughts. Let us demand our own works and laws and worship."

The phonograph theory [I said] has bred the mistaken view that the law is a closed, independent system having nothing to do with economic, political, social or philosophical science. If, however, we recognize that courts are constantly remaking the law then it becomes of the utmost social importance that the law should be made in accordance with the best available information which it is the object of science to supply. Law deals with human affairs, and it is impossible to legislate or make any judgment with regard to them without involving all sorts of assumptions or theories. The issue, therefore, is not between a fixed law on the one hand, and social theories on the other, but between social theories unconsciously assumed and social theories carefully examined and scientifically studied. . . . Hence the lawyer who regards his work as a liberal profession rather than as a commercial trade, must not be satisfied with merely guarding the works which have been handed over to him. He must study the stream of life and be constantly thinking of ways of improving the containing legal forms. We too are men, and now we will live not as pall bearers of a dead past but as the creators of a more glorious future. By all means let us be loyal to the past, but above all loyal to the future, to the Kingdom which doth not yet appear.[1]

I do not think my paper made much of an impression on the audience, but an amusing incident is associated in my memory with its reading. One of my fellow speakers at the meeting was former President Taft. Years later, at the height of the postwar hysteria in which all sorts of violence and illegality were being used against socialists and pacifists, I met him on the street and, taking advantage of our brief contact, suggested that those who upheld, as he did, the supremacy of the courts should speak out against the disregard of law that was manifested in these incidents. He was then Chief Justice of the United States but his reply to me was, "Yes, it is too bad that our side is doing that."

It was in this period from 1913 to 1916 that I wrote two other papers on legal philosophy, "Rule vs. Discretion," for *The Journal of Philosophy* in 1914, and "The Place of Logic in the Law," a contribution to the special issue of the *Harvard Law Review* in 1916 honoring Justice Holmes's seventy-fifth birthday.

All these papers were attempts to get at the basic ideas that could provide an adequate starting point for a liberal analysis of American law and our social order.

It is hard to realize the poverty of American legal philosophy or jurisprudence in the earliest years of the present century. Indeed, in an article in the *Harvard Law Review* for 1914 an eminent judge expressed indignation as well as surprise that anyone in America should venture to study Continental law and legal philosophy. Our activities

---

[1] "Legal Theories and Social Science," *International Journal of Ethics*, XXV (1915), 469; also printed by the New York State Bar Association, 1915.

in the Conference on Legal and Social Philosophy made little impression at the time on judges or practicing lawyers but they did help send a fresh wind through the stuffy air of the law schools and the law reviews. I suppose there are few fields of American thought where one finds so marked a growth over a span of twenty or thirty years as in the field of legal teaching and legal writing. The currents that our Conference on Legal and Social Philosophy started could not help but influence generations of law students and, through them, in the end, public opinion and public life.

The hostile climate of opinion in which I undertook these early studies in legal philosophy and the fact that I was not a lawyer, made it difficult to secure a hearing for the critical viewpoints I sought to put forward on the meaning of law in our social order. But I was sustained by the zest which my students at City College brought to the courses I gave in legal philosophy and by the encouragement and friendly criticism of loyal friends, among them Felix Frankfurter, Judge Learned Hand, Roscoe Pound, Arthur Meyer, Walter Pollak, Sam Rosensohn, Emory Buckner, and Harold Laski. Most sustaining and stimulating of all was the friendship with Justice Oliver Wendell Holmes which grew out of the warm letters in which he used to comment on these early papers of mine. To one who in those years had little to look back upon in the way of achievement and even less in the way of recognition, the glowing words of America's greatest jurist meant a great deal.

While my entry into the Philosophy Department in 1912 gave me a chance to concentrate a larger part of my reading and thinking on legal philosophy, the founding of the *New Republic* in 1914 and the frequent urgings of its editors, Alvin Johnson, Herbert Croly, Francis Hackett, Philip and Robert Littell, and Walter Lippmann, led me to do a great deal of sporadic writing and book reviewing on current social issues as well as on the more enduring problems of law, science and history. I was not always in sympathy with the benevolent aspirations of some of the editors of the *New Republic* to lead the American public in the paths of righteousness, and in later years wrote more and more infrequently for the magazine. But in the years between 1914 and 1921 I was a fairly regular contributor, and twenty-five years later, in gathering a good many of these casual papers together for publication in a volume, *Faith of a Liberal,* I found very few papers which I had any desire to change. Some might view this fact as showing only my inability to learn from the experience of the intervening years. For my part, the test of the years has always seemed to me the best test of the permanent value of the approach which underlies one's day-by-day appraisals of current affairs.

One of the first indications that our Conference on Legal and Social Philosophy had helped to break down the walls between jurisprudence and philosophy came at the end of 1917, when the Association of American Law Schools asked me to join its Editorial Committee, which was engaged in the praiseworthy task of overcoming our American provincialism in jurisprudence by translating into English a number of recent important Continental treatises in the field. I was glad to join in the venture, in which I had already participated informally for some time, for it gave me an added incentive to keep up my reading of the outstanding German, French, and Italian jurists.

I began to feel, finally, that I had forged the instruments for a general attack on the problems of jurisprudence, and had tested them in a long enough series of critical book reviews and articles on current issues. I felt that I could at last undertake a systematic critique of legal institutions in a democracy. This ambition was nourished by the invitation from Columbia Law School to give a course in legal philosophy in the summer of 1927 and by subsequent invitations from St. John's, Buffalo, and Yale law schools. In many of these courses faculty members sat as auditors, and the give-and-take of classroom and after-class discussion gave me some assurance that I was dealing with real problems and not repeating accepted catchwords posing as solutions.

With the framework of a general treatise on legal philosophy in mind and the material of lecture notes and classroom preparation to start from, I managed to get out the essays "Property and Sovereignty," "Law and Scientific Method," and "Justice Holmes and the Nature of Law." In 1930 I collaborated with my son Felix in putting together a source book in legal philosophy for use in my classes at St. John's Law School and City College, there being no available source book in the field. The volume was gotten out in a private and limited edition, with the hope that we could return to the work and some day produce a more ample and useful volume. Such a volume, we hoped, would draw together the most abstract theories and the most concrete problems in the field, utilizing foreign as well as American materials. But there were many distractions in the 1930's that prevented completion of the systematic critique of legal institutions that I had planned twenty years before.

SCIENTIFIC METHOD

The world of science which was revealed to me in my student days at City College loomed as the most distinctive achievement of the modern civilization to which my parents had transported me. The Hellenic ideal of science as a rational inquiry into nature seemed to be the foundation of the distinctive intellectual traits of Western civilization, or of what is sometimes called the modern mind. It was the appeal to nature against conventional taboos and the appeal to reason against arbitrary authority that called modern liberal civilization into being. Unfortunately for the career of liberal civilization, however, various circumstances have brought about a mutual hostility between these two appeals to what are popularly called the heart and the mind. The appeal to nature is frequently a form of sentimental irrationalism, and the appeal to reason is often a call to suppress nature in the interest of conventional supernaturalism.

To understand the true role of reason in nature called for an inquiry into the general meaning of scientific method — that is, of the principles according to which scientific results are obtained and according to which these results are being constantly revised. In developed natural science, reason and nature are happily united. Thus, it seemed to me, no synoptic view of liberal civilization could be adequate which did not include an understanding of science. For years I pursued the dream of producing a philosophical history of science from Pythagoras to Einstein, and though I later came to appreciate that I could never hope to master the many fields of science, I did continue in the effort to get at the basic conceptions and methods utilized in the main fields of science. In this effort I was much stimulated by Wendell T. Bush, one of the editors of *The Journal of Philosophy*, and later by the editors of the *New Republic*, who generally saw to it that I had a chance to review, or at least know about, important scientific books as they appeared.

City College students are not as prone to accept the authority of textbooks (or any other kind of authority) as are the students of some other institutions of learning. Consequently, when I began to teach mathematics in 1902 they, as well as I, did not always find the traditional modes of proof in algebra and geometry, as set forth in the textbooks, logically adequate. This led me to study works on the foundations of mathematics that might throw some light on the nature of mathematical proof and mathematical axioms. My discovery of Russell's great masterpiece, *The Principles of Mathematics,* which had given a foundation to my general philosophical thinking, provided me with the basic tools for my inquiries into the nature of scientific method. In particular, the study of non-Euclidean geometry helped me to see how the growth of science depended on the questioning of traditional assumptions and the precise formulation of possible alternatives. It also showed me how impossible it is to deduce the nature of the world from reason alone, and thus saved me from becoming a worshiper of Kant. For some years, particularly after my return to teaching at City College in 1906, I devoted a good deal of my reading to mathematical philosophy and later to mathematical physics. The second philosophical article I ever published was "The Present Situation in the Philosophy of Mathematics," which was read before the American Philosophical Association in 1910 and published in 1911 in *The Journal of Philosophy.* A similar paper on physics was read before the American Philosophical Association in 1911 and published in 1918. Both these articles I thought of as chapters of a more comprehensive work on scientific method, and both were eventually incorporated into *Reason and Nature.*

Though the essentials of Einstein's theory of relativity were known to the scientific public as far back as 1905, it was only after the astronomical confirmation of its law of gravitation in 1919 that it captured the world's imagination. During the years of the First World War it had been practically impossible in this country to secure copies of the papers in which Einstein developed his generalized theory of relativity, and at the war's end I did my best to make up for lost time. Popular difficulties with the theory of relativity seemed to me to spring from the crudely materialistic conception of things as complete in themselves. These difficulties do not arise if one recognizes the reality of relations, and the fact that opposite relations may inhere in the same object. In a spirited exchange of articles with Professor Lovejoy in 1913 and 1914 I had sought to defend the position that relativity is a characteristic of the real world and not merely a figment of the intellect. The development of Einstein's physical theories seemed to me to give added significance to this philosophical viewpoint.

At the urging of the *New Republic* editors, I wrote several more or less popular articles in 1920 and 1921 on the theory of relativity, hoping to use them some day as bricks in the edifice of a popular volume on the foundations of science. When Einstein came to this country and lectured at City College in 1921, I happened to be the most readily available person who understood both his language and his mathematics, and so I was asked to translate his lectures. This gave rise to the altogether undeserved popular legend that I was one of the unbelievably few people in the world who understood the Einstein theory. I suppose that it was because of this legend that *Vanity Fair* paid me one hundred dollars to look at a movie on Einstein's theory of relativity and comment on it. It was the only movie I had ever gone to. I have often expressed a willingness to go to another movie on the same terms, but have found no takers.

Actually the conversations and the friendship with Einstein that began in 1921 gave a good deal of stimulus to my thinking about science, and gave me assurance that a philosophical approach based on the reality of relations would be serviceable in the understanding of scientific method generally. For if relations are real, then statements which ignore them are incomplete, and apparently opposite assertions that something is near and far, or good and bad, may both be true when properly completed. Such an approach might eliminate many false alternatives and antitheses, I felt, in the social as well as the natural sciences. This conviction was nourished by friends who had done distinguished work in a good many different fields of science, L. Michaelis, the biochemist, A. Fraenkel, the mathematical physicist, Gustave Schultz, a former student and a distinguished figure in mathematical economics, and the anthropologists Boas, Goldenweiser, Lowie, and Sapir, among others.

My dream of publishing a treatise on scientific method had taken on new life in 1919, when Justice Holmes, Judge Mack, Jacob Billikopf and other friends helped me over a period of vast discouragement and financial difficulty by subsidizing a sabbatical year in which I was able to devote myself to reading and writing without the distraction of college classes. In the early 1920's the outlines of my projected volume on scientific method began to take shape. As a prospective chapter of this volume I had done a brief study in political science, "Communal Ghosts in Political Theory," in 1919. Editing a collection of essays of the great American philosophic pioneer and lonely rover, C. S. Peirce, in 1923, helped to illuminate my groping for a systematic view of reason and nature. In 1925 I published a series of papers on reason as the basis of scientific method, and on the rivals and substitutes for reason. Two years later I found the stimulus for completing another chapter of my hoped-for treatise when Professors Ogburn and Goldenweiser asked me to contribute an article on the natural and the social sciences to a symposium volume. There were still large gaps in my treatise. Some were not too difficult to fill. One that gave me much trouble was the chapter on psychology: I had never gotten out of all my studies in psychology at City College and Harvard as much psychological insight as I gathered in the days when I was a merchant — selling newspapers in 1894 between Park Row and the Bowery.

There were other chapters of the projected volume with which I was not really satisfied. But I had made the mistake of telling Justice Holmes back in 1923 that I was hoping to get out my book within a year and that it would be dedicated to him. The years had stretched out, and over many summers, in the leisure between terms I had worked to bring the volume to completion. Beginning in the summer of 1924 I had enjoyed a quiet study cabin in the McDowell Colony, which the inspired widow of the great American composer maintained at Peterboro, New Hampshire, for the use of writers and artists. In later years I spent two or three summer months at another refuge from telephones and daily cares, Yaddo, the Spencer Trask estate near Saratoga. Each day's output was meager, but the accumulation of the years began to assume respectable proportions. Finally, two summers in the company of my eldest son served to bring the book to completion. He had by then not only attained his doctorate in philosophy but had studied law and developed a special skill in belittling the imperfections of my writings and persuading me to publish them and thus discharge my long-standing obligation to Justice Holmes. So it was that in March, 1931, I saw the fulfillment of one of the driving dreams of my life when I presented the first copy of my first book, *Reason and Nature,* to the courageous thinker and loyal friend whose faith in reason had never faltered in the winds of the passing years.

CHAPTER TWENTY-THREE

THE HARVEST YEARS

I HAVE ALWAYS THOUGHT that a philosopher should not publish a book until he reaches full maturity. And yet, although none of my books was published until I had passed the age of fifty, I have been writing books all my life. The first articles I wrote on the philosophy of science, in 1910 and 1911, were conceived as chapters of a volume on scientific method, and the first papers on jurisprudence that I wrote in the years from 1912 to 1916 were conceived as chapters of a treatise on law and justice. Sometimes I made the mistake of publicly labeling an article as part of a projected book, which would, as likely as not, turn into quite a different sort of book in the course of writing. Sometimes I made the mistake of announcing when the book would be finished, and on this I was almost always wrong. But though these dream books changed somewhat in form and content with the passing years, they served to give direction to my reading and thinking as well as to my sporadic writing.

Writing my books in instalments offered many advantages. For one thing, it gave me a chance to profit from the criticisms of colleagues scattered about the country and, in a few cases, beyond the seas, while my thinking on a given topic was still fresh and flexible. Then too, writing books in fragments came naturally to a teacher whose energies, properly wound up, just sufficed for an hour's lecturing. I have never had the sustained energy or exuberant fluency that is needed for long flights of creative writing. The thinking that could be compressed into an hour's lecture or a brief article has always brought me the greatest returns in satisfaction and stimulus — just as browsing in libraries or even glancing through book catalogues has often given me more food for thought than the reading of long-winded tomes.

I confess that after some twenty years of writing volumes, none of which appeared, I began to have some doubts as to the soundness of my method. But I was reassured when, in 1931, the first of my books actually saw the light of day with the publication of *Reason and Nature*. It was not all I had hoped it would be. In the subtitle and in the preface I expressly indicated that it was an essay, that is to say, a fragmentary study, and not a systematic treatise. Yet I felt that, however inadequate it might be in execution, not even the withering refutation of time would prove the effort to be in the wrong direction. For in few earlier ages has the general craving for philosophic light seemed so vast and the offerings of professed philosophers, preoccupied with problems of technique, so unsubstantial. And what I lacked in erudition or originality might be compensated by a stubborn refusal to subordinate the pursuit of truth to other values, to deal in false comforts, to gratify those who crave the confirmation of established prejudices, or to follow the modern penchant for philosophical novelty.

The effort to formulate a more or less integrated view of life and existence without abandoning the painfully critical methods and standards of science was an effort worth making, it seemed, even though the result showed many imperfections. This conviction was strengthened by the reception that reviewers and colleagues accorded the volume. Sweeter than all professional comments, however, was a letter that came to me in 1943 from an ensign who had lost his copy of the book when his ship went down and who sent me a check to procure another copy so that he could continue, against the backdrop of war, to develop what he thought of as "a solid, comprehensive understanding" of his "relationship to man and matter."

Ever since its appearance I have been annotating my copy of *Reason and Nature* with corrections and revisions, hoping to get out a new and amplified edition some day. Still it was good to know that at least one of my fields had come to harvest.

Apart from trying to correct and revise this text, I have, from time to time, tried to complete a companion volume that would deal with the role of unreason in nature. Though I have not in the years since 1931 left the ranks of the rationalists or repudiated any of the basic positions embodied in that first statement of my philosophical standpoint, I have come to feel that the volume failed to deal with a large realm of human life. It seemed to demand a sequel that would do justice to the obstacles that human frailty sets in the path of reason, and would trace the role of myth-making not only in the more personal aspects of human life but also in fields where myth is supposed to have no place, such as science and jurisprudence. My point of view was still that reason is the best weapon we have and that its exercise constitutes the crown of life. But I wanted to give fuller expression to the thought that a rationalist, if he is not to waste his energies or land in cynicism, should not underestimate the power of the many nonrational and irrational roots and sources of human behavior.

The fact that reason is the most valuable of all human possessions does not imply that it is the most powerful of all human forces. The powerful forces of human life which oppose the exercise of reason, the will to illusion that stands in the way of the will to truth, must be understood and evaluated if we are to use reason effectively.

Shortly after the publication of *Reason and Nature* I gave a course of six lectures on this theme at the New School for Social Research, and I hoped to write out my notes and publish the book within a few months, but poor health and later the requirements of the Conference on Jewish Relations and other interests made sustained attention to this topic impossible, and compelled continued postponements.

Once the ice had been broken, friends pressed me to publish the work on law and justice that had been planned in the years of the Conference on Legal and Social Philosophy (1913-17). My son Felix and his bride Lucy insisted that only scissors and paste and a moderate amount of editing and arguing were needed to bring forth the volume that existed potentially in my scattered juristic writings. Since they undertook to wield the scissors and paste and to do a moderate amount of the editing and arguing, I could not refuse. The summer of 1932 in a cottage overhanging a remote corner of Lake Placid was filled with the business of bookmaking. At the end of the summer the gaps in the volume seemed to me greater than ever. In my earlier essays in jurisprudence I had attempted to analyze the nature of legal thinking generally and its relations to logic, ethics, history, and social science. Only in later years did law school lecturing give me an opportunity to wrestle with more specific legal institutions.

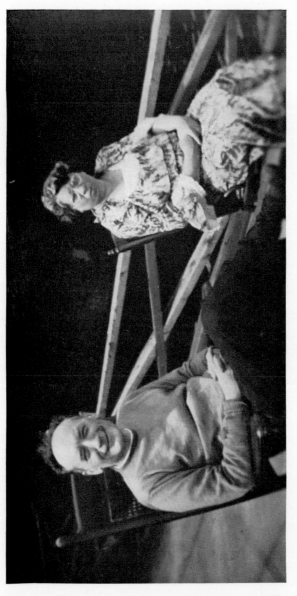

Morris R. Cohen and Mary Ryshpan Cohen

Lake Placid, 1932

Beginning in 1927 I had given a number of lectures and courses at the law schools of Cornell, Columbia, St. John's, and Yale. These contacts with the work of the law schools and with the thinking of several gifted law teachers convinced me that a good many institutions of our legal system — contract, liability, punishment, and constitutional law — called for a deeper philosophical analysis than I or anybody else had made. That, however, might call for a lifetime's work. As a logician I could appraise legal reasoning and analyze its assumptions. As a student of ethics and metaphysics, I could hope to uncover the secret ideals and undisclosed categories of judges and lawyers who had not critically examined their own presuppositions. But I could not deal with the more specific problems that lawyers, judges, and law teachers had long puzzled over without immersing myself in the extensive literature of the subject. This could not be done in brief compass. In the end I compromised by writing a chapter on contracts, as a companion piece to the one on property which I had read at Cornell, and doing a critique of current legal positivism as developed by "realists" like Yntema and Frank. With these additions to things I had said before, the volume *Law and the Social Order* was published in the spring of 1933.

Again, the publication of the volume made me keenly aware of the gaps in it and in my own juristic thinking. An opportunity to fill in some of the worst of these gaps was soon presented by the University of Buffalo Law School, which invited me to deliver, in the following winter, a series of lectures on law and ethics. Accordingly, in January, 1934, I delivered three lectures on crime and punishment, on fault and liability, and on morality and social ethics. I hoped that these lectures would serve some day as the basis of a volume to be called "Law and Justice," supplementing my *Law and the Social Order*. The demands of undergraduate teaching, however, resulted in postponing the projected new volume of juristic studies.

In the autumn of 1938, an invitation from the new dean of the Harvard Law School, James M. Landis, to deliver a series of lectures there, encouraged me to pick up my Buffalo lectures on law and justice and expand on them. In the spring of 1939, when I found that I could not resist the urge to lecture again at City College, where my old friend Professor Mead had become Acting President, I again picked up the growing manuscript "Law and Justice" to use as the subject matter of my course of lectures. And in the following autumn, giving a course in jurisprudence at Yale Law School led me back to this material. The chapter on criminal law I was able to put into shape for publication in the *Yale Law Journal* in April, 1940. But the more I wrote the larger seemed the fields of the law that I had scarcely touched, the

> . . . untravell'd world, whose margin fades
> For ever and for ever when I move.

So it had been, too, with my youthful dream of a book on the development of science. Years of teaching courses at City College on the philosophy of science had underlined my conviction that the understanding of science and of what we like to call the modern mind demands an appreciation of the Hellenic spirit of rational inquiry. As against the caricature of science drawn by the irrationalists — the notion that the Greeks were mere speculators, that medieval thinkers were all sunk in theology and superstition, and that science began in the sixteenth or seventeenth century — I had a driving desire to trace the unending adventures of the human mind from Pythagoras to Einstein which are at the source of all enduring achievements in the history of Western civilization. Articles I had written on relativity and reviews of various scientific works had been conceived as fragments of such a history of science. But just as I was coming to realize how far beyond my powers such a tracing of the development of science from its Greek beginnings would be, I found myself drawn into a co-operative enterprise which offered greater promise of success.

In 1926 the American Philosophical Association undertook to sponsor a series of historical source books in the sciences. What better way could there be of showing the superficiality of the popular legend that science begins with the "get-wise-quick" schemes of Lord Bacon than to have the student of science follow Aristotle as he marshals the evidence from which the sphericity and approximate circumference of our terrestrial globe are deduced? I was enlisted as one of the editors of the series, but even with the collaboration of experts in the various sciences the work moved with geologic slowness. The chief difficulty in such work is that those who are thoroughly grounded in philology and history are seldom familiar enough with the problems of mathematics and science to discriminate justly between genuine science and folklore. On the other hand few scientists have mastered the language difficulties in the earlier Greek and Latin works in their own fields.

The logical man to do a source book in medieval science was my old friend Richard McKeon, and after a little persuading he agreed to undertake that responsibility. Unable to find anybody to take similar responsibility for ancient science, I was reduced to the prospect of doing this myself. But my own knowledge of Latin and Greek was wholly inadequate for that task.

In the summer of 1935 I spent a good deal of time at Long Lake, in the Adirondacks, discussing the problems of Greek science with a former pupil of mine, as bright an all-round student as I ever had, Dr. Israel Edward Drabkin. He had specialized in mathematics at City College and in the classics for his postgraduate work, and was teaching Latin and Greek. I was particularly impressed with a paper on Aristotle's dynamics that he had written which showed a clear grasp of the continuity of the history of physics. It was refreshing in its contrast with the usual attitude of superficial historians who condemn Aristotle for not knowing modern physics — as if a boy were to be regarded as defective because he is not as tall as his father. Here was the sort of collaborator I needed to bring out a *Source Book in Greek Science,* and he generously agreed to enter upon the joint enterprise.

The courses I gave in the philosophy of science at Leland Stanford University in the summer of 1937, and at Chicago in 1938 and 1939, gave me sufficient excuse for what was, in any event, a fascinating journey through the early works in which the method and spirit of science were first developed. About three quarters of the material we selected was available in English translation; the rest had to be put into English by Dr. Drabkin. By the fall of 1941 our book was ready for the press. Then came the war and a publisher's decision that a *Source Book in Greek Science* would contribute neither to the morale of the country nor to the war effort. This meant an indefinite delay in publication, carrying with it a disheartening postponement of the recognition due to my collaborator, whose quiet immersion in classical studies had stood in the way of a recognition that should long ago have been accorded to his distinguished talents.

Even less success attended my efforts to work out a comprehensive analysis of the problems of metaphysics. Such an analysis I had long planned as a treatment of the problems that face us whenever we make the obstinate effort to think clearly about the general significance of the world about us and its elements. It would involve an attempt to treat such categories as time, space and causality from the polar point of view, eliminating false problems, yet pointing out that the inadequacy of all known solutions is no argument against the reality of the problems — that we are thrown against these problems by every intellectual interest in economics, politics, religion, science or history. It would thus be an analysis that would break down the absolutism of the older metaphysical solutions, but also show the inescapable urgency of dealing with these problems, of keeping the windows open on the Beyond without jumping out of them. It would thus help in the cause of a liberalism based not on the belief in necessary progress but rather on sad experience as well as on hopes.

A month or so after my retirement from City College I was asked to give a course in metaphysics at Harvard. I must admit that I was thrilled by the invitation. I have always had a warm sentimental spot in my heart for what I got from the Philosophy Department at Harvard in 1904-6, especially from Josiah Royce. He was, and still is, my ideal of what Carlyle would have called "the hero as philosopher." To give a course in metaphysics in the place where he did was, to me, one of the privileges of a lifetime. And then perhaps, after having been thrown out of gear for continuous philosophizing by the Conference work, I might revive reflective habits of 1904 and 1905 in the quiet Cambridge atmosphere — assuming that one could get far enough away from the Cambridge cars to hear the old quiet.

The course that I gave at Harvard in the fall of 1938 gave me an opportunity to block out a systematic treatment of metaphysical problems, but not to finish the job to my own satisfaction. I tried again at Chicago in 1940. At Chicago a bitter conflict was raging between the positivists, who considered metaphysics to be a refined form of nonsense, and those who worshipped at the shrine of the author of the first treatise on metaphysics, Aristotle. One day both camps had me in the same room and waited for me to take sides. I began my remarks that day by observing that Aristotle was the beginning of all wisdom — to the intense discomfiture of the anti-metaphysical half of my audience. But the smiles on Aristotelian faces faded somewhat when I added, "but not the end of all wisdom." The book on metaphysics, I had hoped, would equally irritate into thought the naturalists and the metaphysicians. I thought of calling it by the paradoxical title "Naturalistic Metaphysics." It would in any event try to establish the inevitability of metaphysical assumptions in the thinking of positivists who deny the possibility of metaphysics, and at the same time seek to demonstrate the utility of the naturalistic method of science in clarifying metaphysical issues. Instead of avoiding controversy by adopting a new vocabulary and avoiding labels, it seemed to me more exciting to rouse the watchdogs of the rival philosophic camps by accepting all the offensive labels at once. "Naturalistic Metaphysics" would do just that. But the prospect of actually completing this treatise seems ever more remote.

Almost the first book I ever rashly promised a publisher was one on contemporary American thought, which was originally planned for publication in 1926 as a volume of the international "Library of Contemporary Thought" that was being published by an English firm. The substance of one of the main chapters in the projected volume, that on American philosophy, had been largely written in instalments for the *New Republic* and published in the *Cambridge History of American Literature* in 1921. But the book I planned would focus not on technical philosophy but rather on the general ideas which are taken for granted in various fields of thought and thus come to constitute the philosophy of a period and a country even before they have been systematically articulated.

Ever since the winter of 1923-24, when Alvin Johnson succeeded in getting the New School for Social Research established and its students elected me to give the first course, I had been lecturing there, off and on, on various aspects of science and philosophy. The course which brought me the keenest response was one on contemporary American thought. I had no difficulty in lecturing on the subject, but the hope that a book could be written from my lecture notes refused to materialize. Perhaps this was because in speaking I could not stop and say, "I'll go and look something up," before continuing, whereas in writing I do that very often. Particularly was this true in a subject like American thought, where meditation cannot take the place of reading, and where the field to be covered grows year by year.

When I retired from undergraduate teaching in 1938, the completion of the volume on American thought was one of the assignments uppermost in my mind. I undertook to lecture on the subject at Chicago in the spring of 1939, and in the course of these lectures managed to get down on paper a series of sketches of American thought on science, history, philosophy, politics, jurisprudence, art, religion, psychology, education, economics, and sociology. These drafts only emphasized the limitations of my knowledge of some of the subjects dealt with. Through the 1939 spring session at Chicago I spent a large amount of time reading up on points in these lectures that needed strengthening. Particularly did I seek to remedy the gaps in my knowledge of early American scientific and economic thought and of American literary criticism and art criticism generally. Reading in the history of American geology, chemistry, astronomy, and physics made me realize how much science was cultivated early in the history of the republic. The work of Franklin in the field of electricity and of Jefferson in geology represented solid scientific research as well as a striking symbol of the common roots of science and liberalism.

In my youth, the ascetic and democratic ideas with which I began to philosophize had predisposed me to view aestheticism as a form of snobbery. Acquaintance with rare paintings or esoteric music could not be a prerequisite, I thought, to an understanding of the depths of human nature or the needs of the human spirit. As a pluralist I could find plenty of anthropological evidence for the view that talk about superior taste may mean a blindness to its natural diversity. Later reflection, however, on the fact that only a few who are highly trained understand the meaning of such scientific laws as that of gravitation, suggested that in the field of art, too, training may make clear what is otherwise vague and indistinct. Later study made it plain that the enjoyment of nature is largely motivated by art. People see or hear what great artists have taught them to see and hear. And so art criticism must be based on understanding of the techniques by which such results are attained. In this train of thought, discussions with Edwin Arlington Robinson and other fellow colonists at the McDowell and Yaddo colonies proved most stimulating.

The more I read, however, on these themes the wider loomed the seas of my ignorance. And the more I wrote on contemporary American thought the farther I was from being up to date in all its fields, much as Tristram Shandy found when it took him seven years to write the first year of his autobiography. Eventually I had to admit to myself that if I ever did complete a book on contemporary American thought it would be out of date by the time it was published. It might be possible, however, to sketch the formative influences or currents that have entered into American thinking without striving for contemporaneity. But even with this limitation the task remained a baffling one.

Better luck attended my efforts to organize my own thinking, in a comprehensive way, in the field of logic. Back in 1918, in an essay, "The Subject Matter of Formal Logic," I had expressed the opinion that of all textbooks those on logic might be considered the most illogical, consisting as they did, for the most part, of a hodgepodge of psychology, grammar, the art of rhetoric, popular science, and recipes for finding out what we already know. The need for an adequate textbook of logic had become increasingly manifest to me in the course of the years of logic-teaching at City College. Finally I found in my brilliant colleague and former student, Ernest Nagel, an ideal collaborator for the writing of such a textbook. Between the two of us — though the major part of the effort was certainly his — we managed after a summer together at Yaddo to get out in 1934 a textbook on logic and scientific method. What we had tried to produce was a text that would find a place for the realistic formalism of Aristotle, the scientific penetration of Peirce (whose philosophical essays I had edited in 1923), the pedagogical soundness of Dewey, and the mathematical rigor of Russell. If we had not entirely achieved this high objective, we hoped that at least we had achieved our minimum demand, which was inspired by the motto with which Florence Nightingale transformed modern hospital practice: "Whatever hospitals do, they should not spread disease." We hoped we had written a logic text that would not infect students with fallacies and confusions as to the nature of valid or scientific reasoning. We were both pleasantly surprised when the book was adopted as a text in various universities about the country, so that it went through five printings in five years. But we were really nonplussed, some eight years after publication, when the Army one day ordered 16,000 copies.

The publication of *An Introduction to Logic and Scientific Method* left me haunted by the things we had left unsaid. Since we had intended only a text, this was not felt a reproach. But the desire to work out the underlying presuppositions of logical analysis remained. I had originally planned to include in my book *Reason and Nature* an analysis of what logic is all about and what its relations to physical and moral realities may be. At the urging of my son, Felix, I decided to leave this for separate treatment. But the desire to come to grips with this problem of the nature of logic grew in my mind from year to year.

This desire was stimulated by contacts at American Philosophical Association meetings and elsewhere with younger logicians, some of them former students of mine, who, with all their technical skill in building upon the foundations that Russell and Whitehead had laid, seemed to me to lack comprehension of what it was they were doing. They were keen enough on details, in our many discussions, but on the main lines I felt no need of lowering my colors. When some of us organized an Association for Symbolic Logic in 1936, we hoped that the journal of the association would bring together more closely the philosophers and the mathematicians, vision and technique. But any progress in this direction was almost imperceptible. This should not have been surprising, for there are few fields in which the last half century has seen so many striking intellectual advances as in that of logic. And periods in which a science is rapidly developing are frequently periods of loose thinking about the foundations of the science itself. (Perhaps the same is true of nations.) It was only natural that logicians busily developing the instruments of the new generalized mathematical logic should be too busy with their new techniques to pay much attention to the meaning of their marks on paper — should even, on occasion, perversely or modestly deny that their marks had any more meaning than a game of chess or tick-tack-toe. But the fact remained that here was a vital source of truth and discovery in all the sciences. Why?

An answer to that question would probe the relations of logic to such fields of study as natural science, ethics, history, and general philosophy. Besides the chapters already written, "The Subject Matter of Formal Logic," "The Logic of Fiction," and "Concepts and Twilight Zones," the book I planned would include treatment of the nature of propositions, the problem of probability, the statistical view of nature, the problem of meaning and implication and the general relation of logic to values and the universe.

Three of the missing chapters I was able to prepare and try out at meetings of the American Philosophical Association in 1932, 1935, and 1936. A fourth of the missing chapters, that on the statistical view of nature, I prepared for the meeting of the American Statistical Association in December, 1935. The course in logic that I gave at Leland Stanford University in the summer of 1937 gave me a chance to test further what had now become the first draft of a book on the significance of logic.

This opportunity for reflecting on the nature of logic in its relation to other disciplines was repeated when, in the spring of 1938, after my retirement from City College, I gave a series of public lectures on logic at the University of Chicago, and a few months later, a course on metaphysics at Harvard. At about this time the crusade against reason in Europe was making the United States the world's center for the development of logic. I found much stimulation in contacts with representatives of the Warsaw school of mathematical logic. Returning to Chicago later to give another series of lectures on logic, I had many occasions to develop and defend my basic viewpoint in argument with the logical positivists, led by Rudolph Carnap. All these discussions helped to clarify my own thinking but also served to emphasize my conviction that logic is more than a game with words or empty forms and that the understanding of logic is the heart of philosophy or metaphysics.

In the midst of this work a series of personal tragedies intervened to break apart my own world. In the autumn of 1941 my wife, who had been my companion and inspiration for the major part of my intellectual life, was stricken with a devastating malady. We had long agreed that the secret of married happiness was that husband and wife should not be ill at the same time. But at the Christmas meeting of the American Philosophical Association at Vassar I suffered what was diagnosed, a few weeks later, as a heart attack. A rest at the hospital was prescribed, and at the hospital I was promptly attacked by pneumonia. After several weeks I was sent home considerably worse not only for the pneumonia but from the consequences of the drugs which killed the pneumonia germs and worked considerable havoc with my general organism. Then a cerebral infarction wiped out all memory for several weeks. When I came to, my wife was dying. Even in her last illness, which she bore with heroic fortitude, she remained my devoted nurse and unending source of comfort. Her passing, on the eve of our thirty-sixth wedding anniversary in June, left me without the support on which I had relied since the days of my youth, with the memory of a singularly beautiful life, and the ache of unshed tears.

For some time I was a completely useless member of society, useless even to myself. I had lost the one human being who gave my life meaning and value. But somewhere in me, too deep for the specialists or the X-rays to discover, was a spark of life which was fanned to flame by the devotion she lavished on me with her last breath. Would that I had a tiny part of her capacity to submerge her own suffering in loving care for others! What was left of my body — it was not very much — she entrusted to an understanding soul, Dr. Mack Lipkin, who had caught a glimpse somewhere of the Hippocratic vision that unites medicine and philosophy. Under his guidance I found my way back to the world of the living. It was a bleak world that I came back to in the summer of 1942, for all who cherished the values of liberal civilization. For me, with the passing of the one whose zest for life had sustained me for so many years, it was a world of dust and ashes. But there were still faithful friends and children who brought solace and rekindled the sparks of philosophical adventure.

Wasted tissues and broken hopes slowly mended in the home of my daughter Leonora and my devoted son-in-law, Harry Rosenfield, who had been my good right hand in the organization of the Conference on Jewish Relations, in the fight over the Bertrand Russell appointment, and in many other adventures. Their moving to Washington assured me of the company of my youngest son, Victor William, who was doing important work in physics for the Navy, and my first-born, Felix, who was legal adviser to Secretary Ickes. Despite their preoccupation with war work, my two sons and their devoted wives, Lucy Kramer and Grace Jonas Cohen, freely gave of the help that a cripple needed to take his place again in the real world. Occasionally some former students would visit or write to me, warming my heart by their accounts of what they thought they owed to me. When, in the spring of 1943, I began once more to participate in the meetings of the New York Philosophy Club, I found myself no longer an intolerable companion. And my spirits took a decided leap upwards when the University of Chicago invited me to return to the campus — even though I had to defer acceptance. Apart from a few blank spaces where recollections of the spring of 1942 might have been, I felt that my memory had recovered its old strength, and while my speech was too thick for lecturing it sufficed for a moderate amount of dictation.

Having thus managed to gather together enough strength and courage for a renewed assault on the problems of philosophy, the completion of my half-finished volume on the nature of logic was my first task. With some editorial assistance from my son Felix and a faithful former student of mine, Charles Biedermann, the work was finished in the summer of 1943 and published in January, 1945, under the title, *Preface to Logic*. For years I had planned to call the book "Prolegomena to Logic" but my son and my publisher objected, and remembering how, at the urging of my wife, I had substituted *Chance, Love and Logic* for "Tychism, Agapism and Synechism" as the title for my collection of Peirce's philosophical essays — to the vast relief of the publisher — I yielded to the protests and accepted the simpler-sounding title. The volume was a "preface" only in the sense that one might properly ask what logic was all about before beginning to study it. To show that logic deals with all the world—with ambiguities as well as clarities, fiction as well as truth, probabilities as well as certainties, value opinions as well as the facts of history and the universal propositions of science — seemed to me a service in dispelling the mists that envelop a good deal of contemporary philosophizing. And thus to view logic, not as something narrower than the world of reality, but as an indispensable instrument for the exploration of yet unrealized possibilities might make plain the role of logic as an indispensable element of liberal civilization and free thought. That, at least, was the faith in which this volume was presented.

By May of 1944 I had completed the work on American liberalism begun in the days of the First World War. The essays that made up my volume, *Faith of a Liberal*, had been published or written, with few exceptions, in the years from 1915 to 1941. Three new chapters and minor amplifications of older articles that I added helped to round out the outlines of a *Weltanschauung*. My studies in philosophy had long ago led me to a rejection of all absolutisms, including the absolutism of inevitable progress and the absolutism of Marx or of doctrinaire communism. Not believing in an inevitable universal progress, I have not had reason to change my views because of the First World War and the reaction which has followed it. Nor has the Bolshevik Revolution made me change any of my convictions. I feared from the beginning that a dictatorship of the proletariat would become a bureaucracy different in ideology, but not differing much from the method by which the old bureaucracy ruled Russia. For this unpopular view I was prepared by the reading of Michel's *The Sociology of Political Parties*. Philosophically distrustful of all panaceas, and confident that the spirit of inquiry, motivated by reason and good will, will always be needed in meeting our social problems, I felt that the temper which underlay these scattered essays was as relevant to the current scene as to the years in which they were written. The public reception that was accorded to the volume on its appearance in the spring of 1946 was deeply gratifying.

By the spring of 1944 I had recovered enough of my health and strength to tackle the work that loomed as the main objective of what might remain of my life. In November of 1940 I had been honored with the appointment to deliver the Carus Lectures before the American Philosophical Association. I had been devoting an increasing share of my reading and reflection to history, in part as an incident to editorial duties which I had assumed on two new scholarly journals. Of one of these, *Jewish Social Studies,* I was editor, and I had contributed to its first issue, in January, 1939, an essay on "Philosophies of Jewish History." I had also agreed to serve as one of the editors of *The Journal of the History of Ideas.* The founding of the latter periodical in 1939 had been made possible by a research and publication fund established by the Class of 1912 of the College of the City of New York and increased by Mark Eisner of the Board of Higher Education. Here was one of the first contributions of my college to the world of scholarly periodicals, an attempt to bring together scholars of many different fields on the basis of a common concern with the history of ideas. A gifted former student of mine, Dr. Philip Wiener, had undertaken the arduous job of managing editor of the new magazine and I had been promising him some articles on the philosophy of history. In particular I had promised, and done a good deal of reading and writing on, a study of the various interpretations of the history of science. In line with these currents of my interest, I undertook to make "The Meaning of Human History" the theme of my Carus Lectures.

To this subject I devoted the major part of my energies throughout the year 1941. After the tragic interruptions of 1942 and after I had finished putting the final touches on the *Preface to Logic* and *Faith of a Liberal*, I turned in the spring of 1944 to pick up the broken threads of what I had come to regard as my *magnum opus*. The work was finished in 1945.

Custom prescribed that before publication the author read three chapters of his book at a meeting of the American Philosophical Association. Two obstacles stood in the way. I had become afflicted with a serious speech defect that made it impossible for me to read anything loudly and distinctly enough to be heard by an audience. And the American Philosophical Association could not, under the wartime transportation restrictions, hold its planned Inter-American Congress of Philosophy, for which my lectures had been scheduled. Both obstacles were side-stepped. The officers of the Association called a special meeting of Association members and guests living in and about New York, to be held, much to my delight, at the City College. They also accepted my plea that while it would be a strain on me to read the lectures it would be no strain on the audience to listen to my son's reading of them. And so the two of us left Washington on a sunny day in May, 1945, and made the journey back to our college, after a long absence. My thoughts turned back fifty years to the day of my admission to the City College and to the tears of joy in my mother's eyes when I brought her the news. Now the tears were in my eyes as my son's voice came to the end of the last lecture:

While it is true that brute power can for a limited time crush the human spirit, history also shows that the spirit of truth has a superior vitality and thus truth, even though for a time crushed to earth, rises again. The Hellenic spirit has outlived the Roman conquest, and Napoleon could not permanently wipe out the ideal of Liberty, Equality, and Fraternity. . . . The tragic view of human history widens our sympathies and prevents us from becoming dull to the finer possibilities which wiser conduct or a different turn of events might have realized. Above all, it enables us to do our best in an actually imperfect world, and if it warns us that in the language of Kant man is a crooked stick and that we cannot build a perfect kingdom of heaven on our own limited earth, it also provides us with the vision of an ideal which, even though not completely attainable at any one time, illumines the direction in which our efforts should be exerted if the history of the future is to be brighter than the history of the past.

When, seven months later, in December, 1945, I sent to the publisher the finished manuscript of the Carus Lectures volume, *The Meaning of Human History,* I breathed a deep sigh of relief. This was one race with death I had not lost.

Not all the dreams of writing had come true. None of my books had proved all that I had hoped. And there were still half-written manuscripts of books on "Metaphysics," "Roads to Philosophy," and "The Will to Illusion."

All these half-finished volumes had a right to reproach me for starting them and not finishing them.

Nevertheless, as an old-fashioned physicist I have never rejected the principle of entropy, that is, that the processes of physical nature cannot be reversed and that we cannot stop the process of aging. My right hand had become unfit to perform its writing duties during my illness in 1942, and the difficulty with my speech left little hope that I could ever finish these half-written volumes.

I had brought to completion a fair share of the work I had put my hopes on, and one could echo Goethe's *Prometheus*:

> Wähntest du etwa,
> Ich sollte das Leben hassen,
> In Wüsten fliehen,
> Weil nicht alle
> Blütenträume reiften?

There was still work to be done that I could do, though crippled, in the gathering together and organizing of volumes that were already written in substance and needed only editing and supplementing. I had, I felt, reached the years when I could no longer produce anything new. But there was still harvesting to be done. And there were loyal former students like Ernest Nagel, Kenneth Arrow, Stanley Nehmer

and David Spitz, and secretaries like Mrs. Minor Fisher, Miss Ma-
thilde Rosenblüth, and Mrs. Ruth Beebe, who were glad to co-operate
with my children in these editorial tasks.

First to demand my attention was a considerable volume of papers
on philosophy and scientific method written in installments over
thirty-five years, and another potential book on juristic philosophy,
nearly as long in the making, that seemed worth publishing. Though
neither was systematically complete they embodied my more mature
reflections on the two phases of philosophy — scientific method and
jurisprudence — that had always been at the heart of my thinking.

I also had on hand a collection of papers on Jewish problems,
planned since 1937, that the Conference on Jewish Relations undertook, in the summer of 1946, to publish. Among other pieces, the collection would include a Biblical dialogue I had written in the summer
of 1938 on the rise of the United Hebrew Commonwealth as seen
through the tragedy-filled eyes of Saul's daughter Michal, the first
wife of David. The story had gripped me with such dramatic intensity
that I was forced to sketch it out literally in one sitting as it appeared
to the mind's eye. Later, in our quiet retreat at Blue Mountain Lake
in the Adirondacks I put the play into shape, reading to Mary and
the children every night what I had written in the course of the day,
and finding in this unaccustomed occupation a philosopher's holiday.
And though I was painfully aware of my own incompetence to write
the drama that might be written on this theme, the result seemed to
me, despite its literary inadequacies, to have some significance as an
account of the interaction between historic movements and personal
experience.

Above all, there was the challenge to complete my autobiography
— if an autobiography ever can be completed. Since my adolescent
years, but especially since the death of my father in 1934, I had been
consumed with a desire to write an autobiography that would tell the
epic or odyssey of my parents' coming to this country and my own
journey from the medieval to the modern age — the journey of a
dreamer who never worshiped the goddess of practicality. Sometimes
I would cross-examine myself, "If some Spirit were to stop you and
say, 'What would you care to do most of all?' what would you say?"

"My autobiography."

"Then why don't you do it?"

"Well — there are the articles for the various law reviews and the book on law and justice."

"But is not that a mere excuse? Could you not, if you had the energy and determination, put in many bits from time to time?"

I had to admit that I could, and with that admission in July, 1935, began the jotting of notes that might, some day, serve as the raw material for an autobiography. Talks with my mother, who retained a remarkable photographic memory down to her last days in November, 1936, helped me to relive the days of my childhood in the Old Country and of my adolescent and most impressionable years in the New World. On occasion the doubt would arise: Why bring to life wearing emotions, the *Wehmut* of stirring memories, and the hopeless effort to communicate their flavor in writing? Why not just relax and enjoy the free air and sunshine? But enjoying laziness proved a wearisome occupation whenever I tried to stick to it for any length of time. And so I would return to the autobiography whenever the completion of some more pressing task left me with a vacant space in my intellectual life.

Once in 1937, when I was teaching for the summer at Leland Stanford University in California, my son Felix chided me for neglecting what seemed to him more important enterprises, like the volume on metaphysics, to indulge in the writing of an autobiography. I tried to defend myself in a letter I wrote him on July 25, 1937, my fifty-seventh birthday:

Physically, this day is like any other day in this pleasant climate. Still I am fifty-seven years old and I have distinct memories of fifty-four different winters, and I am conscious of the fact that I will not see as many more. My gray hairs are not the only signs that there is a winter coming that will know no spring.

. . . You have doubtless often wondered why I do so little writing. In the first place writing requires sustained energy, and I have very little of that. In my youth I seldom had much consecutive time to myself, hence I got into the habit of writing fragmentary cryptic notes — rarely in full sentences and never followed out completely.

. . . I suppose I must have written out volumes of such hints of thoughts that have passed thru my mind and which a little more energy could have embodied in essays or books. There is however another side to that, and that is that I do not have the linguistic gift.

. . . My speech is seldom fluent or felicitous, and it is often awkward.

Mary Ryshpan Cohen and Gene Maura Cohen, 1940

It is only the large store of information and reflection and the painstaking effort not to be the victim of conventional views or phrases that gives my conversation or lectures their go. But when I come to write, the inadequacy of the written words before me is most discouraging. Moreover, I am dependent on new stimuli from conversation or reading. My thought does not feed itself for long sustained flights. I need to alight frequently and to get new starts, just as a sick man needs frequent, if scant meals.

There is still another factor in the case. My childhood was an unusually lonely one and largely given to day-dreaming. From my tenth to my fourteenth year I lived largely on romances, first in Yiddish, then in English. I thus have a large sentimental streak in me and I always had a great craving to write something appealing more to the hearts of men than my philosophical disquisitions (logical or juristic) can possibly achieve. Actual attempts have convinced me that I have no more gift for producing imaginative literature than for creating music. I have, however, for over forty years nourished the hope of writing the story of my life as an illustration of the various forces which have met or found expression in my life, especially of currents which have molded Jewish history and which are vividly illustrated in the heroic struggles of my father and mother, under diverse conditions, to earn their daily bread and to bring up their children in decency. You, and the men of your generation seem to have no conception of the magnitude of this struggle and the immense fortitude which sustained it. I thus have a burning desire to do what so few people that I know can do, namely, outline the basic facts of the great epic — the odyssey, if you like — of the generation which cut its roots in the old home and crossed the ocean into a strange land without any resources other than their own unconquerable fortitude.

. . . I feel about it very much as Proust must have felt about his *A la Recherche du Temps Perdu*. It is the vehicle by which almost all that my life has meant can be expressed — even all that my philosophic reading and reflection have meant to me.

If my son was not wholly convinced by this defense at the time, I think he was persuaded three years later when I presented the first installment of the autobiography to his year-old daughter, my first grandchild, Gene Maura. And in later years I know he came to share my feeling that while I could leave to others the completion of half-thought-through systems of metaphysics or jurisprudence, I could not do this with the development of my own life and thought, as seen from within. Certainly he came to my aid in a heart-warming way when the tragedies that crowded my life in 1942 left me so largely dependent on that aid to realize whatever might be left to me to realize. With his help the tangled notes and thoughts could be put together, edited, and hammered into some recognizable shape. And what could be more natural in the half-light of dusk, when the tasks of the midday sun are over, than to look back to the half-light of dawn, when we were young and eager and the world had alluring freshness, when there were so many things to be done, and ours was the opportunity.

BOOK SEVEN

JEWISH SOCIAL STUDIES AND
AMERICAN DEMOCRACY

I N THE WINTER OF 1890 there had been some question as to whether my mother, my sister and myself should go to join the rest of the family in America, and I wrote a letter to my father expressing my fear of the irreligious surroundings to which I should thus be subject and my hope that he would allow me to continue my pious studies where I was. But my father's efforts to establish a livelihood for himself and his family in the following months in Minsk were doomed to failure. And when my mother, my sister and I traveled to America two years later, my youthful fears of what would happen to my religion in the irreligious atmosphere of America were borne out by events. It was only a few months after we had arrived that my childhood faith was broken on the sharp edge of Mr. Tunick's skepticism. The questions our old neighbor asked of my father and my father's inability to give a rational answer shocked me to the quick. The angels that guard us, recited in every prayer, had been very real to me. I had lived in strict conformity to the tenets of Jewish Orthodoxy. But I could not forget Mr. Tunick's questions: "What proof have you that there is a God and that he told anything to Moses? And why should I believe that Jews are the only ones that have the truth? And are there not other people just as intelligent as we, and can we prove the Jewish religion is superior to all others?"

After some soul-searching I came to the conclusion that I had no evidence that could effectively answer these questions. I have not since that day ever seen any reason to change that conclusion.

The loss of the religion of my childhood brought no suffering in its train. It seemed to me that the restraints from which I was freed outbalanced the consolations that were lost. Perhaps that is because

211

not all of the consolations were lost. Rational argument could never wholly efface a natural clinging to the joys of Friday night. Much less could it efface the larger spiritual patterns and values of my childhood religion. Indeed, in my youthful rejection of the Orthodox Jewish observances, I did not feel that I was cutting myself off from religion. I knew that the rejection of ritual is itself deeply rooted in the Hebraic tradition. I could not forget that the Hebrew Prophets, from Amos to Jeremiah, the founders of spiritual monotheism, all made Jahveh despise the ritual with which Israel believed it served Him. Says the God of Amos — and his command is repeated by Micah, Isaiah and Jeremiah:

> I hate, I despise your feast days,
> And will not delight in the day of your solemn assemblies —
> Put thou away from me the noise of thy songs —
> But let justice run down as waters,
> And righteousness as a mighty stream.

If I was a heretic, at least I felt that I was erring in good company. As with ritual, so, I felt, with creed. The essence of religion, it seemed to me, was not in the words uttered with the lips but rather in the faith which shows itself in our moral life. I could not bring myself to think that a just God would condemn the upright and spiritual-minded men I knew in all churches, and outside of all churches, merely because they did not pronounce the right formulas. Beyond any divinity of creed, it seemed to me, there was a God of morality, but even beyond this there was a God of nature. Or to put it in other words, man is a spiritual being in relation not only to his equals, other men, but also in relation to the whole universe. Here again I found myself in company with the Hebrew prophet Micah who strikes at the root of the matter when he says:

> And what doth the Lord require of thee,
> But to do justice and to love mercy,
> And to walk humbly with thy God.

Something more than mercy and justice are required, for one may be just and merciful and still be an intolerable prig. What is needed beyond these in a character that we can revere is humility. This does not mean that we are to bow down before God as we do before a petty tyrant. It means that we need to recognize that we are in a universe which contains a reality which is and always will be beyond all our knowledge and power; with that reality the spiritual faculty seeks communion. It means, too, that we must all be prepared to suffer and be punished for the sins of others; otherwise we are not entitled to the benefits which we all do derive from the virtues of others.

My youthful rejection of the claims of the Jewish religion to absolute truth was subsequently reinforced by philosophical reflections which led me to reject all forms of absolutism, the source of all fanaticism, and all forms of monism — including monotheism. The essence of monotheism is an emphasis upon the harmony of the universe, which seems to me to be most unfortunate in that it tends to dull the sense of resentment against the injustices of the world. I have never been able to reconcile the reality of evil and of the struggle against injustice with the idea of a benevolent and all-powerful deity.

If evil is real, and I am as persuaded of that as of anything else in this world, then God is either the author of evil or else He is defeated by other forces. However comforting the thought of an all-good and all-powerful deity may be in cultivating a wise resignation in the face of evils we cannot surmount, I found myself unable to follow my revered teacher, William James, in considering the comfort that flows from a doctrine any sign of its truth. And making a God in man's image has seemed to me the height of arrogance.

On the other hand I have hesitated to violate ordinary understanding by using the word "God" to refer to an ideal of holiness that enables us to distinguish between the good and evil in men and thus saves us from the idolatrous worship of a humanity that is full of imperfections. Such a conception of God has seemed to me valid, but since I do not generally know what other people have in mind when they ask whether I believe in God, I have generally replied, "That depends upon what you mean by God." This usually brings forth a denunciation of metaphysical quibbling.

There have, of course, been many attempts by rabbis who are not complete strangers to science to formulate a concept of Judaism that may free the Orthodox creed from its incrustations of superstition. But these efforts to rationalize the Jewish faith, and similar attempts to rationalize other historic faiths, have not impressed me. I do not believe that there is any such thing as Judaism as an abstract doctrine — which is what an "ism" is — upon which all Jews can agree. I have heard many definitions of Judaism and they all seem hollow. I know of no religious belief that is common to all Jews, and I know of no belief held by any substantial number of Jews which is not to be found also, in some measure, among other people. Jews are people first, and only Jews incidentally. I have never believed that the Jews, as a people, have to justify their existence. Jews exist because they are human beings, and human beings have a right to exist.

I do not know of any religious doctrine which I share with any large number of my fellow Jews, and certainly there is no political or economic doctrine which unites all Jews. I have always been a Jew because I was born and brought up in a Jewish family. When, in 1899, I was in a position to order my own life, I ceased to observe the traditional Jewish code of ritual practices. This, however, did not carry with it any loss of respect for those who maintained the old observances where such observances represented the expression of an inner conviction. I have always had the highest reverence for those who, like my sainted parents, have a genuine and abiding faith that God listens to their prayers and that His actions are influenced by their petitions and oaths. I have never had any missionary zeal to convert anyone from his own views on religion, or to engage in any polemics with those among whom I was brought up. But I must, in the interest of truth, record my observation that the number of those who outwardly profess Orthodoxy is much greater than of those who really let it influence their lives.

I remember as a boy having a talk with the late Joseph Jacobs. He asked, "Why do your young people on the East Side keep away from the synagogue? Don't they believe in religion?" I replied, "Going to synagogue or not going is a minor matter, Mr. Jacobs. We take religion more seriously than you do." I think that was the truth. True religion must be an expression of the inner soul and cannot be forced on anyone merely because he happens to have been born of a certain ancestry. It seemed to me that in the friction between the older generation and the younger generation which the religious question brought to the fore in the days of my youth, both sides were at fault. The older generation was at fault in not distinguishing between ritual forms and true religious faith. It was lacking in human sympathy with the honest views of the younger generation. It could not learn that the real vitality of a religion does not show itself in the power to resist the advance of new truth but rather in the capacity to adapt itself to whatever new light it can get.

On the other hand there was a certain superficiality in the attitude that many of my generation took towards religion. We used to read accounts of a conflict between science and religion in which, we were told, science had gradually conquered. This, however, seemed to me to leave out of consideration the realm where science cannot rule, where neither the telescope nor the microscope can penetrate, the realm of ideal expression. Appropriation or rejection of science thus did not solve the problem of religion. Those who called themselves atheists seemed to be singularly blind, as a rule, to the limitations of our knowledge and to the infinite possibilities beyond us. And those who called themselves materialists appeared to me to be shutting themselves off from philosophy, wisdom, and the life of the spirit, which are certainly not material things. Those of my circle who rejected religion *in toto* seemed to me to be casting away the ideals that had sustained our people through so many generations before we had fashioned guideposts to our own lives that could stand up against the sort of buffeting that the old guideposts had withstood. In this some of us lost sight of the larger view that Thomas Davidson had taught, that we have no right to break away from the past until we have appropriated all its experience and wisdom, and that reverence for the past may go hand in hand with loyalty to the future, "to the Kingdom which doth not yet appear."

The ideal of intellectual integrity compelled me and many others of my generation to reject superstitions that had been bound up with the practices of our Orthodox parents, but it did not prevent us from cherishing the spiritual values which they had found in those practices, and which many others have found in the practices of other older and younger religions. The struggle between Orthodoxy and active opposition to all religion seemed to me, like so many of the passionate struggles of life, to overlook possibilities and values which a more tolerant and rational outlook could find.

Indeed I marveled then, and have never ceased to marvel, at the fact that on matters where knowledge is readily demonstrable — such as cooking or chemistry — discussions show little of the heated mood of the zealot and fanatic, whereas, in matters on which it is much more difficult to arrive at the truth, such as questions of religion, we are inclined to be very sure of ourselves. Perhaps we try to make up by our vehemence for the lack of demonstrative evidence.

Of course, if you claim to be in possession of a special revelation, then you have a mortgage on the truth of the universe, the other fellow can have nothing true to tell you, and the thing to do is to hold on to your revealed truth with all the ardor that is in you. But then the other fellow is just as certain that he alone has all the truth and there is no use in any argumentation. But if you take your stand on human history and human reason, and recognize, for example, that the claim to the possession of a special revelation of the Jew is, as such, not a bit better than that of the Christian or the Mohammedan, or any of the ten thousand other claims, then, it seemed to me, you must grant that each possesses both truth and error.

Having once made up my mind that the whole truth of the matter did not lie with either side, I saw the religious problem of my own intellectual generation as a problem calling for creative thought rather than simple loyalty. "Before we can appropriate the religion of our ancestors," I wrote in an article on the religious question on the East Side, in June, 1902, "we must build it over again in our own hearts. This holds good not only of religion but of all the products of civilization. Whatever thou hast inherited from thy ancestors, earn in order to possess. Only that which we have worked out ourselves is truly ours."

Twenty years later I was still seeking for a way of uniting naturalism in science with piety towards that which has been revered as noble and sacred in the spiritual history of man. Of all philosophers, it seemed to me that Spinoza had most clearly developed the rational and tolerant attitude to the values of religion for which I had been searching. In my addresses before the American Philosophical Association in 1922 on "The Intellectual Love of God," I undertook to defend the validity of the Spinozistic ideal, "amor Dei intellectualis," as a beacon that may illumine the problems of modern life and thought. Naturalism, for Spinoza, did not import that worldliness which wise men in all generations have recognized as a state of spiritual death. Nor did he conceive of love as a passive emotion. The quest for understanding, Spinoza saw, is an activity, often a breathless activity, that even apart from its practical consequences, is the most divine of human enterprises.

It is true that Spinoza rejects the idea of an anthropomorphic God who will respond to our flattering prayers, reward us for our unsuccessful efforts, and in general compensate us for the harshness of the natural order and the weaknesses of our reason. If, however, religion consists in humility (as a sense of infinite powers beyond our scope), charity or love (as a sense of the mystic potency in our fellow human beings), and spirituality (as a sense of the limitations of all that is merely material, actual or even attainable), then no one was more deeply religious than Spinoza.

And while Spinoza has little regard for the immortality which means the postponement of certain human gratifications to a period beyond our natural life, he does believe in the immortality which we achieve when we live in the eternal present or identify ourselves with those human values that the process of time can never adequately realize or destroy. He thus showed me the path to that serenity which follows a view of life fixed on those things that go on despite all the tragedies and depressions which frighten hysterical people. Above all, Spinoza made clear to me the vision that saves us from the worldliness that drowns out life. We are all like the waves tossed high up by the ocean and breaking on the sands of actuality. If we are to attain true human dignity, we need some sense of our continuity with the past and the future, a consciousness of ourselves not as temporary flies but as waves of a human ocean larger than our own lives and efforts.

Spinoza, like the other great religious teachers and the morally wise men of science, teaches the great lesson of humility — that there are always vast realms beyond our ken or control, and that the great blessing of inner peace is unattainable without a sense of the mystery of creation about us and a wisely cultivated resignation to our mortal but inevitable limitations.

These limitations men surmount only as they learn to subordinate their separate individualities to the interest of families, social or religious groups, nations, races, or that humanity whose life is the whole cosmic drama of which, as thinkers, we are spectators.

In the days of my first youthful revolt against the Jewish observances, I was inclined to regard cultus, prayer and ritual as of little importance in comparison with belief or faith. This was certainly the view that my teacher William James took of the matter. The conclusion he drew from this was that the religious experience of the great mass of people, who follow in the steps of great masters, is of little significance. My own studies of the great historic religions led me, however, to see that ritual, what men do on certain occasions, is a primary fact in human religious experience, and that the beliefs and emotions associated with ritual are more variable than ritual itself, as is shown by the diverse explanations and justifications of the Hebrew Sabbath and the Easter ceremonies. Indeed the character of the founders of the great religions, as we know it, is largely a product of tradition.

Men cling to sanctified phrases not only because of the insights they contain but even more because, through ritual and repetition, they have become redolent with the wine of human experience. For each of us the symbolism of our childhood offers paths to peace and understanding that can never be wholly replaced by other symbolisms. For me the ancient ceremonies that celebrate the coming and going of life, the wedding ceremony, the *b'rith*, and the funeral service, give an expression to the continuity of the spiritual tradition that is more eloquent than any phrases of my own creation. The ritual may be diluted by English and by modernisms, but the Hebraic God is still a potent symbol of the continuous life of which we individuals are waves. So it is, too, with the celebration of the eternal struggle for freedom, in the family service of the Passover.

Like vivid illustrations in the book of my life are the prayers of my parents, the services at their graves, the memory of an old man chanting funeral songs at the *Jahrzeit* of my dear friend Dr. Himwich, the unveiling of the monument to the beloved comrade of my life's journeys, and the celebration of the continuity of generations in the Passover services in the home of my parents and in the homes of my children. And though I have never gone back to theologic supernaturalism, I have come to appreciate more than I once did the symbolism in which is celebrated the human need of trusting to the larger vision, according to which calamities come and go but the continuity of life and faith in its better possibilities survive.

CHAPTER TWENTY-FIVE

THE JEWISH HERITAGE IN AMERICA

M Y FIRST ATTITUDE toward non-Jews — *Goyim* — was that they were not fully human beings. Those I saw were ignorant peasants and I heard of generals and *pritzim* (lords) who were our persecutors. I did not understand their ways and they did not understand mine.

Yiddish was my mother tongue. In it I was brought up, and though long years of inactivity have made me tongue-tied when it comes to speaking Yiddish, no other language ever entirely replaced it in the expression of intimate affection.

The first language in which I read was Hebrew. The studies of my youth were directed to the great Hebrew classics — the Old Testament and the Commentaries, the Babylonian and Palestinian Talmuds, the Shulchan Auruch and the Kav Hayosher. My grandfather, who had charge of my early education, saw to it that no Yiddish literature reached me. It was only after I left his household and returned to Minsk that I began to read Yiddish — or jargon, as it was called. And it was not until after my twelfth year, when I came to America, that I began to read English and to come into active, intellectual contact with non-Jews. Even then what chiefly helped me in attaining an understanding of the ways of my adopted country was the Jewish press, principally the old *Arbeiter Zeitung*, which Abraham Cahan, Feigenbaum and Kranz edited and to which the old grandfather of the Jewish socialist movement, Winchevsky, frequently sent letters from England. I owe a good deal of my education to the Yiddish press. It taught me to look at world news from a cosmopolitan instead of a local or provincial point of view, and it taught me to interpret politics realistically, instead of being misled by empty phrases.

As I look back on the Yiddish and the English press in the last decade of the nineteenth century I cannot help feeling that the former did more for the education of its readers than the latter. Having no army of reporters to dig up sensational news, the Yiddish press necessarily paid more attention to things of permanent interest. It tried to give its readers something of enduring and substantial value. I therefore have never been able to share the views of my fellow citizens who look upon the very existence of a foreign press as a sort of treason, who would make the speaking or writing of a foreign language a crime. These people are doubtlessly influenced by patriotic motives, but their conception of Americanism is narrow and unworthy of the great traditions of American liberalism. The patriotism of these people is a narrow nationalism copied from, or in imitation of, European nationalism. The American tradition is federalism, which allows for diversity instead of dull uniformity. The very name "United States" and our motto, "E Pluribus Unum," express this.

America has been settled by many peoples and each has contributed freely to the common stock — the Germans have contributed their love of music, the Italians have contributed their love of nature, gardening, and certain household arts. Why should not the Jews contribute their specific gifts? The idea that all immigrants should wipe out their past and become simple imitations of the dominant type is neither possible nor desirable. We cannot wipe out the past. And we make ourselves ridiculous in the effort to do so.

All great civilizations have resulted from the contributions of many peoples, and a richer American culture can come only if the Jews, like other elements, are given a chance to develop under favorable conditions their peculiar genius. The Yiddish press has prepared millions of Jewish people to take a worthy part in American civilization while also promoting the natural self-respect to which Jews are entitled because of their character and history.

Apart from the Yiddish press, the major intellectual contacts of my adolescent years were those with my fellow students at the College of the City of New York, and, in later years, my intellectual life was largely wrapped up with my students at the College. The vast majority of them, especially in latter years, were Jewish.

My readings in anthropology early persuaded me that the superiority of the Jewish brain is a myth, but the social differences between

Jewish and non-Jewish family life remain a reality. In general the Jewish student, as I have known him, takes his studies more seriously than does his Gentile comrade. The latter is quite often discouraged from studying by his environment; at any rate, he is less likely to share the atmosphere of reverence, the traditional love for learning, which the Jewish boy imbibes from childhood. At Harvard a "C" man is considered a perfect gentleman, while a mark above that stamps one as a "grind." But, due to centuries of poverty and persecution in Europe where a Jew rose in the esteem of his fellow man only in proportion to his learning, the Jewish student is generally more devoted to his studies. The Jewish lad who is only a generation or two removed from the Talmudic tradition has been brought up, in most cases, by parents eager to give him the finest of education. His environment is, dominantly, intellectual, and to that extent it is natural for him to be openminded, eager to examine new ideas and new points of view. Other students are more likely to come to college with firmly fixed opinions and prejudices. New ideas often bewilder them and unconsciously they resist them.

A somewhat similar situation exists in the world of science. Certainly there is no aptitude for science that is characteristic of the Jewish people as such. We do not, for instance, find the Jews making any contribution to science in Biblical times. In Talmudic literature, to be sure, some knowledge of current astronomy and some familiarity with astrology and medicine can be found, but in the main no one can say that the Jews made any notable contribution in the field of science before Saracen culture began to flourish. Even then the great names of Maimonides, Ibn Gabirol, and others belong more to the field of philosophy than to that of science. Not until the end of the eighteenth century do we find Jews making outstanding contributions to European science. This, of course, was not the result of any racial factor but rather a consequence of certain historic changes in the position of the Jew.

So long as the Jews were shut up in their ghettos and excluded from the universities they had no chance to make significant contributions to the life of science. But when ghetto gates and university doors were opened there were special factors which led the Jews to make extraordinary contributions to the development of modern science.

In the first place the pursuit of science depends to a large degree on communal respect for the scientist. In this the Jews have the advantage of a highly favorable tradition. Ever since the synagogue has taken the place of the temple the Jews have always regarded the scholar with great reverence. This traditional respect for scholarship readily transforms itself under new conditions into a respect for intellectual life, of which the pursuit of science is a part.

A second element in the scientific endeavor is the element of zest or adventure. The Greeks, when they made their great contribution to science, were a commercial people traveling from one country to another and thus liberating their minds from complete subservience to customary or inherited views. So it has been with the Jews, who since the end of the eighteenth century have been a people on the move. Breaking away from old routines, the Jews have been spiritual explorers ready to appraise and enter new realms of thought. It is thus that they entered the field of science as a result of the enlightenment which began with Mendelssohn. It is thus that the Russian Jews in the liberal days of Alexander II flocked to the universities. Something of this sort is now going on in this country despite many obstacles, external and internal.

In this connection it is interesting to note the prominent part that Jews have taken in new and revolutionary movements in science. Jews such as Einstein, Levi-Civita, Minkowsky, Michelson, and Ehrenfest, in relativity, quantum and statistical mechanics, and atomic research, Jacques Loeb in biology, Peano and Sheffer in mathematical logic, Boas, Lowie, Sapir, Kroeber, Goldenweiser, Durkheim and Lévy-Bruhl in anthropology, Ricardo and Marx in economics, and, in the fields of jurisprudence, Brandeis, Cardozo, Ehrlich, Stammler, Kantorowicz, Hohfeld and Freund, are not merely great names but identified as explorers in hitherto uncharted realms.

Such being the fact, and believing as I do that science has done much to lighten human life, spiritually as well as physically, I have not been able to embrace the assimilationist idea that Jews should give up as quickly as possible all those characteristics which distinguish them from their non-Jewish neighbors. Of course if all Jews were to retire to farms their "visibility" in American life would diminish and points of irritation leading to anti-semitism would also diminish. If we should cease to value higher education, the number of Jews in the professions would decline and a common source of rabble-rousing would lose whatever statistical base it now has. But why should good Americans object to our Norwegian immigrants, with their great maritime tradition, supplying more than their proportionate numbers to American shipping? Or why should we object to the concentration of Scottish immigrants in the engineering profession, or to the fact that the Irish have more than their proportional share in our police forces, where their loyalty and courage contribute conspicuously to the public good? If the traditional Jewish love of learning is of value to a liberal civilization, is it not better for the Jews to maintain it, and perhaps transmit it to other portions of the population, rather than retreat from it as a source of danger?

I have always sympathized with the feelings, if not with the arguments, of those who oppose assimilation as an ideal. Of course everyone living in this country and seeking to share fully in its life and in the responsibility of citizenship must try to assimilate American ways of earning a living, dressing, eating, recreation, newspaper reading, and use of the English language. Even conservative Jewish rabbis have introduced the sermon as a regular part of their religious services, though that was not the custom of the Orthodox before they came to this country. In that literal sense of the word we are all assimilationists. On the other hand, it seems an entirely vain and undignified attitude to attempt to imitate the manners or mores of those about us, if that means ignoring our own past experience and traditions which have molded us. Not only does self-respect militate against such an attitude but we can be better Americans, if, instead of being blind imitators, we approach American civilization critically and try to contribute something distinctive to the general fund of its spiritual goods.

What that contribution shall be cannot be fixed in advance. I am myself inclined to believe that the Jewish tradition of high respect for, and internal interest in, the intellectual life for its own sake — derived from the Hebrew idea that study is a form of divine worship — is a valuable influence mitigating the American acquired habit of glorifying narrowly practical values. Others think that the Jewish zeal for social reform or social justice, or for the arts and sciences, will probably be our most valuable contribution. But this issue can be resolved only by time. Today we can only say that if the Jew has any distinctive gifts or historically inherited traits, he will show them to the best advantage if he has an opportunity to choose freely from the elements of both the Jewish and the American traditions.

To the extent that such opportunity is held open, the process of assimilation is, to quote a phrase of Justice Holmes's, "only a necessity and not a duty." Assimilation is a poor ideal, but it cannot be denied as a fact, at least a long-range fact.

I am no longer shocked to see a Reform rabbi eat ham. Nor am I shocked by intermarriage, which so many of my Zionist friends exemplify. Yet I am less than enthusiastic about a good many of the changes in Jewish attitudes that mark the process of assimilation. For two thousand years the Jews have admired scholarship and have looked up to the *Talmud Chocham* (the scholar or searcher after wisdom) as a leader in the community. It seems to me that this Jewish tradition, under which you find scholars among shoemakers, is worth preserving. The people of Neshwies, in the days of my childhood, wore rags on their feet and ate white bread only on the Sabbath, but no child went without schooling. That subordination of material things to spiritual values has made it possible for Jews to survive unprecedented calamities with dignity and self-respect. But in this country, which has relatively recently been conquered from nature, and where people have had to build anew the physical basis of civilized life, it has been the practical man who has been most admired. The result is that the scholar, the contemplative person, is often regarded as a nut (I think that is the official name).

I remember a professor of my college — to be sure, a professor of military training, but I think he was typical of American instructors — addressing the student body one day and saying, "If you want to be a he-man, go in for football; if you want to be a nut like Einstein, stick to the books."

Practically, this means that in American national life scholars are not accorded a very high place. We do not even trust them to run our educational institutions, but usually put men of property on the supreme governing boards. A recognition in recent years of the need of scholars in government was quickly followed by a reaction against "brain trusters."

We Jews in imitation of American ways have gone much farther and have made no room at all for the scholar in our communal affairs, leaving the communal will to be determined entirely by gifted orators, journalists, or men of affairs whose philanthropies give them deserved distinction. I do not doubt that many of these leaders are possessed of a good deal of shrewd wisdom. But a man may be a persuasive orator or well informed and wise in business affairs and yet not have the requisite insight into issues that require long historical and other study. Moreover, while we cannot ignore the lessons of experience which men of affairs accumulate, it is not good to be guided in practical affairs entirely by practical people. For the man who has his nose to the grindstone in the marketplace cannot usually see far enough. We need also other-worldly people who look ahead and are not too enmeshed in the immediate situation. This, historically, has been the role of the rabbi. But today the Jewish people are divided with regard to religion, and even those who derive comfort from the rabbi's ministration will often question his authority to pass on the crucial social, political and economic problems which face us.

Despite the process of assimilation, the Jews will, for a long time to come, continue as a distinct group. This is inevitable because of the natural force of social cohesion. Jews are more likely to associate with other Jews than with Gentiles. The majority of Jewish boys are likely to keep company with and marry Jewish girls and thus group cohesion will continue and group traditions be perpetuated. The highest rate of intermarriage ever known in the heyday of German liberalism was fourteen per cent. Even if centuries of assimilation in an atmosphere of tolerance were unbroken by waves of anti-semitism, it would probably be at least eighty generations before the Jews would disappear as a distinguishable people upon the American scene. It is probable that for many centuries the Jewish group will continue to show some characteristics which will differentiate it from the rest of the population, and so long as there are differences between groups there are bound to be elements of friction. I do not regard this as necessarily evil. It is, according to the liberal philosophy, a good thing for a Christian community to have its faith challenged, as my revered teacher Thomas Davidson used to put it, by the presence of those who hold that the tradition of the Old Testament has been properly continued in the Talmud rather than in the New Testament, and vice versa, just as it is good for both to be challenged by the presence of agnostics and atheists. It might be even better if all of these were challenged by the resurgence of some form of polytheism such as William James preached at times, to which as a pluralist I am benevolently inclined. The Greeks were able to make their unprecedented contributions to civilization precisely because there were so many differences among them. The Jews as well as the Scots resemble them in this respect. The cause of liberal civilization in twentieth-century America will not be served by wiping out the cultural values of any minority.

As a solution to American problems the ideal of political Zionism has appealed to me as little as the ideal of assimilationism. I should like to see Palestine, and all its inhabitants, prosper. I have the deepest admiration for the brave and wise efforts through which Jewish pioneers have rescued the soil of Israel from centuries of neglect and abuse. I should like to see the racial or religious discriminations with which the British exclude Jewish immigrants and restrict Jewish land ownership broken, just as I should like to see similar discriminations in our own land broken. I should, above all, like to see the Hebrew University become a beacon of light throughout the world, and from time to time I have done what I could to help those who, like the head of that great institution, my old friend Judah Magnes, have worked to make that aspiration a living reality. I have hoped that all these things may be accomplished without introducing into the political structure of Palestine discriminations against non-Jews which would undermine the struggle of all oppressed minorities for freedom and equality.

When I defended this position in a *New Republic* article in 1919 I was promptly labeled an anti-Zionist and, in some quarters, an anti-Semite. But I said then, and said again in 1945, that Zionism has served a high purpose, that the older nineteenth-century ideal of assimilation had degenerated into an ideal of blind aping of Gentile ways, and that Zionism has rendered the supreme service of increasing men's self-respect, and has helped men to realize that they must be ready to give of their own past experience as well as to accept.

I have never outgrown the thrill that I felt as a child at reading of the idealized glories of King David or Judas Maccabaeus. Nor have I ever lost a childhood love for the land which was the cradle of the Jewish people. And all who have a spark of human feeling must sympathize with the refugees who are bravely trying to build a home on the wasted soil of the old land of promise. To all this must be added natural pride in achievements which a lover of soil like Lowdermilk so graphically depicts — the triumph of mind and soul over the desert. But as a lover of truth I cannot let these feelings obscure the dangers that inhere in political Zionism, dangers which inhere in all forms of nationalism or tribalism. I am still disturbed by the concept of a Jewish State — perhaps because of the vagueness of the concept. Is a Jewish State a racial state based on mystic ideas of "blood and soil"? Will all non-Jewish inhabitants have equal rights in such a state? Will it be possible for non-Jews to hold public office? Will a Moslem, for example, find no legal obstacle to becoming President of the Republic? If Jews are permitted to immigrate will Arabs be excluded from immigration on equal terms? Certainly I could never bring myself to support efforts to establish a Jewish State which would not be in accord with the democratic principles of separation of Church and State and equality of civil, religious and economic rights to all inhabitants regardless of race and creed. Perhaps Zionists will some day devise a Constitution and Bill of Rights that do not violate the conceptions on which Jews throughout the world base their claim for equal status. But if they have done so already, I have not seen the evidence.

Be that as it may, I return to the proposition that from the point of view of those who face life here and now in this land of ours, Zionism is a distraction, or at best a side issue, not a solution of American problems. To my way of thinking the realities before us here and now, where our practical efforts are likely to be most effective, are actual human beings, boys and girls who are our children, who live here, who must adapt themselves to the conditions of American life, and who want to make their lives fuller and richer. A few of them will go to Palestine and cease to be Americans. A few will stay here and cease to be Jews. But the great majority, for generations to come, will be American Jews and, out of self-respect, will want to make the greatest contributions to American life which their heritage, their training, and their individual efforts make possible. For them, as for those of us whose hopes as parents and as teachers are bound up with theirs, the problem remains: What can we, with our age-old heritage, contribute to the fullness of American life?

The promise of America is the promise of freedom for the development of human energy, liberated by free education and the abolition of hereditary class distinctions. This promise rests on the liberal faith in separation of Church and State, in the subordination of the military caste to responsible civil authorities, in the value of the individual regardless of race, creed, or previous condition of servitude. It was this liberal faith that broke the gates of ghettoes and welcomed me and millions of immigrant boys like me to a share in the life of America. There is no future for the Jews of this country that is not bound up with the fortunes of liberal democracy. Under its sway Jews have gained full political and civil rights. Jews have become governors of our principal states, justices of our highest courts, cabinet officers, and ambassadors. While we are not all international bankers —indeed our representation in the banking field is considerably lower than our proportions in the total population—our economic position in relation to other groups is not markedly unfavorable. We are not forced, as many Jewish communities of Europe were forced, to look to Palestine for freedom. We are not a homeless people. We helped to build our American homeland. The overwhelming majority of Jewish immigrants and their descendants in this country have committed their lives to the basic principle of American democracy—that here in these United States men and women of many different backgrounds may co-operate, bringing each his contribution to a greater civilization than has yet existed. The dynamic principle of American Jewish life is to be found neither in the wiping out of special gifts nor in a withdrawal to the desert but rather in the fruitful bringing together of Jewish and non-Jewish cultural values in the common enterprises of liberal democracy.

This liberal faith stands in grave peril today, threatened by many forms of racist and nationalist fanaticism. Nothing that we can contribute to America as Jews can be of enduring value unless it helps to strengthen the American faith in freedom and tolerance. Therefore, whatever our inner differences regarding religion, Zionism, Diaspora nationalism, economics, and politics, we must cultivate the tolerance of liberalism in our own councils before we can strengthen it in the world about us. Only by helping to keep alive the liberal temper can we hope to conserve for our children the opportunity that our parents won for us of contributing to the fullness of American life.

CHAPTER TWENTY-SIX

THE PIETY OF AN AGNOSTIC

SANTAYANA DEFINES PIETY as "reverence for the sources of one's being." In this sense, if not in any more orthodox sense, piety has always seemed to me a necessary corollary of the Socratic maxim "know thyself."

None of us are self-made men, and those who think they are, are generally no credit to their makers. The language in which our thinking moves, the ideals to which our hearts are attuned in the formative years of our childhood, our habits, occupations, and pastimes, even our gestures, facial expressions and intonations, are so largely the social product of generations of teaching, that no man can understand himself and his own limitations unless he understands his heritage; and it is very difficult to understand one's heritage, or anything else, unless one approaches it with a certain amount of sympathy.

No ordinary human being deliberately chooses the country or household into which he shall be born. Hence none of us justly deserve any credit for the deeds of our remote ancestors any more than we can be blamed for their misdeeds. Nevertheless we are born not only as individual men and women but also as members of historic groups; and we are brought up to take pride in the achievements of any one who in any way belongs to our race, nation, or family. Such pride sustains our self-respect, by supplementing the poor record of our individual lives with the glories of the larger unities with which we identify our being; and in some cases this spurs heroic achievements on our own part. The members of any hereditary group which, like the Jewish, is regarded as in some way inferior by dominant opinion are apt, by way of reaction, to intensify this pride. But in some cases they naturally wish to escape their handicap and become absorbed in the dominant group, if not for their own at least for their children's sake. I have never joined the outcry against such individuals as "traitors," or "deserters." I see no justification for condemning intermarriage or the conversion of Jews to Christianity. (It is of course contemptible to crawl into any church for your belly's sake, but this applies also to many of those who remain in the church of their fathers.) Still a realistic view shows that for the most part we must accept our heredity and do the best we can with it. In any case we cannot achieve self-respect if we are afraid of self-knowledge, of knowing the history of our ancestors and how we came to be what we are.

One of the most serious consequences of the declining influence of the synagogue is that the great mass of Jews has lost contact with the traditional substance of Jewish education. Not only those who wish to forget their Jewish origins but others remain ignorant of the historic background which has molded their own being. This has produced, most regrettably, the type of Jew interested in everything except his own history. Because none of us can escape the influences of our ancestry and the traditions in which we are brought up, it is important for a Jew living in a predominantly non-Jewish world to understand the actual history of his own people, the conditions which have brought about his present position, and the main factors that are effective in maintaining or changing these conditions. In other words, to lead a dignified self-respecting life, a Jew must know the history of his people, not merely in the Biblical period, which is generally just as well or even better known by his non-Jewish neighbor, but also in Talmudic and more recent historic eras. He must know enough to understand the real sources of the difficulties which he will encounter and to meet those difficulties with understanding rather than with blind resentment or cowardly complacency. And for an American Jew it is important to understand the large role which the Hebraic tradition has played in the development of American thought and American democracy from Puritan times to the present day.

The history of the Jews has always had, for me, a peculiar fascination. Even in the years when I was most consciously rejecting the supernaturalism of Orthodoxy I was devoting a large part of my thinking to Biblical history, Biblical criticism, and comparative religion. Beginning in 1899 and for many years thereafter as a volunteer teacher of the Thomas Davidson School, I gave courses in the Book of Job, the Hebrew Prophets, and other religious subjects. When I entered the Graduate School at Harvard, courses with Woods and G. F. Moore in the Hebrew religion and the history of religions formed a major part of my studies. In later years a considerable part of my reading and lecturing was directed to Jewish problems. The literature of the Old Testament which I studied as a child has never ceased to grip me, and in days of depression when I have had little energy for writing or study I have found the books of the Bible and Old Testament criticism most absorbing reading.

Interest in Jewish affairs, however, has never been for me a purely intellectual matter. At all periods of my life I have seen fellow human beings, sometimes dear friends, close relatives and cherished students, suffering and facing all sorts of perplexities because they were of the Children of Israel. This was not always a matter of creed. Anti-semitism, in its modern as in its more ancient forms, does not generally draw distinctions between Orthodox, conservative, Reformed, agnostic, atheistic, or even converted Jews, between conservative Jewish bankers and fanatical Jewish revolutionists. The blows of oppression, contempt and discrimination generally fall on all Jews alike, even unto the third and fourth generation. Out of this reality comes a call to rise to the defense and help of one's fellows.

To the sensitive humanitarian this call may sound across all the gulfs that separate peoples and civilizations. I have always had the greatest admiration for Gentiles like John Haynes Holmes who have come to the defense of Jews as of any other oppressed people. And I have always felt the same admiration for Jews like Julius Rosenwald, Louis Marshall, Walter Pollak, Osmond Fraenkel and Nathan Margold, who have enlisted gallantly in the struggle for the rights of other oppressed racial and religious minorities. But such sympathy is a rare flower of civilization. The eighteenth-century philosopher who said, "The world is my country, to do good my religion," expressed an ideal which few humans have ever achieved. For most men the cumulative force of social tradition and the enormous difficulty of overcoming the momentum of social institutions limit the horizon of effectiveness, even of effective sympathy. He who would call upon the better nature of his fellow men must recognize these human limitations.

Humanitarianism can become a potent force in the real world

only as it builds outward from group relations in which sympathy is normal. He must be narrow-hearted indeed who cannot feel for those with whom he grew up, whose heritage is his heritage, whose misfortunes are his misfortunes. Humanitarianism ceases to be thin and other-worldly when it is bound up with men and women whose roots are intertwined with one's own. When, in the days of the Russian famine of the twenties, a distinguished American Zionist warned that "man does not live by bread alone," that "Palestine was the only salvation," and that it was "useless to give bread" to the Jews of Russia, I could not forget my own cousin, who starved to death before help from this country could reach him. Massacres in Czarist Russia or Nazi Germany are very close when one knows that, but for the good luck or unconquerable fortitude of parents or grandparents, he and those who are dearest to him might be among the victims. When, in the months before our marriage, Mary Ryshpan headed a drive to aid the victims of the Russian pogroms of 1905, who of us did not recall the words of the Puritan who said, when he saw a man led to the gallows, "There, but for the grace of God, go I."

So it was again in the years of the First World War, when on the Eastern Front every Russian defeat and every German defeat was blamed and visited upon the Jews, and when every Russian or German victory was celebrated with an offering of Jewish blood or a bonfire of Jewish homes. So it was again in the days of Hitler. In the face of these realities I have never been ashamed to identify myself with fellow Jews who suffered, and I have tried not to let differences of religious belief or politics or other ideologies stand in the way of practical co-operation in the struggle against injustice or in the endeavor to relieve suffering. After all, what is distinctive about a civilized man is that he can work with others who have different ideals, so long as there exists an underlying human sympathy.

Still, it is sometimes hard to live up to the civilized ideal when one's fellows resort to the attacks on character and integrity with which we Jews so often embellish our differences of opinion. Perhaps this habit is evidence of a peculiar capacity for hatred; perhaps it is but a modernization of the art of cursing, which was already highly developed in Old Testament times but certainly reached a pinnacle of perfection on the East Side of my youth. It has sometimes seemed to me that we need a special Anti-Defamation League to protect Jews

against the libels and slanders of their fellow Jews. In fact some
fruitless efforts in this direction were made in the days of my youth
by my godfather, Reb Meier — a *rov*, who never accepted any fees
for answering ritual questions, or other service, and who always when
solicited for advice urged women to refrain from cursing. Cursing
was not only a form of attaining relief from their many troubles
but it developed into a fine art, and I do not know of any language
that is as rich as Yiddish in that respect.

A single story that I heard from one of my teachers may illustrate
the possibilities of cursing as a fine art. There was a contest among
three men as to who could invent the most terrific curse. The first
man started off with the following: May you have as many sores as
there have been perforations in all the *Matzoths* which the Jews have
eaten since they left Egypt. (To prevent fermentation in the dough,
every *Matzoth* has many rows of thin perforations in it.) The second
contestant then produced the following: May you be as rich as Korah
(the Jewish equivalent of Croesus) and may all that money be spent
on salt to rub into these sores. Whereat the third countered with the
decisive one: May you have all that fools have wished on themselves.

Many of these curses contained strange words that had no definite
meaning, but were all the more terrifying for it. I remember the rage
I felt when my sister in angry quarrel with me called me "Brahman"
— a word of whose meaning I had no idea whatsoever. But perhaps
these childhood experiences helped to inure me to the epithets that
would be hurled at me in later years by men and women who deemed
themselves endowed by God or Lenin with authority to solve all
human problems and to smite unbelievers with the wrath of His indignation.

I do not believe that there is a "Jewish Question" or a "Jewish
Problem" any more than there is a "Christian Question." Indeed
when I was scheduled once to speak on "The Jewish Problem" at a
meeting of the Menorah Society, I rose and said, "Gentlemen, there
is no Jewish problem." Then I sat down. After having shocked the
audience into thinking, I did rise and explain why I thought that
there is no "Jewish Problem." There are, of course, many human
problems, of which Jews, as human beings, have perhaps more than
their share. But these problems, traced to their ultimate roots in
reality, are also the problems of other minority groups, and what

group of human beings is not a minority in one situation or another?

For most of these problems I know no answer. But I believe that one of the essential elements of civilization is the division of labor. I have faith that some problems which are beyond my powers and beyond the powers of any one of us may be solved by the co-operation of many. In the words of Rabbi Tarphon, "The day is short and the task is great. It is not incumbent upon thee to complete the whole work, but neither art thou free to neglect it." And so, for each of us who is able to recognize his own limitations, comes the question, "How can I best contribute to that which is beyond my power to complete?"

To me the choice of ways in which to express my respect for the sources of my being has always been very simple. Never having been afflicted with wealth, I have never had to trouble myself seriously about what causes or institutions I ought to endow or support. I have never had the talents for raising money in good causes which my dear friend Jacob Billikopf has put to such good use. I have never had the strength to address and fire large crowds. All that I have ever been able to offer to my people is that which a teacher and scholar can give.

In my younger days, such offerings as I could hope to make on the altars of social understanding were fired by the dream of Thomas Davidson of a school or movement which would combine the underlying insights of religion with the knowledge of science and the wisdom of philosophy. In the first articles of mine that ever found their way into print, articles published in 1901 and 1902 in the old *Alliance Review,* I struggled with these problems — the problem of religion and science, the loyalty that we owe to the past and the loyalty that we owe to the future, the problems of a lost or liberated generation on the East Side, which are, seen in true perspective, the problems of every generation in a changing world. And for some seventeen years after Davidson's death I did my best to keep alive the rare combination of intellectual study and spiritual communion that had taken shape in the Thomas Davidson School at the Educational Alliance.

When in 1902 I began to teach at City College, and for thirty-six years thereafter, I naturally shared in the struggles of my students against the discrimination that faced so many of them as they sought to establish their careers. And as a citizen I could not be silent in the face of the great campaign to repudiate the declaration that all men are created equal which culminated in the racist immigration laws of 1922 and 1924. Along with Jane Addams, Isaac Hourwich, Felix Frankfurter, Father John Ryan, and other unregenerate liberals, I joined in the battle to expose the false science on which this anti-semitic and anti-Catholic legislation was based. Our efforts in 1921 to raise money and to enlist scientific bodies to support studies and publications in this field came to naught in the face of the postwar hysteria with its nightmare of an immigrant threat to 100 per cent Americanism.

In later years there were other ventures in the field of Jewish scholarship and education to which I could not refuse what small contribution I might offer. As Chairman of the Talmudic Library in 1928-29, alongside Dr. Chaim Tchernowitz, I did my best to bring into being an encyclopedia that would make the Talmud intelligible to all readers. But the prevailing cult of unreason had made of "Talmudic disputation" a popular term of contempt—even among Jews. It was hard to find among Jewish intellectuals the sort of enthusiastic support for this project that we obtained from non-Jews — among them Dean Roscoe Pound, Dean Shailer Mathews, Professor Dewey, Professor Torrey, and my old teacher of religious history, George Foote Moore of Harvard. At all events, I was unable to persuade more than a handful of my fellow citizens that the Talmud is a unique achievement in the history of civilization and one that throws a white light upon the historic value and general significance of Jewish contributions to world civilization. The Talmud had been my first teacher. Now the Talmud was in low estate, and it would have been gratifying had I been able to repay it in the only coin a teacher values.

Not quite so hopeless were the efforts in the field of vocational education that my wife, the devoted companion of so many of my labors, and I put into the development of the work of the Ort. To both of us, as old teachers, Ort presented a continuing challenge: What could vocational training, administered with sympathy and understanding, do to help oppressed people to surmount the degradations of poverty and hatred?

With the help of my son Felix my philosophical outlook had been formulated in *Reason and Nature* in 1931, and the bearing of this philosophy on law and society had been fairly outlined in a volume published in 1933 under the title *Law and the Social Order*. With the help of my colleague and former pupil, Ernest Nagel, the implications of my philosophical approach for the teaching of logic had been reduced to what was later to prove a "best seller," as logic books go, *An Introduction to Logic and Scientific Method*. Our work on this was drawing to a close in the spring of 1933. I could now look forward to retirement from college teaching with a feeling that what I had to contribute to the world of philosophy would not entirely perish with me. With this sense of relief, I could look about me to see what, if anything, the meager offerings of a logician could contribute to the future of my people here and abroad and to the cause of human freedom, with which the fate of the Jew has been so intricately bound for so many centuries.

CHAPTER TWENTY-SEVEN

JEWISH SOCIAL STUDIES: A CONTRIBUTION TO AMERICAN DEMOCRACY

WHEREVER WE FIND anti-democratic forces arrayed against liberal civilization, we find anti-Jewish measures a major part of their program. This is no accident. Those opposed to the modern movement of liberation, which led to the American and French revolutions, must oppose the emancipation of the Jews, which was one of the distinctive achievements of the liberal regime. Those of us who are the objects of the various anti-semitic movements have more opportunity than most of our fellow citizens to become aware of their character. We thus have the teacher's supreme obligation, that of sharing knowledge. We cannot contribute as we should to the common good of the larger community of which we are a part unless we are willing to say to fellow Americans in the face of dark and fateful forces that loom before us, "These are the things that threaten to destroy us — and after us, you."

The world-drama in the spring of 1933 showed the unmistakable signs of impending catastrophe. The attacks on the Jew in America were mere pinpricks in themselves, and the accession of Hitler to power had not been accompanied by a wholesale slaughter of German Jewry. That was to come years later. But here, for all who could read, were written the most dire prophecies that any lover of freedom had read in more than a century.

For me, the harvest years had come. I had finished, or was finishing, the books closest to my heart. Like many others of my generation I was reaping American fruits that had ripened under the warm sunlight of liberal democracy. Now there was the feel of winter in the air. Should we not set aside some part of our harvest as seed for the future, for our children and theirs, who in their lifetime would face realities that were just becoming discernible?

The friends of freedom were rallying on many fronts as the modern apotheosis of violence and irrationalism in Europe became clearer with the passing months. This was particularly the case among Jewish and non-Jewish men and women who understood the pattern of blood and reaction that begins with anti-semitism. In these circles there was a quick response to appeals for aid to the victims of persecution fleeing to America or to the ancient land of Israel, and to the anti-fascists who stood their ground and fought back as best they could. Organizations dedicated to combating intolerance and strengthening political and industrial democracy in our own country multiplied their efforts. Leaders and humble workers in several of these enterprises were close friends and former students who spoke so warmly of what I had done to equip them for the fray that I felt that I was, even in the lecture room, a participant in the battle.

Yet there was something missing. Nowhere, in all the roster of worthy organizations fighting the rise of intolerance, did I find one that had mastered the Talmudic precept, "Teach thy tongue to say, 'I do not know.' " There was not one that frankly confessed the vast ignorance that is ours concerning the position of the Jew in the modern world and frankly appealed to men and women equipped by training and interest to contribute to the growth of knowledge and understanding. It is easy to say, "Why bother about more facts when we know we are right?" In a world where almost everyone was an amateur physician, confidently prescribing the sovereign remedy for the ills of Israel, as for other ills, a teacher of logic and scientific method could not be sure of avoiding the fate of Socrates if he tried to call attention to the need of careful diagnosis before attempting any prescription. Discussion of Jewish problems is generally full of references to ideals, and it is important to remember that ideals are great motive forces in human affairs. But no solution of any difficulty is possible without thoroughly facing the actual facts. To do this is a very disagreeable task and most people not only dislike to do it themselves but they also dislike those who do it for them. Facts are messy and do not conform to what we should like them to be. But the physician or engineer who keeps his eye on the ideal and ignores the actualities is worse than useless.

The problem of intolerance is one that is not solved simply by emotional appeals to human sympathy. It demands, as well, devotion to the long-range weapons of study and scientific research. The forces that in the early 1930's proclaimed their purpose to destroy the Jewish people and liberal civilization were obviously well organized. Behind the outward show of Hitlerism, with its lurid resurgence of medieval bigotry and brutality, there were long-range planning and research agencies. The world's greatest library on Jewish problems was being built up in Nazi Germany. Were we to face a cunning enemy with bare breasts and a blowing of trumpets, or could we make use, in the cause of freedom, of the tools of science that freedom of thought had called into being?

This question many sensitive men and women faced in the spring of 1933. Out of a common concern grew a common resolve to do what none of us alone could accomplish, namely to enlist research and science in the struggle against intolerance, at what seemed to us to be, if not the most critical sector of that struggle, at least the sector we were best equipped to man.

Opinions differed, of course, as to the worth of research and science in meeting the threat to civilization that the rising tide of world anti-semitism carried. Endeavors to base activity in Jewish affairs on accurately ascertained knowledge rather than on prejudice and guess-work continually encounter the objection that this is dangerous and that its result may be to bring out facts that are unsafe. Indeed, one met this objection even from intelligent physicians who would be shocked if anyone suggested that people should not go to a doctor for examination lest they thus find something wrong with them. What, indeed, should we think of the captain of a boat who, with dangerous rocks ahead of him, shuts his eyes and steers blindly?

To me, our failure as Jews to understand our own situation and our own problems — we who have been called the "People of the Book" — has long seemed a deep disgrace and disaster. Our very lack of unitary authority emphasizes the need for research in Jewish affairs, motivated by a genuine desire to get at reliable and verifiable facts that all can recognize. We have no pope or political leader who can speak for all the Jews with any authority. No one today really believes that all the Jewish community can be united as a religious body. I happen to be one of those who do not expect the synagogue to go out of existence in any near future. It has weathered the storms of over two thousand years and it still has a great deal of vitality as a center for Jews — just as the church is still a natural center of the social life of Christians. Nevertheless, it is vain to hope that all Jews can be united in the synagogue or Reformed temple — there are a great many who can not or will not subscribe to Judaism as a religion or even to any form of theism. You may read them out of the fold, as the Jewish community of Amsterdam excommunicated Spinoza, but they and others will consider them Jews and nothing will be achieved by the excommunication except to make it a little more difficult later to gloss over the fact that there was no place for Spinoza in the Jewish community.

The unanimity that we cannot find in religion we certainly cannot find in political and economic affairs. Some years ago Israel Zangwill wrote, "Hear, O Israel, the Lord our God is One, but we, his people, are dual and so undone." I do not agree with Mr. Zangwill. I think the fact that the Jews are not a unitary organization, that there is a great diversity among them on almost all issues of religion, politics, economics and the like is a good thing. It is good for the Jews; it has tended to develop them spiritually by fostering individuality instead of dumb military obedience. And it has guaranteed our security by enabling us to adapt ourselves to most diverse conditions. And yet some sort of unity we need in order to ward off the dangers which threaten us. In a world in which the spirit of strife is becoming more intense, we must look after our interests, and we must relate them to the interests of all men of good will. In the words of Hillel, "If I do not look after myself, who will? But if I look after myself alone, what do I amount to?"

As I looked about me at the bitterness of Jewish ideological conflicts, and saw the vehemence with which Jews themselves attributed the sufferings of the Jewish people to the assimilationism or non-assimilationism, religion or irreligion, Zionism or anti-Zionism, nationalism or internationalism, capitalism or communism, of fellow Jews, it seemed to me that the only possible basis of unity was the basis that gives unity to the disagreements of scientists, a common acceptance of the need for demonstrable knowledge, based on nonpartisan scholarly studies. The authority of the facts is, as the history of science shows, sufficient for practical purposes. Dictatorships are not necessary in medicine or in methods of hygiene. In any case, it seemed worth while to try to mobilize intellectual forces for study of the present and prospective situation of the Jewish people and to put the findings of such research at the disposal of all men of good will. Human knowledge and understanding may not enable us to solve all the problems of the Jew in an unjust world, but abandoning the effort to understand the underlying causes and to avoid foreseeable errors is intellectual cowardice.

Research, of course, is not enough. Facts must be brought to focus in practical activities inspired by good will. But of such activities the Jewish community in America never lacks. There is no shortage of good will in the outpourings of Jewish charity, and the administration of this charity has generally found able hands — certainly hands much more competent than my own would have been. What has been lacking, however, on the American scene is long-range use of the results of research. This demands scientific periodicals and other publications, conferences for the interchange of ideas and facts, and all the other instruments that help to bring harvest from seeds of insight. Above all it demands, as does any great educational or commercial enterprise, institutions that will outlast individual lives. Of this the deaths of the honored and lamented Louis Marshall and Max Kohler gave us striking evidence. Both of these men devoted their lives to the defense of Jewish rights in various fields, in accordance with the American idea of fair play to all. In the course of their work they amassed an enormous amount of useful knowledge. But there was no institutional recording of their experience and its lessons, and no organization to ensure continuity of attention to these problems and to profit by cumulative experience.

There were many agencies of good will, Jewish and non-Jewish, to disseminate and utilize generally accepted facts — and sometimes generally accepted myths — in all sorts of Jewish affairs, from vocational guidance to the defense of civil rights. But it was dismaying to see what poor, makeshift data most of these agencies had to use as the factual starting point of their work. And no one of them was devoting its primary efforts to the task of operating an effective intelligence service for the Jewish people in their fight against the forces which would degrade them and deprive them of their human rights.

So it came about that a handful of men and women to whom this task seemed of first importance met in June, 1933, to take counsel. We met at the New School for Social Research, which had, under the inspiring leadership of Alvin Johnson, become for many of us a reincarnation of Glenmore and of Thomas Davidson's liberal faith in learning without academic trappings. Some of us were teachers, some were doctors, lawyers, economists. Most of us were accustomed to working with our heads rather than with the larger muscles of arm and thigh. Some of us were old cronies from Thomas Davidson days, others were strangers drawn together for the first time by a common sense of need and a common urge to use whatever strength we had in a common enterprise. We might disagree among ourselves on many issues, but we were united in thinking that in days of bitter stress for the Jews over most of the world there was a great need for an organization that would be devoted primarily to the business of fact-finding so that our attitude and policies might be based on the most reliable information and not on cant or illusion or on the guesswork or impressionism that is so dangerous in time of panic and hysteria. We realized that the necessity for an armory of scientific knowledge in the struggle against the forces that would degrade us would be appreciated only by men and women who understood the value of knowledge. This did not necessarily limit our membership to professional scholars — a Jewish laundryman once gave me as clear a formulation of the fundamental ideas of our undertaking as I have ever heard — but it meant that we could not hope to develop a mass appeal. We did hope that a sufficient number of men and women accustomed to working with facts might conceive it to be their special duty to support our enterprise and thus give it a chance to demonstrate its worth.

Out of this meeting in June, 1933, there emerged, after a few months' gestation, the Conference on Jewish Relations. We were, in fact, a continuing conference, not tied to any cause or creed less universal than the old, simple faith that the search for truth is an essential part of any progress towards a more humane and tolerant world. As a pluralist in philosophy I had long maintained that any human problem of major dimensions can be fully grasped only through a diversity of approaches and perspectives. The outcome of our efforts left me more than ever convinced of the creative significance of differences of background and interest even where men are co-operating for a common goal. Among our number were Orthodox and Reformed, religious and irreligious Jews, Zionists and non-Zionists, socialists and individualists. Yet we found it possible to work together with a reasonable amount of mutual sympathy and a common concern for the gathering of knowledge and the promotion of a better understanding of the position of the Jew in the modern world. Ideological differences between our Zionist and non-Zionist members never prevented us from reaching agreements about the research tasks that we could most usefully undertake. Here, as in many other fields, it was much easier to agree on specific tasks and solutions than on abstractions Even institutional rivalries — many of our members were affiliated with the American Jewish Committee and many others with its chief rival, the American Jewish Congress — never obstructed the progress of our work. Within a short time our working membership included some of the most distinguished scholars of the country in the fields of economics, statistics, history, law, medicine and other sciences. Among our first members were Professors Einstein of Princeton, Wolfson and Frankfurter of Harvard, Sapir of Yale, Sharfman of Michigan, Perlman of Wisconsin, Kandel, Baron, Michael and Israel Wechsler of Columbia, Dean Klapper of the City College, Dean Loeb of George Washington University, and Vice-President Deutsch and Professor Max Radin of the University of California. As these and many others of our active workers were living on professors' salaries, we would not have been able to do our job but for the financial aid of members and friends who had the vision to see completed works in our architect's plans. A thousand-dollar contribution to the Conference from its first treasurer, my life-long friend Arthur S. Meyer, started a wave of enlightened generosity which, while never large enough to remove our financial worries, gave us at least the wherewithal to demonstrate the worth of our plans.

One of the first problems to which we turned was the problem of bringing before the world's conscience the character and dimensions of the German assault upon Jewish, and therefore upon human, rights. The passing years have made it hard to realize how strenuously and successfully most Americans in the first years of the Third Reich refused to face the facts. But we can see the scope of this wilful blindness by turning back to the pages of the Spanish Civil War, when a military insurrection with the aid of Moors, Fascist Italians, and German Nazis attacked the Spanish Republic, and we practically joined the attack by prohibiting our citizens from selling arms to a sister republic with which we were at peace.

Those of us who saw and understood what was happening in Europe had to present the facts to the American people in terms that could not be mistaken, before the sands of time ran out. In the summer of 1935 we arranged to send one of the world's outstanding authorities on minority rights, Professor Oscar Janowsky, to Europe to prepare a comprehensive legal and factual report on what was happening to guaranteed "minority rights" in the various European countries. A year or so later, one of the moving spirits of our Conference, James N. Rosenberg, persuaded Mr. James G. McDonald, the High Commissioner for German Refugees, to make of his proposed "Letter of Resignation" a documented analysis of the Nazi crimes against humanity. To our Conference fell the job of gathering the facts. The resulting document stimulated a great growth of consciousness here and abroad as to the relation between anti-semitism — which many at the time were disposed to consider only a curious form of insanity — and the Nazi threat to world peace and liberal civilization.

One of the first of these studies, embodying materials compiled for a petition to the League of Nations, was the volume, *International Aspects of German Racial Policies,* published in 1937 and written by Professor Oscar Janowsky and Melvin M. Fagen, the brilliant young secretary of our Conference. In 1938 we published, under the title *A People at Bay,* Professor Janowsky's report to the Conference on the situation of the Jews in Eastern Europe. At the same time we undertook a series of studies of the problem of multinational states, with particular reference to minority rights. We hoped that these studies, directed to the history of Switzerland, Belgium, and other multinational states, would throw important light not only on the problems of Europe but also on the central problem of Palestine. In these and other studies of the situation of overseas Jewry we felt that our tiny efforts were reaching the hearts and clearing the heads of millions of fellow Americans. And in the course of doing that we were demonstrating that it is possible, even in situations which pull one's heartstrings, to press an inquiry into roots and causes and thus to contribute towards that understanding which is the indispensable condition of any possible humane and effective remedy.

We were unfortunately less successful in our equally strenuous efforts to expose and break down prejudices and misconceptions that barred half-empty lands of plenty to the homeless freedom-seekers of Europe, all through our hemisphere, from Alaska to the Argentine.

The old ideal of the New World as a haven of refuge, and the workings of that ideal in the development of a liberal civilization, had become obscured by foolish fears. We found few allies in our efforts to overcome these fears by exposing them to the light of the facts. But even in this emotion-ridden field we hoped that careful studies of economic opportunities and legal barriers in North and South America would some day bear fruit. And in later years were were gratified to find that our studies were being put to very practical use in fitting refugees, here and abroad, into situations where their contributions to the country of their adoption would arouse good will rather than hatred.

On the domestic front the problem of anti-semitism and of discrimination in economic and academic fields set the focus of most of our studies. Anti-semitism seemed to most of us to be a symptom of several diseases that needed to be diagnosed before we could be at all sure that the current nostrums did more good than harm. The starting points of such a diagnosis we attempted to bring together in December, 1935, in a scientific conference on the historic, anthropological, and legal phases of anti-semitism. Organizing an extended conference in those days, when we had no office staff, was a hard job and most of it fell on the capable shoulders of my wife. The result was more than we had a right to expect. The participation of eminent scientists and scholars, Professors Boas, Sapir, Hans Kohn, Baron, and many others, gave us intellectual give-and-take of the highest order, and provided the material for a significant volume of *Essays on Anti-Semitism*, published by the Conference seven years later.

One of the promising specific studies that we succeeded in carrying out in this field was a psychological study of racial attitudes among college students. The results of this study, carried on by Dr. Eugene L. Horowitz, in co-operation with Pi Lamba Phi fraternity, tended to establish the proposition that intolerance towards Jews is closely correlated with general intolerance towards other groups, even nonexisting groups. The question, "Would you be willing to have Piranians for next door neighbors?" proved a key to the irrational factor in race prejudices. Out of these scientific beginnings, we hoped, there might develop a new diagnosis and therapy that would make the present well-meaning efforts to cure these social ills appear to future generations like the work of witch doctors and children.

One thing that all our studies of anti-semitism made clear was the fact that anti-semitism is a symptom of a deeply irrational trait in human nature, known of old as xenophobia, that is, the aversion to the stranger or to anyone who is different from ourselves. In times of peace this, though ever present, may be subdued by rational considerations which make for liberal civilization. But in time of stress it breaks out in violent forms. It is futile to fight symptoms while the source of the disease is active, just as it is hopeless to try to get rid of mosquitoes while their breeding grounds flourish. Jews, here and abroad, are a small minority and cannot by themselves remove the cause of the world distress. So long as the latter prevails, anti-semitism and other evils will remain. Jews cannot expect to receive justice in an unjust and sick world.

Of course, it is possible to mitigate the evil of some of the adventitious forms of anti-semitism. Jews must, I suppose, refute false charges. Only so is it possible to prevent fair-minded but uninformed people — and we must remember that a large part of America still knows the Jewish people only by hearsay — from believing these charges. And only by meeting false charges with demonstrable facts can we prevent irresponsible people from producing ill-considered replies, dictated by indignation rather than knowledge and understanding. Yet when this is fully admitted, it is still true that much evil results from answering every scoundrel who wishes to attract public attention by denouncing the Jews as the cause of all human distress. Such answers add to the publicity that such scoundrels crave; and in the long run it is bad for the morale of the Jews, who are the principal readers of such attacks and replies. The man who broods over his own wrongs and always expects to be unjustly dealt with is not a pleasant neighbor even to himself.

A far more important argument against throwing too much of our energies into the fight against anti-semitism is the difficulty of avoiding sinking to the moral level of those who attack us, of avoiding "fighting fire with fire." It is very difficult to refrain from answering an opponent in kind. But the one fact that stands out unmistakably in the history of the Jews is that they have never been able to beat their enemies at their own weapons and on the ground chosen by them. In the long run the Jews have survived, like any other people in similar circumstances, by developing inner moral strength that has enabled them to bear contumely and misfortune and to do so with quiet courage and the dignity of self-respect.

As I look at the world from the point of view developed by fifty years' study of its history, I see grave troubles ahead for America and, therefore, for the Jews in it. Instead of wasting our energies by concentrating exclusively on the fight against anti-semitism, we can do better by studying our resources and taking thought as to how best we can be prepared to do our share as Jews in the fight for humanity. To do this we must join the liberal forces everywhere, help them in the crucial battles ahead on behalf of all oppressed minorities, and prepare ourselves to bear the inevitable wounds and hardships. In olden days the strength to do this came from religious conviction. Today we Jews are no longer united as a religious brotherhood. But we can and we must do all in our power to strengthen our resources by a campaign of educating or enlightening our fellow Jews as to where we stand and what we may reasonably expect. Above all, we need to face and solve, with courage and intelligence, the special economic problems that are the outgrowths of anti-semitism. But such problems, we must realize, cannot be accurately formulated, much less solved, unless we have scientifically reliable information on such factors as the numbers, birth rate, death rate, and occupational distribution of our Jewish population. And beyond this, we need to know the truth with respect to physical and mental disease, and to what extent, if at all, American Jews differ from their non-Jewish neighbors in intelligence and conformity to legal and other social or moral standards.

On all these subjects, we found an appalling reliance upon guesswork and rumor even in the most high-minded of practical endeavors. Indeed the more practical the endeavor the more likely were its sponsors to resent factual inquiry with the warning that this was a time for vigorous action and not for study. But Jewish problems like other problems cannot be satisfactorily dealt with on the basis of preconceptions, rumors, or the policy of muddling through. And we found that the basic data on Jewish population, age groups, and occupational distribution were nowhere available. Indeed we found that the basic figure which is a factor in every generalization about American Jews, namely their total number, was not known with any degree of accuracy. Some of our studies indicated that past estimates of this total had been considerably exaggerated. This lack of accurate knowledge was reflected in all sorts of local enterprises. Thus a well-meaning community might make large charitable contributions to the building of a home for the aged that could not be filled — we saved the Jewish community of one city about $1,000,000 by pointing this out — or, with all good will, a community might waste its righteous indignation on occupational discriminations that were imaginary and fail to act on some that were real, or might direct vocational guidance work into fields that could not be fruitful and overlook other fields where slight effort could bring large results.

We soon decided that it was necessary to inaugurate a series of factual studies of the composition of the Jewish population and its place in the economy of the country, to serve as a basis of welfare programs, vocational guidance, and intelligent answers to the problems of discrimination. Some years later, in 1943, several of these studies were compiled and edited by Sophia Robison under the title *Jewish Population Studies*.

One of our first enterprises was a study of the place of Jews in the legal profession in New York City. By dint of much pleading and a little browbeating, I managed to enlist an able committee, largely from the ranks of old schoolmates and students, and one of my old college teachers, Judge Galston. Our committee included Justice (then Professor) Frankfurter, Judges Lehman, Mack, and Shientag, Professors Michael, Gray, Handler, and Schiller, and many distinguished leaders of the New York bar such as Simon Rifkind (later Judge Rifkind), Carl Austrian, Louis Fabricant, Leo Gottlieb, George Medalie, David Podell, and Sol Stroock. Most of the spadework in this enterprise was done by Samuel Klaus and Melvin Fagen. The result, later published, was to make available, for the first time, reliable data regarding the number, training, type of practice, clientele and income of this vocational group as compared with the profession as a whole. Among the striking data revealed by the survey was the fact that, as of 1937, only half of the Jewish lawyers of New York earned as much as $2,426 per year, and that it took Jewish lawyers between seven and eight years of practice, on the average, to reach this income level.

A rather comprehensive study of the position of Jews in the medical profession was carried out by a group of physicians led by

Doctors A. A. Rongy, Reuben Ottenberg, Israel S. Wechsler, J. J. Golub, Leonard Blumgart, J. A. Goldberg and Aaron Brown. This study served to disprove many current ideas as to the percentage of Jews in the medical profession. It also showed the large number of cities without any Jewish physicians — a fact which served, later, in aiding the effective placement of Jewish refugee physicians. Finally our study brought into clear focus the various forms of discrimination faced by Jewish practitioners, students, internes, and teachers of medicine.

In law and medicine, as well as in teaching and other occupational fields that we studied, we were able to find facts that needed to be faced by Jewish young men and women planning their careers, and by those who sought to give these young men and women vocational guidance not based on wishful thinking. One of our earliest efforts at community economic analysis was a study of the occupational distribution of the Jews of New York City. Recognizing, however, the shift of Jewish population from seaboard cities to interior and smaller towns and the significant changes in birth rates and occupation that accompany this shift, we directed major efforts to small town studies.

A good many different Jewish communities quickly recognized the practical significance of such information and began to appeal for the help of the Conference in organizing such studies. Out of these studies emerged a growing awareness of what they could contribute to more effective charity, vocational guidance, and social welfare work — the first result of our first community census study was a doubling of the available mailing list for local and overseas relief and a doubling of contributions for these worthy causes.

Thus there developed in the spring of 1939 a lusty offshoot of the Conference, the Jewish Occupational Council, sponsored and supported by a number of organizations that were not used to finding themselves contributing to the same enterprise — among them the American Jewish Committee, the American Jewish Congress, the Ort, B'nai B'rith, Hias, the Jewish Agricultural Society, the Jewish Labor Committee, the Jewish Welfare Board, the National Refugee Service, the National Council of Jewish Women, and the Union of American Hebrew Congregations.

I soon came to look upon the Jewish Occupational Council as

my favorite child. Not only was it doing competent work in a field of first importance, but the co-operation of so many organizations in sponsoring its work was the best possible proof of my hunch that, with patience and good will, traditional and hereditary differences between organizations, as between individuals, can be subordinated to a common enterprise devoted to the ascertainment of objective truth. For only an organization committed to the search for objective truth could give to those who stood at the threshold of their careers the help they needed to chart useful and rewarding journeys at a time when the shadows of discrimination were lengthening throughout the land.

The spring of 1939 marked the fruition of another enterprise that had long been close to my heart. My retirement from undergraduate teaching in the spring of 1938 had made it possible for me to devote a good deal of my time to the development of a scholarly journal that would advance the social, economic, and political studies and discussions which were the life of the Conference. It is almost impossible to promote scholarly studies in any field today without some special organ for their publication, notice, and review. Such an organ for the publication of detailed scholarly and documented studies seemed essential if we were to make a contribution to human understanding worthy of what was becoming, by the grim processes of history, the strongest Jewish community in the world. Thus I helped to float the first issue of *Jewish Social Studies* in January of 1939 with a contribution on "Philosophies of Jewish History," and wrote a good many book reviews in later issues. The laboring oars in this enterprise were wielded by my indefatigable co-editor, Professor Salo Baron, and by the journal's talented managing editors, first Professor Koppel Pinson, then Dr. Joshua Starr, and later Dr. Theodor Gaster.

All these ventures depended for their realization on the voluntary contributions of our members and friends, and I soon found myself in a role I had always dreaded, that of a practical administrator and professional beggar for good causes. My deficiencies in these roles have always been noteworthy. I never have had the executive ability to induce others to do things to which they are not otherwise inclined. This proved a real handicap to our organization, as well as to the philosophical work that I tried to carry on between agitational tours. I remembered the amazement that a writer for the *Jewish Tribune* in 1927 had expressed that a professional philosopher such as myself should spend so much of his time discussing and thinking over such problems as Zionism, nationalism, and anti-semitism. At the time, I had answered him, cavalierly enough, "A philosopher should be interested in every phase of human life." But now I was beginning to realize the difficulties entailed by such an ambition. And even the faithful services of a first-rate corps of executive secretaries and assistants — Mark Hirsch, Melvin Fagen, Harry Rosenfield, Joshua Starr, Theodor Gaster and Mina Wagman, could not blind me to my own administrative shortcomings. Yet it may be that our very lack of aggressiveness or popular appeal made it easier for us to work in close co-operation with older and larger or richer organizations.

They were glad to make use of the insights and researches of a research or intelligence service, so long as they did not have to worry about us as a rival body threatening their sources of funds and their membership. Indeed we deliberately chose to forego much needed revenue by not presenting ourselves as the effective agency to fight anti-semitism.

The close co-operation which the conference found in its work with other organizations was naturally reflected in my own life. As the President and chief travelling salesman of the Conference I found it difficult to decline invitations to head or help direct many other worthy organizations and enterprises with which the Conference was co-operating. Within a few years I had accepted such offices in at least half a dozen organizations, in addition to the conference and the Jewish Occupational Council — among them the Jewish Academy of Arts and Sciences, the Jewish Social Research Council, the Joint Distribution Committee, the American Jewish Committee, the Ort Economic Research Committee, and the American Palestine Fund. The rounds of talks, conferences and committee meetings soon assumed dismaying proportions.

In the first months of the Second World War, the Conference had inaugurated a series of discussions and studies devoted to postwar problems. Some of our more practical-minded brethren regarded it as a wholly unrealistic expenditure of time and effort to study postwar problems while the outcome of the war itself was still uncertain and the structure of the postwar world unpredictable. Yet it seemed to us that it was none too early to study the conditions of a desirable peace and the position of the Jews in it. Only so could we be sure that at the war's end we would have the pertinent data needed for conducting a competent defense of basic human rights for those Jews who should survive a war in which mass hatreds would also survive hostilities. And only by plunging without reserve into the long-range tasks before us could we hope, in calamitous days that filled the heart with horror at unparalleled atrocities and pity for the helpless victims, to guard against yielding to panic or hysteria or falling into helpless and benumbing despair. In days when almost every bit of news made one sick at heart it seemed more than ever necessary that we not only strengthen our hearts to face the dangers ahead, but also clear our vision.

I reported the sense of many colleagues in the Conference when, in my last presidential report, in June of 1940, I observed, "When the European war ends, Hitler's war against the Jews is not likely to be terminated. And in any case acute problems of relief and migration will face us, for which preparatory studies must be instituted now." I felt that we had prepared the way for such studies in the day-to-day work of the Conference. The most important thing we have achieved so far is that we have kept the faith and in doing so have impressed others with the need of clear and courageous vision into the basic realities of our situation without letting our attention be diverted by passing incidents.

The work we started was, as usual, larger than our resources though not larger than our faith. We were gratified when other organizations, better financed, notably the American Jewish Committee, came to our aid and set up the Research Institute on Peace and Post-War Problems on a solid basis — even though this meant abandoning my hope that our institute could function as an autonomous nonpartisan agency equally serviceable to all of the established Jewish organizations. We could expect now that other institutes would be set up under other auspices. But I have never shared the popular horror at a plurality of research agencies. Certainly a merger of all of New York's colleges would be highly undesirable. If other institutes of Jewish research were established, we could only offer them our fullest co-operation. Our real danger lay in lack of thought and research, not in any superabundance of these commodities.

France had fallen and the battle for Britain was approaching its climax. Under the pall of these events many regarded consideration of postwar problems as illusory. Yet it was becoming increasingly plain, even before the entry of America into the war, that all the human rights which had been built up by the modern movement of liberation that produced the American and the French revolutions were at stake. It was becoming increasingly plain that the winning of the war could not be divorced from the hammering out of principles which would assure the people of all lands that there was a peace, as well as a war, to be won. And in the face of these great issues it was becoming plain that Hitler would soon have the power to destroy a large part of European Jewry and that the responsibility for defending the survivors of Hitler's butchery would fall increasingly on American shoulders.

Of course there were many worthy organizations in this country interested in mapping the conditions of an enduring and endurable peace. But none of these groups was, at the time, giving any special thought to the position of Jews in the postwar world. None of them, indeed, seemed fully aware of the extent to which guarantees of human rights to European Jewry had broken down even before the outbreak of the war. Something more than a return to the *status quo ante* was called for, and we could not expect non-Jews to solve this perplexing problem if we ourselves ignored it.

As those who are not Jews do not as a rule study the Jewish problem, they do not often realize the various peculiar factors that enter into it. The July, 1940, issue of the *Annals of the American Academy of Political and Social Sciences*, for example, was devoted especially to a comprehensive survey of the conditions of a lasting world peace. It never even mentioned the Jews. When I called this to the attention of a colleague who is justly regarded as one of the best informed specialists in international affairs, he quite naïvely remarked that the Jewish problem would solve itself if the democratic powers win the war and equal rights are extended to all citizens. While this answer states a consummation devoutly to be wished, it utterly neglects our actual past experience in countries like Poland and Rumania. After the First World War, they did solemnly pledge themselves to that ideal and still managed to degrade their Jewish citizens and to deprive them of many necessary means of subsistence. In Poland this occurred with hardly a single law on the statute book avowedly discriminating against the Jews. It was all brought about by administrative measures with the co-operation of private non-Jewish organizations. Clearly it is impossible to understand the actual conditions under which human beings live if we rely only on legal prescriptions.

Nor can we reasonably expect many of our fellow citizens to be acquainted with the actual conditions under which Jews are living abroad if we do not provide them with adequate and thoroughly authenticated and reliable information.

In the autumn of 1940 I was asked to prepare blueprints for a series of Jewish studies of peace and postwar problems. My starting point was the premise "that as the war against the Jews began long before the present European conflict, it is likely to continue after peace between Germany and England is declared. It is not likely that the torrents of hatred let loose against the Jews by the powerfully organized Nazi propaganda will at once completely disappear on the signing of any treaty . . . The Jews will be in a worse plight than the rest of the population not only because, even before the present war, they lost a major part of their means of subsistence but also because they have become the object of intense nationalist suspicion and hatred that will take more than a generation to dissolve. War always leaves wounds and suffering which are not conducive to good will."

From this starting point it became clear that three groups of problems would confront us at the end of hostilities: problems of relief and rehabilitation, of migration, and of the vindication of Jewish and human rights.

The problems of relief and rehabilitation at the end of the war would, in all likelihood, be of an unprecedented scale, measured in human distress.

The problems of migration would also assume unprecedented proportions — the problem of how to help those who cannot possibly remain in Europe but must emigrate. Here we would have to study the natural resources, climatic and health conditions, economic opportunities, legal, political and social affairs of the countries of immigration. The problem contained the seeds of bright hope and grave peril.

The record of many failures at colonization [I wrote], e.g., by the British in the West Indies, shows the necessity of taking all factors into account, the economic and ethnographic as well as the geographic. On the other hand, the record of Jewish colonization in Palestine, in Argentina and in Southeastern Europe shows that with proper selection and training Jews can make excellent colonizers. It is important that American Jews, as well as men of good will everywhere, should get rid of the myth that Jews have always been traders or in the professions and entirely unfit for pioneer labor.

It is also important to show the economic fallacy which, especially in time of large unemployment, has in many lands served to shut the gates against immigration, viz., that the newcomers will take away jobs from the natives. This, like the old wage fund theory, is based on the false assumption that there is a fixed and unchangeable number of positions, so that an increase of population means a large number of unemployed. This ignores the fact that a larger number of people can create a larger market or demand for goods, and that the principal wealth of a nation is in its human resources. History shows that countries like Holland, England and America have been made great by the immigration of vigorous peoples.[1]

Finally, we had to look forward at the war's end to keeping up the perennial fight to which not only we, as Jews, but all good Americans and indeed all who value humane civilization must devote themselves, and that is the maintenance of the fundamental rights of human beings irrespective of their race or creed. There is no safety for anyone in a world in which such rights are ignored.

In the days just before Pearl Harbor I wrote to the newly elected President of the American Jewish Committee, Maurice Wertheim, urging that he help to rededicate that organization to the high objectives of its founders, who sought, in defending Jewish rights, to maintain the traditional American conception of equality and freedom which has made this country a sanctuary of peace and tolerance:

I think we must emphasize the fact that we fight as American Jews for the maintenance of the fundamental basis of humane civilization, which liberated the Jews from the ghetto and gave them the opportunity to enjoy the glorious privileges which our country offers, because it is based on a philosophy of freedom. The enemy of civilization today is not merely the man Hitler or some of his stooges in this and other countries. The enemies of liberal civilization are all those who wish to overthrow faith in human personality and its free development; faith in equal opportunity for all, because, forsooth, they believe in some racial or nationalistic idol which

[1] "Jewish Studies of Peace and Post-War Problems," *Contemporary Jewish Record,* IV (1941), 110-125.

like Moloch demands human sacrifices. We must fight the old fight for justice which the Hebrew prophets fought in their day and which all lovers of mankind have fought for through the ages. We must do it, of course, in the light of the present situation in the world. But we must do it in a way to arouse men and women by appealing to their imagination. Only in that way can we arouse the enthusiasm which liberates men's energies and makes real achievement possible.

Within this general postwar agenda there were hundreds of reports and studies to plan and to organize. I felt, however, that a philosopher's task was done when the problems and modes of attack were formulated. I had already turned over the active management and presidency of the Conference on Jewish Relations to my faithful collaborator, Salo Baron, and the continuance of its vital activities helped me to feel that I could return to my first love, philosophy, knowing that the work I had helped the Conference to start would be carried on, and that I could henceforward best serve the Conference as a critic of ideas rather than as an organizer or director of its practical activities. Now it was with a feeling of deep relief that I turned over the guidance of the Jewish peace and postwar studies to the capable hands of Max Gottschalk, at the end of April, 1941. I could not wholly dissociate myself from this work, any more than I could divorce myself from the Conference, and I was glad to write the foreword to one of these studies when what had been outline topics grew to reality four years later. It was good to know, in 1945, that there were solid answers to some of the questions we had formulated four years before. What had once been a plea for research could now become a plea for action based on knowledge. It was in this vein that I wrote, by way of foreword to Siegfried Goldschmidt's study, *Legal Claims against Germany*:

On the threshold of a long and difficult period of world readjustment it behooves us to examine with some care the techniques which have been developed in centuries of thought and action for the righting of situations intolerable to the consciences of civilized men. Though we cannot bring back to life the uncounted victims of Nazi blood lust or blot out from the record of history the bitter cries of those whose careers, homes, and families have been destroyed, there is much that we can do to bind up the wounds of a tortured humanity and to see that the evil that has been done does not long outlive the regime by which it has been perpetrated. Millions of surviving victims of the Nazi holocaust, Jews and non-Jews, will stand before us in the years to come. What can be done to restore to these, our fellow human beings, the basis of self-respect and self-support? How far can we devise and execute plans for restoring to them the things of which they have been robbed?

In meeting this challenge we shall need all the intellectual resources of civilized thought, not the least of which is the body of thinking on the morality of nations which has been called, in hope, I think, rather than in summary of achievement, international law. For law is one of the means by which man tries to control his fate, and it is only fitting that our efforts to control the fate of the world in the coming generaion shall take studious account of successful and unsuccessful attempts in the past to right wrongs that have shocked humanity.

In retiring from active management of the Research Institute on Peace and Post-War Problems just as its planned studies began to assume the garb of reality, I felt that I had done what a logician could be called on to do in a time of crisis. It was time for a philosopher to return to his philosophical labors. Indeed, as I returned to the writing of the Carus Lectures on "The Meaning of Human History," in the spring of 1941, it was with a sense that the struggle for freedom in our own generation would be effectively waged only as we saw it in all its perspective in the history of the struggle for liberal civilization, to which so many peoples in so many ages have contributed. In a very real sense the development of this vision might be the most enduring contribution I could make to the cause of human liberty and human tolerance in the native land of my children and my grandchildren. Such at least was the sustaining hope that shone through years that brought to me, as to so many of my fellow men, personal tragedy unrelieved against a background of cosmic disaster. In dark days this hope gave strength to faltering hands.

Liberalism and the toleration of differences are the fine flowers of civilization which prepare the seeds of material and spiritual freedom. All our material comforts and present intellectual resources are derived from the spirit of free inquiry and the taming of fanatical group intolerance. The cultivation of such liberalism has throughout the ages called forth heroic labor and at times martyrdom. But when the chill autumn blasts and cruel wintry frosts come, the sacred plant which bears the fine flowers and seeds of the life abundant, becomes neglected and despised. Only its faithful guardians seek to preserve it until the warm spring sunshine comes again.

BOOK EIGHT

WHAT LIFE HAS MEANT TO ME
(Fragments)

CHAPTER TWENTY-EIGHT

ON LIFE AND DEATH

I CANNOT AGREE with Spinoza that the free man thinks of nothing less often than of death (which is nothing in itself). The thought of death — or rather of the annihilation of the life of those that are most vivid in my memory, my mother especially — is ever present in my mind. This life that meant most to me — indeed my own past life and that of Felix who is now a man of thirty — is it all of such an evanescent sort? And yet so gripping? I ought to be writing my autobiography now when I am relaxed and my memory has not become dulled or overcoated by the technical things which I plan to write. (Diary note; July 18, 1937.)

Walked in afternoon to Palo Alto and the vegetation suggested the simile of how much our death and spiritual disintegration forms the soil from which our successors grow. (Diary note; August 29, 1937.)

A printed volume can never replace the
touch of a vanished hand,
And the sound of a voice that is still.

Yet some part of the spirit that we once knew in the flesh does speak to us in the pages of this book. It is well that we cherish it as long as we can. And while I have no vain desire to minimize the sense of loss to those in whose lives he was an integral part, I may urge that it was a genuine privilege to have known him. Apart from all speculations as to what he might have attained had he lived longer, there stands the fact that he was a glorious youth. The somewhat grim saying of the Greeks: "They whom the Gods love, die young," is true if we take *young* in the wider and nobler sense—independent of the physical years. (From the Foreword to Alvin Bruch's *Poems and Letters*, 1928.)

261

I am finding life more restful though obsessed with the idea that my mind is drying up. I am feeling the mystery of the coming and passing of consciousness and animal life as vividly as ever. (Diary note; February 14, 1935.)

I feel that my mind is now sufficiently active to warrant my doing a little more constructive writing. This period of relative health, a freedom from pain and depressed feeling of debility, cannot last very long, and if I do not do something I shall have less to look back upon, to buoy me up when the twilight sets in, wherein I shall not be able to stand up. (Diary note; May 9, 1937.)

I shall not be dead. For the dead [body] will not be I. The dead body of what was my mother is not the Bessie who lived, suffered and yet kept a masterful grip on life. Death is the absence of life where it once was. There is no evil in it — there is evil only in thinking of being deprived of the enjoyment of living. But the dead are not deprived of anything. And when the living are deprived of suffering they are relieved. Blank annihilation may be preferable to a life in which the balance is on the side of torture. (Undated note; c. 1940.)

The whole world will disappear so far as I am concerned for since there will be no I as subject after my death, there will be no object to it. But I live with the idea that my children or other people will continue, that my books perhaps will be read, that my body, changed, will continue in some form, etc. (Diary note; undated.)

Still it is depressing to think that it [forgetfulness of familiar names] indicates that in the remaining years of my life I shall not be able to achieve much of my intellectual program. Of course, the reflection is present: Why worry about the number of books I leave behind? What difference will it make when I am no more? But after all my whole life has been geared for formulating certain important ideas, and it is not pleasant to think that they will die with me. I often console myself with the thought that if I read more I should find in others, in even ancient writers, ideas to which I arrived as a result of my own thoughts. Every sentiment that I have felt has probably been felt by countless others, some of whom gave it expression. Yet even to gather such ideas into the genuine expression of one mind is a service to humanity — of the kind that makes friendly communication with our fellow men mean so much to us, and makes a sort of affection between writer and reader which has a distinctively human note. (Diary note; May 29, 1940.)

CHAPTER TWENTY-NINE

ON BOOKS AND READING

How MARVELOUS IT IS to pick up an old book and feel that you are communicating with a man who has long passed away, that you are getting at his mind, his feelings, and way of expressing himself! This is more marked in handling copies printed centuries ago, when spelling and manner of writing were different; for example, the old *Transactions of the Royal Society* — for then you feel these very books were read and handled by those who no longer exist. We are apt to form vague conventional views of what the men of the seventeenth century were, felt, and did. The actual things they handled and read make their life more vivid to us. (Diary note; May 1, 1939.)

Read a good deal of Herder and Kant's review of Herder. What a gentle reviewer Kant was of a book with which he differed so radically! I was not up to snuff when at Harvard I wrote in my thesis on the effect that this review had on Kant. For I did not notice that the review came after Kant's own essay on universal history which was still pre-critical, i.e., naturalistic, so far as ethics was concerned. (Diary note; July 20, 1941.)

I have also been reading Santayana's *Last Puritan* — not much of a novel; the characters are not much alive.

Yet the reflections are not without a vital interest. To be too detached — to walk this life like a ghost would not give us anything at all to see. (That is why only bad ghosts wander at all.) We see those things in which we have some interest. (Diary note; March 6, 1936.)

Is Hitler's achievement due to his not having been spoiled by education?

Have just read Hazlitt's essay on "The Ignorance of the Learned" and have been surprised at the lack of care in his reasoning. It is of course true that learning is not the same as general intelligence, and certainly experience shows us many learned men who are pedantic fools. But this does not prove that the reading of books makes men ignorant or stupid — though in moments of tiredness men may prefer to read rather than to think. Certainly the acquisition of knowledge through books does not make men ignorant.

Perhaps it is to some extent true that people who rely on the authority of books (or any other authority outside of their own experience and reflection) are likely to make mistakes that more naïve or unlearned folk will not. But it has not been proved that book knowledge (or any other knowledge) dulls our judgment and makes us stupid. The foolishness of some learned people is not necessarily due to their learning. And when Hazlitt points to the unlearned Shakespeare, it does not prove that the great poet's wisdom was due to his not knowing much Latin or Greek. If ignorance were the cause of greatness, how many great men we would have. (Diary note; July 31, 1940.)

It is not always the great books — the works of the master — that give us most insight. They very often teach us nothing except what we already know. But often the work of some insignificant writer, whose knowledge and power is even inferior to our own, forces us to rethink life. His very mistakes force us to see the truth. (Undated note; c. 1910.)

CHAPTER THIRTY

THE CHARACTER OF M.R.C.

I AM NOT AS STUPID as I look, but neither am I as bright as you sometimes think me to be. Hence, my remarks are not always as significant as they may sound. (Undated; probably c. 1900.)

The offerings of poor people — I mean poor (such as myself) in the resources of genius — are meager in themselves, but to one who looks into the mind of the one who makes the offering, the widow's mite, it has a value of its own. (Diary note; July 21, 1935, at Triuna Island.)

Read Santayana (on Hamlet).
The great, sheer abundant, and overflowing vitality of Santayana by contrast to the thin, readily fatigued and exhausted, me.
Yet the latter has a coherence or tenacity of its own.
Tenacity is the key to my life as well as to that of my parents and of the Jewish people. Little overflowing energy — whether or not because of unfavorable circumstances or constrained opportunities — there is an intense self-absorption which stands in the way of disintegration. (Diary note; October 22, 1936.)

It is easy to stand by your conviction through thick and thin without compromise if your convictions are clear cut and have an absolute definiteness. But when reflection begins to wear away their artificial boundaries, compromise, accommodation and adjustment ceases to be a sin. On the contrary it becomes the alternative to fanaticism. Why should those who oppose physical war, because they recognize common interests of humanity, favor intellectual war between rival principles which are part of a common truth? Naturally war is inevitable in both realms so long as we remain partial, but in truth war is not superior to peace, no more than intellectual harmony can dispense with conflict. . . . Emerson concludes the essay with the observation that the loss of wife or children may make one mature and a source of comfort to others. But it may deprive one of all the support that makes life effective or dignified. (Diary note; June 23, 1935, at Triuna Island.)

Show by your life that you do not care for success — that you do not care for the approbation which comes of trifles — that you are determined not to set great value on baubles simply because the multitude does so, and you will be rendering a greater service than by conforming to society's petty regulations for the sake of getting the favor necessary for success.

Conform to details, says Davidson, because, although details, they mean so much in society. But must we not protest against society's emphasis on these small matters, if they are small? (Undated; probably c. 1899.)

Decided not to go to Yosemite. Why should I tire myself with riding six hours or so, sleep or fail to sleep at a high altitude, having the dizzy feeling when I look down from great heights — all to see some sights which I can well imagine without going there? Reed said to me, "You seem to enjoy only the things of the mind — you do not crave experience." But I, "Staying home is also an experience. Seeing the earth and sky around here is fascinating if you have the energy to enjoy the elements. It is only when we are exhausted that we need the stimulus of novelty. There is enough novelty in the constant changes of the sky, clouds, and diverse aspects of the scenery around us — just as a healthy taste can find satisfaction in simple food. The sight of people, clean faces, sparkling eyes, elegant figures — are all attractive wherever you are. . . ."

I feel rested and relatively free from strain and I look back upon my past life and wonder how little of it was devoted to the pursuit of enjoyment or to play. That is partly the influence of my grandfather and the life example of my father and mother to whom life was always a tense struggle where every penny counted and had to be eternally watched and fought for. Then there was the tension of sex, of work, of worry over ill health, etc. How few of the things I craved for as a young man, beauty of surroundings, health, etc., were accessible to me! Then there was the valley of the shadow from 1905-06 and the valley of humiliation of 1906-11, the poverty of 1918-19 (the first time in my life when money matters began to worry me) when I was steadily falling behind ($1280 in debt with no prospect of being able to pay it), and as a climax the confusion of 1926-31 and the hard work under failing health of 1934——. (Diary note; August 25, 1937.)

One of the wisest sayings in the Bible is the statement that "The undoing of the poor is their poverty." It requires means to institute any system of economy, so that the poor cannot afford to economize. This showed itself early in my life when I wasted time and energy to save a few pennies, e.g., to use scraps of paper of various sizes instead of some uniform pad and to clutter up all the room available to me with papers and books which could economically have been thrown away since taking care of them, keeping them in some order, and looking through them for the things wanted consumed more time and energy than would have been involved in rewriting and repurchasing.

The great example of inefficiency is the habit of saving money on carfares, porters' tips, etc. The persistence of that habit after I had plenty of means, is the cause of the strain on my heart to which I subjected myself on that cold day in Chicago, in the spring of 1939, when I hurried home after my lecture instead of taking a cab.

From another point of view the greatest source of inefficiency in my life has been the habit of elaborate preparation. Instead of tackling a thesis directly at once, and proceeding to do as much as I could about it, I got into the habit of making most elaborate preparations, like the Dutchman, who wishing to leap over a ditch, started to run from such a distant point that he got tired before reaching the ditch. In my case it has been worse because I made many starts from different directions to accomplish things which were not worth while so that my life has been filled up with fragmentary efforts in most diverse fields instead of concentrating on some one line of activity. I suppose that it all arises out of the fact that when I start anything I soon get tired, and in that state it is easier to tackle something else. (Diary note; c. 1940.)

Though I rejected this asceticism intellectually, it dominated as a habit. not only my own life but communicated itself to my children who thought it sinful to spend more money than was necessary — though in that respect it may also be the fact that I always took the children into my full confidence as to my financial situation and let them have whatever was necessary. (Diary note; c. 1940.)

CHAPTER THIRTY-ONE

M.R.C.'S INTELLECTUAL EQUIPMENT

HOMER SAID of a famous bard that the Muse loved him greatly, so she took away his sight and gave him the gift of song. If that be the way of the Muse, she certainly does not love me at all. For she gave me the gift of sight but took away the power of song. (Note; August, 1923.)

Not insensitive but trained to look for the repeatable elements — the average rather than the distinctive. Good memory — but lack of vigorous following through. No bold strokes but in constant brooding and returning to the point of departure. None of the vitality and flare of genius of James or Santayana, the fruitfulness of Peirce or Royce or even the solid substantiality of Dewey. Yet withal a tenacious clinging to truth. Never linguistically endowed. Not resourceful in playing chess. Better second thoughts. (Undated.)

Since the days of my youth I have been troubled by the fear that I have lost the characteristic quickness of perception (grasp) and thought, as well as that tenacity of memory which characterized me when I first met Thomas Davidson. At any rate it seemed I no longer had that free mind, ready to give itself up to any new thought with all its might and main. There were always, it seemed, preoccupying thoughts, even if only in the background of consciousness, and not that large free force of thought available in the days of my youth. (Undated.)

Writing down one's ideas robs them of the glamor which all ideal beings have so long as they are not fully within our grasp. I have a brilliant idea, proceed to write it down, and behold — it is but a poor little commonplace. Is it because writing is a kind of prose translation of the poetic idea, sacrificing its rich aura for bare accuracy of outline, or is it that the poor idea is like the peasant maid, charming in the distance, but dull and prosaic when seen at close range? Perhaps there is no real conflict between these two explanations. (Undated.)

There are those whose mental life is like a plane — everything on the same level. Every day so many pages of fairly uniform worth or worthlessness. Mine is like a desert with oases — sometimes high peaks and illusive play of clouds about them, sometimes such clear sunlight as to make me feel that I have seen clearer than any other creature. But for the most part it is dry desert sand — getting my nourishment from reading. I am, however, most stimulated by conversation with those who are intelligent but not too obstreperously critical or unsympathetic. Contradiction opens fresh faucets in my mind, but I also need some appreciation that the flow is worth something. (Diary note; August 19, 1936.)

When I muse my thoughts seem to be grandly significant with large vistas. When I speak them the inadequacy of my expression to the idea is sometimes heavily felt. But the spoken word is gone and there is nothing that can be done about it. But the ineptitude of the words and sentence structure then first occurs to me, becomes a challenge and an insult to me when I look at it, and the natural hestitation about deciding which expression really gives my thought soon makes me feel that the thought itself is not accurately conceived. (Diary note; November 30, 1936.)

To draw me out fully, to release most fully the flow of my thoughts, I need the stimulus of conversation with certain kinds of people, people with enough intelligence to appreciate the meaning of what I say even if they do not agree. Indeed, relevant objections are most stimulating provided the objectors are not too bumptious or vessels whence irritable and irritating tones overflow.

This raises a question: Why can't I when I write look into my mind and find the thoughts and knowledge that I possess when I lecture or converse? Of course there is no store of ideas or knowledge

in my mind — it is simply an ability to write or say inwardly or outwardly certain things and perceive what they mean. Still it is a puzzling
situation. Most of our ideas originate in what we have heard or read.
Yet they sometimes come out of us in a form which no one ever saw
before. (Undated note; c. 1938.)

Most of my life has been spent daydreaming. Never very active
physically, seldom engaged in social play, reading and occasional conversation have been my principal occupations. In these as well as in
my more elementary classes, the activity of my mind has always been
in large part aloof. The topic on the page or of the conversation generally suggested reflections beyond the immediate topic. Except in
heated argument, I was a spectator in my own conversation, sometimes
approving and more often regretting that I had not put it in a better
way. That is why writing has almost always been a very difficult enterprise for me. The sight of what I have written down brings out the
critical impulses which hinder the flow of words if not that of thought.
I suppose that classroom routine has made it easier for me to overcome
my hesitation in speech, my ill-constructed sentences, and my ineptitude in finding the exact word. But writing reveals the incomplete-
ness of my thought. (1939.)

CHAPTER THIRTY-TWO

WHY DO PEOPLE so wise in their advice to others fall down in their own lives?

Advice depends on penetrating analysis, but action depends upon energy especially in the last or finishing touch. Many things, properly planned and started, fail because at the last moment the energy is not there to carry it through properly. (Diary note; June 16, 1934.)

The condemnation of the speculative life as an "escape" — "epistemologic chess as an indoor sport" — need not be taken seriously by an intelligent being who is not afraid of epithets. (For nothing is changed by them.) Escape from suffering is what we all try to effect. In some instances we can escape by changing the external social conditions. But human power or the power of any one individual in this respect, is very limited. The other way is to cultivate within ourselves those adjustments that will enable us to lighten the burden. The two ways are not always compatible but they are not always mutually exclusive. And in any case a wise man will use both ways.

Of course life involves, or forces on us, various choices. And when someone chooses the opposite, I may have to fight him. But a fight is not an argument or proof. You may say, I do not care to prove it, but will kill you instead. But you cannot thereby prove that I am wrong.

You can prove things in a defined world, but not in regard to the actual world, which is not defined. (Diary note; August 10, 1937.)

Why don't I relax and deliberately plan to enjoy my remaining years? Why do I plan agitational tours and activities for the Conference? And why above all do I urge myself to write when writing comes so difficult for me? One cannot, of course, readily change the pattern and rhythm of a lifetime. (Diary note; July 5, 1937.)

Why do I persist in wasting my few remaining years by reading stupid books, when I should be writing less stupid ones myself? (Diary note; June 22, 1938.)

Why, oh, why can't I concentrate on the important things to write and drop the less important details or instrumentalities! My memory is failing and soon I shall be through, with all the accumulated reflections on life dying with me. Yet, paradoxically enough, what I can offer of most value to my fellow creatures is the lesson of peace through abandoning the constraints of unnecessary obligations and irrationally passionate drives. (Diary note; July 4, 1938.)

I am fortunate in every respect in which the world counts fortune. I have a devoted wife and children of whom any parent can well be proud. They are thriving in every way and a source of almost continual satisfaction. My income is more than adequate for my needs and my work is in the main so pleasant that I would miss it if I had to go without it. With all, I have admiring as well as devoted friends and the seemingly genuine respect of a large public. But while I am fairly at peace, I am certainly not happy. Why not?

In the first place happiness is physical. While my health has been fair recently, and I have been relatively free from distressing symptoms, I have not enough energy for real enjoyment. I have so long had to take care lest I overstrain myself and get too tired, that I have acquired the habits of a permanent invalid and I am conscious of it — which is a humiliation. It is humiliating to see things undone or done poorly by others when a little better organization of my life would have enabled me to do them much more in conformity with my ideals.

The real evil, however, can be put in psychologic terms by saying that I cannot get myself to abandon certain ideals of writing or other achievements, such as the Conference, and yet I cannot devote myself wholeheartedly to the achievement of these objectives. I am distracted not only by different objectives but also by perpetual doubts as to whether it is all worth while and whether it would not be better to ease up and live to enjoy myself in my own quiet way, in reading, out-of-door walking and intellectual converse with friends, and thus pass the rest of my days in as much peace and comfort as the opportunities afford. Why should I, of all men, try to run a practical affair like the Conference? Yet how can I abandon it? And that is the case with all my interests. I cannot drop enough of them and yet I cannot concentrate to bring any of them to ripe fruition. And so most of my life seems wasted. (1939.)

A QUIET, not highly productive but on the whole restful and satisfactory day. From five to seven wrote on the divergence of philology from logic. Dictated letters and notes nine to ten-thirty. Lecture on romantic and rational philosophies of history — elements of nationalism and anti-nationalism in nineteenth-century historians.

Entertained Dr. S. of the Sociology Department of Columbia at lunch — a profitless time between twelve and two.

Saw Mrs. B. in regard to Ittelson.

Then rested and prepared lecture on American ethics.

New light of idealist philosophers on "My Station and Its Duties" — e.g., Holmes.

Home before eleven. (Diary note; December 1, 1936.)

I felt very much encouraged by this visit [to Dr. Herzstein]. By concentrating more on my work I shall free myself of anxiety neuroses. (Diary note; June 30, 1940.)

And yet although I have done practically no work I feel at times that my mind is as clear as ever — that my analysis of the war, of the reasons for Germany's military victory (as expounded to Joe Willen and to Bardin) and the inner difficulties of liberals like MacLeish, Lewis Mumford, etc., is deeper and truer than what most writers realize. I need a little more courage to write and to abandon other enterprises.

There are modern novels much better than classic ones that will not live as long. A modern work has more competitors and thus attracts relatively less attention. *The Vicar of Wakefield* published today would receive rather little attention and would be forgotten within a few years, as, for instance, Jack London's *The Sea Wolf*, or *The Call of the Wild*.

Such reflections dampen the ardor for writing. What can I produce that will make a relatively enduring impression on the sated and blasé world? My wisdom is not of a romantic or revolutionary character but the distillation of old common sense passing through a skeptical sieve.

When I conceive some book or essay, I may be stirred by the grandeur of the conception. But when I begin to write it down it looks prosaic and sapless and I am halted by doubts as to the proper formulation or order of exposition — yet when, years later, I read any writing of mine I have no such feelings but am rather carried on by its current. There is then the stimulus to more writing until the feeling rises, Oh Hell! *Cui bono?* Why toil? Why not enjoy the passing dream and the *dolce far niente?* Is it when a conception is far advanced in development that it presses to be let out into the world? Or is it rather when it is first conceived that it arouses most energy in us? (Diary note; June 26, 1940.)

OF COURSE, I AM against any military clique that stages a rebellion against a democratically elected government. What American, loyal to the principle of government by the people, enunciated by Jefferson and Lincoln, can take any other position?

General Franco and his cohorts are not only traitors to their country by inviting Moors, Italians, and Germans to shoot down their own Spanish people, but also traitors to humanity by the way they make war on defenceless women and children. (Comment in *Writers Take Sides*, March, 1938.)

Mrs. Carnap yesterday remarked how tired I looked and I had to admit that I felt that way. I have tried hard not to let the horrible progress of the war affect me too severely, but it does depress me. I know that even the triumph of Hitler in the whole war will not upset the whole trend of civilization — that his domination of all Europe cannot last, so long as the nationalist feeling in other countries is fanned by his kind of Germanism. Besides, as a philosopher, why worry about this change in history more than about the fall of Greece, or Judea, or the Roman Empire, or the Saracen civilization? Still Hitler embodies so much of what is hateful to me that his triumph depresses me perhaps more than did the death of my father in 1934. The latter event made life seem peculiarly vain and empty and unreal. But father had lived to a ripe old age and his sufferings the last few months made death a great relief. (Incidentally, the noble life, hard toil, and terrific suffering of my father make the notion that the world order is just seem a bitter mockery.) But the progress of German arms annoys me almost every other minute. Everyone talks about it, the headlines hit me in the face and I cannot induce May to stop buying newspapers or tuning in on the radio reports. (Diary note; May 26, 1940.)

The Western Philosophical Association adopted a strong resolution unanimously urging the lifting of the embargo on arms to Spain. This is the first time in the history of the Philosophical Association that any resolution of a political nature was even proposed. There was some doubt as to the propriety of it, but I argued that it is better to do the right thing now and take care of "precedents" later. I was not responsible for the introduction of the resolution (at the time it was introduced I was not a member of the Western Division) but I think that my argument helped to make it unanimous. (Diary note; April 26, 1938, Chicago.)

T HE DREAM —

Occasionally I meet former students who by their mere appearance bring home to me very vividly the picture of their presence in my classroom decades ago. Sometimes this passing of time becomes poignant when they are accompanied by sons of the same age as their fathers were when they sat before me. (Undated.)

To be reminded of one's youth is like being refreshed by a mild breeze from a fragrant field. Oh, for the days when we were young and eager and the world had alluring freshness, when there were so many things to be done and ours was the opportunity! But to dwell in the past is to stop work and what is life without any tasks which drive us? (1939.)

I have grateful memories of the Educational Alliance ever since 1892, when it was called the Hebrew Institute.

It was there that my father and mother regularly went to hear the Rev. Masliansky preach in my parents' native tongue, Yiddish.

It was there I drew books from the Aguilar Free Library and thus began to read books in English. The Educational Alliance afforded me the opportunity to join a club of my fellow students at C.C.N.Y., called the Young Men's Literary Society; and the reading room supplied me with the opportunity to become acquainted with English periodical literature.

It was there that the woman who afterwards became my wife and mother of my children received the vital part of her intellectual development under the guidance of Edward King and the first superintendent of the Educational Alliance, Isaac Spectorsky. I myself attended the meetings of the Comte Synthetic Circle, led by Mr. King, which was attended by my wife, her younger sister, Mrs. Spectorsky, Leonora O'Reilly, and a number of other keenly intellectual and very attractive young women.

It was there too that I first met Thomas Davidson who became a light of my life and of my intellectual development, as well as that of my wife and a host of other young people who afterwards formed the Thomas Davidson Society. The Thomas Davidson Society became Branch B of the Educational Alliance and for many years received support from it. To this day the Davidson Society holds its memorial meetings in the Educational Alliance.

Through Davidson I met and enjoyed the friendship of the first president of the Educational Alliance, Isidor Strauss. He and Mrs. Strauss became my personal friends, and our first wedding gift was a beautiful set of chinaware from Mrs. Strauss.

Through Davidson I also met Mr. and Mrs. Cyrus Sulzburger, remarkably cultivated and public-spirited people.

In connection with my work as chairman of the Executive Committee of the Thomas Davidson Society I came in contact with Judge Greenbaum, the second president of the Educational Alliance, who loyally supported my efforts.

My work at the Educational Alliance also brought me into contact with that remarkable leader of the Jews and of the American people, as well as of humanity in general, Louis Marshall, whose friendship and courage proved sustaining to me in troubled times.

A window of my life opening up on the soul-strengthening vista of humanity will always be dedicated to the Educational Alliance. (Note on Anniversary of Educational Alliance; October 19, 1943.)

CHAPTER THIRTY-SIX

MY PARENTS

IN ALL I KNEW of my father he conformed to the old conception of a saint. He was kindly, sympathetic, just in all his dealings, and never harming anyone, pained at the presence of any injustice or inequities, and always hoping for the triumph of good causes. (Note; 1935.)

Read Mrs. Stillman, Samuel Butler — impressed with fact that this antagonism of children to parents and the tragedy of frustrated children, etc. is all bunk — if I may judge by my own experience. My grandfather beat me unmercifully and unjustly and humiliated me beyond measure; yet I loved him and my general attitude then and now is one of gratitude. (Diary note; June 24, 1935.)

Election Day. Caught earliest train, not knowing whether I should find Mother dead or still alive. Walked with May from the station to the hotel. When I entered my sister Florence's room and saw the candles, I experienced no shock. I was prepared for the end. Went to the sea beach twice before taking three forty-five train home. (Diary note; November 3, 1936.)

The life of my mother is going through my mind. The prosaic (or commonsense) question of my father when he first came to see her: "Don't bother about hats! Do I please you?" And the sixty-seven years' devotion — she realized my father's limitations as regards wisdom and often resented his inability to see her point of view and his narrow-sighted insistence, his irritability, etc. Yet no one had a more faithful and devoted companion. And for the twenty-seven months after his death the word most often on her lips was Motinke (the endearing diminutive of Mordecai).

Did she really grow in wisdom in her later years or did she have more leisure and more opportunity to impress people with her sagacity? Wherever she went she held court — all recognizing her remarkable and vigorous intelligence at her age (though she did not look her age because her hair remained reddish, with but a little fringe of gray).

My last two years with her made me appreciate her qualities more than I did in the years when I saw little of her.

If I had to make a speech, I would have spoken of the spiritual importance of the Neshwieser Verein — how it enabled the hardy pioneers to adjust themselves to the new land, to keep people in self-respect and to make a home for the new generation; how the traditional learning was a light — not like the modern electric but like the ancient candle or torch — which enabled people to interpret the new life. (Diary note; November 5, 1936.)

It is curious that while my father's death left me with an overpowering feeling of the shadowy character of life, the loss of mother who was so much closer to me for the last two years has had no such effect. It has, however, made me look more in the past, to repeat:

"Oh, for the touch of a vanished hand and the sound of a voice that is still."

All the dreams of my life, my long communings with myself directly or indirectly connected with her, seem to be endowed with some of her tenacious vitality despite physical frailty.

Was her superior intellectual vigor due to the fact that she was not distracted by many conflicting considerations so that she could concentrate with all her strength on the issues of the moment? In comparison with her, I seem to be an intellectual weakling. (Diary note; November 30, 1936.)

If I had the opportunity to write the epitaph of my father's and mother's grave —

Here lie the remains of two brave souls
Who were born in obscurity and poverty,
Whose courage was never daunted by hardships,

And whose fidelity to the ideals of honesty, piety, and devotion to all those dependent on them never faltered.

They were married throughout sixty-seven years and remained absolutely faithful even when separated for years.

She never uttered anything foolish and he never did or said anything base. (November, 1941.)

CHAPTER THIRTY-SEVEN

ON WRITING AN AUTOBIOGRAPHY

T HE FULLNESS OF LIFE — the many people whom I have met whose lives meant a good deal, the many more about whom I read — the stories, biographies, the scenes of beauty and grandeur. (1939.)

I thought of some incidents in my biography and wondered why autobiographies are so much devoted to the early years of one's life. Of course the reminiscent moods occur most often when we are not very actively in pursuit of some practical end, and in the earlier years we are more impressionable, and the impressions are more vital and stick more. But to this must be added the fact that autobiographies are written when we are in or nearing our second childhood, and the active events of our middle years no longer grip us and we do not think them sufficiently romantic. The midday is enjoyed but not the subject of a good deal of romantic fantasy. (Diary note; January 1, 1938.)

How vivid at times are our early memories. These events will never happen again — nevermore will I hear my mother read the Tzenou V'renou — but never again will some of the events of today recur; but the events of the past are practically isolated in memory, deprived of the dross that surrounds our active experiences. Also in youth fewer things occupy our minds and they write these impressions on clearer tablets. The psychophysicists used to say that the brain is softer in youth and therefore more impressionable. But be that as it may, it is a fact that we remember the first lines of poems, of books, such as the Bible, Dante or Xenophon much better than the rest. Everyone who has ever read Caesar knows "Gallia est omnis divisa in partes tres" and few remember the next sentence.

Why then do I not tackle my autobiography? There is the old snare of more research to perfect my source book of Greek science. And yet I know it is a snare — that I shall never become a master on the subject of Greek science. But it is easier to read than to write. (Diary note; June 26, 1940.)

CHAPTER THIRTY-EIGHT

ON MARY RYSHPAN COHEN

WE ARE GATHERED TOGETHER by the ever sacred memory of one of the noblest women who trod this earth of ours, one who combined the perfection — so far as perfection is ever granted to humans — of a perfect wife, mother, relative and devoted friend to all who came under her beneficent influence. We cannot by anything we say or do bring to life again her illuminating presence. The adamantine jaws of death close irrevocably on all we hold dear to us, but we owe it to the light which she shed on our lives to hold her memory forever dear to us and our children and our children's children forever. Brief is the life of man, and fragile are all his works. But the echoes of a noble life will go on as long as human life lasts.

Throughout all her life Mary Cohen was an ardent admirer of George Eliot, whom she took as her model of womanly courage. And it would be most fitting on this occasion to recite George Eliot's famous lines in "The Choir Invisible":

Of those immortal dead who live again
In minds made better by their presence: live . . .
In deeds of daring rectitude, in scorn
For miserable aims that end with self,
In thoughts sublime that pierce the night like stars, . . .
That watched to ease the burden of the world, . . .

Unfortunately, I do not remember all those lines and I do not have a copy to read to you today, but I may add a reference to a poem which another hero of my life and hers, Thomas Davidson, often recited. It is from Swinburne's "Super Flumina Babylonis":

Whoso takes the world's life on him and his own lays down,
    He, dying so, lives.
Whoso bears the whole heaviness of the wronged world's weight . . .
    How should he die?

(June, 1943.)

EPILOGUE

by

Felix S. Cohen

The writer of this autobiography once expressed the hope that it might be "the vehicle by which almost all that my life has meant can be expressed — even all that my philosophic reading and reflection have meant to me." Seen against that purpose, the present volume is a thing of shreds and patches, mute testimony to the fate that crushes human hands in the midst of their work. It was with a keen awareness of life's brevity and of the uncertain duration of man's handiwork that Morris R. Cohen penned the prologue to this autobiography in the summer of 1940. And yet there went with that keen awareness of impending fate — keener than most of us knew — a mystic faith in the "echoes from soul to soul" that outlive our individual lives. It was natural that one in whom such a faith burned should entrust the completion of this volume, the dearest child of his brain, to the hands of a first-born son of his own and of the woman he loved unto death.

The task of completing this manuscript did not seem an impossible one. He to whom it was assigned had served as Socratic midwife in other labors. Most of the task of editing was done under the guidance and direction of the manuscript's author. All that appears in this volume was already in manuscript, though the manuscript was sometimes only scattered cryptic and fragmentary notes. But in the end the hands to which the task fell — even with the help of many loyal and devoted friends, students and colleagues of the author — proved incapable of filling the gaps, and incapable of telling what the writer had hoped to tell of "the fullness of life — the many people whom I have met whose lives meant a good deal, the many more about whom I read — the stories, biographies, the scenes of beauty and grandeur." Not only is the last book of the autobiography fragmentary, but several of the preceding books and chapters which were not finished before the author's death on January 25, 1947, are equally fragmentary in substance, if not in form.

Yet it must be said that what impels the presentation of this unfinished work is more than loyalty to a filial promise. High in the wisdom which Morris R. Cohen handed down from an older generation of teachers were the words of Rabbi Tarphon: "The day is short and the task is great. It is not incumbent upon thee to complete the whole work, but neither art thou free to neglect it." Recognizing the unfinished character of all human efforts has made it easier to see in this volume, fragmentary though it be, something of enduring worth — words through which the living flame that was Morris R. Cohen will continue to rekindle "efforts after things that are of perennial value."

Some day a writer who has known all the mansions in which Morris R. Cohen lived—perhaps one of his many extraordinarily gifted students — will piece together out of the materials of this autobiography, and out of a larger mass of jottings, letters and human memories, a fuller story of the life on which this volume throws fugitive light. Until then this brief story of his life, told in his own words, must stand as the avenue through which may travel men and women who seek to share in the adventures of the spirit that made up this "Dreamer's Journey."

BIBLIOGRAPHY

of the Published Writings of Morris R. Cohen

1901-1902

"Amos and his Disciples," *Alliance Review,* II, 392.
"The East Side," *Alliance Review,* II, 354, 449.
"Some Ideals and Characteristics of Thomas Davidson," *Alliance Review,*
   I, 258; II, 290.
"The Story of Some Remarkable Societies," *Alliance Review,* II, 324.

1908

Review of Bax, *The Roots of Reality,* in *Journal of Philosophy,* V, 78.
Review of Ormond, *Concepts of Philosophy,* in *International Journal of
   Ethics,* XIX, 385.

1910

"The Conception of Philosophy in Recent Discussion," *Journal of Philosophy,* VII, 401.

1911

"Court of Appeals" (letter), *Survey,* XXVI, 569.
"The Present Situation in the Philosophy of Mathematics," *Journal of
   Philosophy,* VIII, 533; reprinted in *Reason and Nature,* 1931.
Review of Natorp, *Die Logischen Grundlagen der Exakten Wissenschaf-
   ten,* in *Journal of Philosophy,* VIII, 693.

1912

Review of Boas, *The Mind of Primitive Man,* in *Current Anthropological
   Literature,* I, 93.
Review of Shuster *et al., A History of the Cavendish Laboratory, 1871-
   1910,* in *Journal of Philosophy,* IX, 79.
Review of Miraglia, *Comparative Legal Philosophy,* in *Harvard Law Re-
   view,* XXVI, 383.
Review of Whitehead and Russell, *Principia Mathematica,* in *Philosophi-
   cal Review,* XXI, 87.

1913

A letter, in *Journal of Philosophy*, X, 27.

"Jurisprudence as a Philosophical Discipline," *Journal of Philosophy*, X, 225.

Review of Holt *et al.*, *The New Realism*, in *Journal of Philosophy*, X, 197.

"Supposed Contradiction in the Diversity of Secondary Qualities," *Journal of Philosophy*, X, 510.

1914

"History vs. Value," *Journal of Philosophy*, XI, 701; reprinted in *Reason and Nature*, 1931.

"Intellectual Leadership in America," *New Republic*, I, 16.

"Philosophy," *Cyclopedia of Education*, IV, 685. New York: The Macmillan Company.

"Process of Judicial Legislation," *American Law Review*, XLVIII, 161; reprinted in *Law and the Social Order*, 1933.

"Qualities, Relations and Things," *Journal of Philosophy*, XI, 617.

Review of Croce, *The Philosophy of Giambattista Vico*, in *Philosophical Review*, XXIII, 677.

Review of Kohler, *Moderne Rechtsprobleme*, in *Journal of Criminal Law*, V, 618; reprinted in *Law and the Social Order*, 1933.

Review of Von Jhering, *Law as a Means to an End*, in *Philosophical Review*, XXIII, 557.

"Rule vs. Discretion," *Journal of Philosophy*, XI, 208; reprinted in *Law and the Social Order*, 1933.

1915

"The Bill of Rights Again," *New Republic*, II, 272.

"The Bill of Rights Theory," *New Republic*, II, 222; reprinted in *Law and the Social Order*, 1933.

"Legal Theories and Social Science," *International Journal of Ethics*, XXV, 469; also printed by New York State Bar Association; reprinted in *Law and the Social Order*, 1933.

"The Legend of Magna Charta," *New Republic*, III, 136; reprinted in *Faith of a Liberal*, 1946.

Review of Brunschvicg, *Les Étapes de la philosophie mathématique*, in *Philosophical Review*, XXIV, 81.

Review of Chamberlain, *Immanuel Kant*, in *New Republic*, IV, 79.

Review of Emery, *Concerning Justice*, in *New Republic*, II, 107; reprinted in *Law and the Social Order*, 1933.

Review of Parry, *The Law and the Poor*, in *New Republic*, IV, 25; reprinted in *Law and the Social Order*, 1933.

Review of Riley, *American Philosophy*, in *New Republic*, IV, 106.

Review of Russell, *Our Knowledge of the External World*, in *New Republic*, III, 338; reprinted in *Faith of a Liberal*, 1946.

Review of del Vecchio, *The Formal Bases of Law*, in *American Political Science Review*, IX, 799; reprinted in *Law and the Social Order*, 1933.

"Shall the Judges Make the Laws?," *New Republic*, III, 31.

"Thomas Davidson," *Cyclopedia of Education*, II, 255. New York: The Macmillan Company.

1916

"Charles Peirce and a Tentative Bibliography of His Published Writings," *Journal of Philosophy*, XIII, 726.

"Josiah Royce," *New Republic*, VIII, 264.

"Jus Naturale Redivivum," *Philosophical Review*, XXV, 761; reprinted in *Reason and Nature*, 1931.

"Neo-Realism and Josiah Royce," *Philosophical Review*, XXV, 378.

"New Leadership in Law," *New Republic*, VI, 148; reprinted in *Law and the Social Order*, 1933.

"Place of Logic in the Law," *Harvard Law Review*, XXIX, 622; reprinted in *Law and the Social Order*, 1933.

"Real and Ideal Forces in Civil Law," *International Journal of Ethics*, XXVI, 347; reprinted in *Law and the Social Order*, 1933.

"Recent Philosophic-Legal Literature in French, German and Italian," *International Journal of Ethics*, XXVI, 528; reprinted in *Law and the Social Order*, 1933.

Review of Botsford and Sihler, *Hellenic Civilization*, in *New Republic*, VI, 221.

Review of Dewey, *Essays in Experimental Logic*, in *New Republic*, VIII, 118; reprinted in *Preface to Logic*, 1944.

Review of Guthrie, *Magna Charta and Other Addresses*, in *New Republic*, IX, 18; reprinted in *Law and the Social Order*, 1933.

Review of Huss, *The Church*, in *New Republic*, VII, 23.

Review of Michels, *Political Parties*, in *New Republic*, VIII, 303; reprinted in *Faith of a Liberal*, 1946.

"The Use of the Words, Real and Unreal," *Journal of Philosophy*, XIII, 635.

1917

"The Distinction between the Mental and the Physical," *Journal of Philosophy*, XIV, 261.

"Interests Served by the Law and the Methods of their Evaluation," *Journal of Philosophy*, XIV, 189.

Review of Boutroux, *The Contingency of the Laws of Nature*, in *New Republic*, XIII, 191; reprinted in *Faith of a Liberal*, 1946.

Review of DeMorgan, *A Budget of Paradoxes*, in *Journal of Philosophy*, XIV, 107.

Review of Galileo, *Dialogues Concerning Two New Sciences,* in *New Republic,* XI, 85; reprinted in *Faith of a Liberal,* 1946.

Review of Root, *Addresses on Government and Citizenship,* in *New Republic,* X, 109; reprinted in *Law and the Social Order,* 1933.

Review of *Modern French Legal Philosophy* (Spencer, ed.), in *American Political Science Review,* XI, 137; reprinted in *Law and the Social Order,* 1933.

Review of Stone, *Law and Its Administration,* in *New Republic,* XI, 227.

1918

Editorial on Emile Durkheim, in *New Republic,* XIV, 187.

"Hermann Cohen," *Journal of Philosophy,* XV, 587.

"Mechanism and Causality in Physics," *Journal of Philosophy,* XV, 365; reprinted in *Reason and Nature,* 1931.

"The Need for a Modern University," *New Republic,* XVII, 130; reprinted in *Faith of a Liberal,* 1946.

Review of More, *Platonism,* in *New Republic,* XVI, 143; reprinted in *Faith of a Liberal,* 1946.

Review of Wigmore et al., *Science and Learning in France,* in *Illinois Law Review,* XIII, 136.

"Subject Matter of Formal Logic," *Journal of Philosophy,* XV, 673; reprinted in *Preface to Logic,* 1944.

1919

"A Slacker's Apology," *New Republic,* XXI, 19; reprinted in *Student Outlook,* II, no. 4, p. 10; reprinted in *Faith of a Liberal,* 1946.

"Baseball as a National Religion," *Dial,* LXVII, 57; reprinted in *Faith of a Liberal,* 1946.

"Communal Ghosts and Other Perils in Social Philosophy," *Journal of Philosophy,* XVI, 673; reprinted in *Reason and Nature,* 1931.

"On American Philosophy—1. The Idealistic Tradition and Josiah Royce," *New Republic,* XX, 148

"On American Philosophy—2. William James," *New Republic,* XX, 255.

Review of Adler, *An Ethical Philosophy of Life,* in *New Republic,* XIX, 254; reprinted in *Faith of a Liberal,* 1946.

Review of *American Problems of Reconstruction* (Friedman, ed.), in *New Republic,* XVIII, 155; reprinted in *Faith of a Liberal,* 1946.

Review of Heine, *Sämtliche Werke,* in *New Republic,* XX, 15; reprinted in *Faith of a Liberal,* 1946.

Review of Lewis, *A System of Physical Chemistry,* in *New Republic,* XX, 65.

Review of Read, *The Abolition of Inheritance,* in *New Republic,* XX, 129; reprinted in *Law and the Social Order,* 1933.

Review of Young, *Portugal, Old and Young,* in *New Republic,* XVIII, 426.

"Zionism: Tribalism or Liberalism?," *New Republic*, XVIII, 182; reprinted in *Faith of a Liberal*, 1946.

1920

"American Philosophy," in *On American Books*. Francis Hackett, ed. New York: B. W. Huebsch, Inc.

"Einstein's Theory of Relativity—I. Time and Space," *New Republic*, XXI, 228.

"Einstein's Theory of Relativity—II. The Law of Gravitation and the More General Theory of Relativity," *New Republic*, XXI, 341.

"Judas Iscariot" (a letter), *New Republic*, XXI, 172.

"On American Philosophy—3. John Dewey and the Chicago School," *New Republic*, XXII, 82.

"On American Philosophy—4. George Santayana," *New Republic*, XXIII, 221.

Review of Hall, *Morale, the Supreme Standard of Life and Conduct*, in *New Republic*, XXIV, 126.

1921

"Dante and the Modern Reader," *New Republic*, XXVIII, 303.

"Dante as a Moral Teacher," *New Republic*, XXVIII, 181; reprinted in *Faith of a Liberal*, 1946.

"Impressionism and Authority in Literary Criticism," *New Republic*, XXVIII, 252; reprinted in *Faith of a Liberal*, 1946.

"Later Philosophy," *Cambridge History of American Literature*, III, 226-265.

"Philosophy in the Modern Curriculum," *City College Quarterly*, XVII, no. 3, p. 4; reprinted in *Faith of a Liberal*, 1946.

"Questions in Einstein," *New Republic*, XXVIII, 136.

Review of Frazer, *Studies in Comparative Religion, Legend and Law*, in *New Republic*, XXVIII, 51, 112; reprinted in *Faith of a Liberal*, 1946.

Review of Holmes, *Collected Legal Papers*, in *New Republic*, XXV, 294; reprinted in *Law and the Social Order*, 1933.

"Roads to Einstein," *New Republic*, XXVII, 172.

"The Significance of Napoleon," *New Republic*, XXVI, 311; reprinted in *Faith of a Liberal*, 1946.

1922

A letter in *Journal of Philosophy*, XIX, 278.

Introduction to Pierre de Tourtoulon, *Philosophy in the Development of the Law*. New York: The Macmillan Company. Reprinted in *Law and the Social Order*, 1933.

"Liberalism and Irrationalism," *New Republic*, XXX, 333; reprinted in *Faith of a Liberal*, 1946.

"Remarks on Immigration," *Foreign-Born*, III, 168.

Review of *Bibliotheca Chemico-Mathematica* (compiled by H. Z. and H. C. S.), in *Journal of Philosophy*, XIX, 275.

Review of Curtis, *Science and Human Affairs*, in *New Republic*, XXXII, 255.

Review of Fisher, *Studies in History and Politics*; Duguit, *Law in the Modern State*; Laski, *The Foundations of Sovereignty*, in *New Republic*, XXXI, 111; reprinted in *Law and the Social Order*, 1933.

Review of Gray, *The Nature and Sources of the Law*; Cardozo, *The Nature of the Judicial Process*; Pound, *The Spirit of the Common Law* and *Introduction to the Philosophy of Law*, in *New Republic*, XXXIII, 4; reprinted in *Law and the Social Order*, 1933.

Review of Pound, *An Introduction to the Philosophy of Law*, in *Columbia Law Review*, XXII, 774; reprinted in *Law and the Social Order*, 1933.

Review of Rogers, *English and American Philosophy Since 1800*, in *New Republic*, XXXII, 204.

Review of Windelband, *An Introduction to Philosophy*, in *New Republic*, XXXII, 341.

"Ways of Current Philosophy," *New Republic*, XXXII, 341.

1923

"Amor Dei Intellectualis," *Chronicon Spinozanum*, III, 3.

"Einstein in the Movies: A Note on the Exposition in the Films of the Theory of Relativity," *Vanity Fair*, XX, 48.

Introduction to *Chance, Love and Logic: Essays of C. S. Peirce*. Morris R. Cohen, ed. New York: Harcourt Brace & Company, Inc.

"Liberalism and the Russian Mind," *Survey*, XLIX, 731; reprinted in *Faith of a Liberal*, 1946.

"On the Logic of Fiction," *Journal of Philosophy*, XX, 477; reprinted in *Preface to Logic*, 1944.

Review of Dewey, *Human Nature and Conduct*, in *American Review*, I, 360.

Review of Krabbe, *The Modern Idea of the State*, in *Philosophical Review*, XXXII, 97, 349; reprinted in *Law and the Social Order*, 1933.

Review of Hoover, *American Individualism*, in *New Republic*, XXXIII, 353; reprinted in *Law and the Social Order*, 1933.

Review of Pound, *The Spirit of the Common Law*, in *Journal of Philosophy*, XX, 155; reprinted in *Law and the Social Order*, 1933.

1924

"Legalism and Clericalism," *New Republic*, XLI, 15; reprinted in *Law and the Social Order*, 1933.

Review of Abbagnano, *Le Sorgenti Irrazionali del Pensiero*, in *Journal of Philosophy*, XXI, 554.

Review of Conger, *Theories of Macrocosms and Microcosms in the History of Philosophy*, in *Journal of Philosophy*, XXI, 556.

Review of Madariaga, *The Genius of Spain*, and Unamuno, *The Tragic Sense of Life*, in *New Republic*, XXXIX, 278.

Review of *Rational Basis of Legal Institutions* (by various authors), in *Yale Law Journal*, XXXIII, 892.

Review of Thorndike, *A History of Magic and Experimental Science During the First Thirteen Centuries of Our Era*, in *Journal of Philosophy*, XXI, 456.

1925

"Have Ideas Prestige among Us?," *World Tomorrow*, VIII, 202; reprinted in *Faith of a Liberal*, 1946.

"The Insurgence against Reason," *Journal of Philosophy*, XXII, 113; reprinted in *Reason and Nature*, 1931.

"The Intellectual Love of God," *Menorah Journal*, XI, 332-341; reprinted in part from *Chronicon Spinozanum*; reprinted in *Faith of a Liberal*, 1946.

"The Myths of Popular Science," *City College Quarterly*, XXI, 203.

Review of Bradley, *The Principles of Logic*, in *New Republic*, XLIV, 148; reprinted in *Preface to Logic*, 1944.

Review of Lowie, *Primitive Religion*, in *City College Quarterly*, XXI, 86.

Review of Pound, *Law and Morals*, in *Harvard Law Review*, XXXVIII, 1123; reprinted in *Law and the Social Order*, 1933.

"The Rivals and Substitutes for Reason," *Journal of Philosophy*, XXII, 141, 180; reprinted in *Reason and Nature*, 1931.

"Social Policy and the Supreme Court" (letter), *New Republic*, XLIII, 195.

1926

"Evolution as a Biological Law," *City College Alumnus*, XXII, 118.

"Myth about Bacon and the Inductive Method," *Scientific Monthly*, XXIII, 50.

"Professor Cohen's Reply [to the Case for Military Science]," *Lavender* III, no. 6, p. 12.

1927

"A Story of Philosophers" (letter), *New Republic*, L, 20.

"Concepts and Twilight Zones," *Journal of Philosophy*, XXIV, 673-683; reprinted in *Preface to Logic*, 1944.

"Positivism and the Limits of Idealism in the Law," *Columbia Law Review*, XXVII, 237-250; reprinted in *Reason and Nature*, 1931.

"Property and Sovereignty," *Cornell Law Quarterly*, XIII, 8; reprinted in *Law and the Social Order*, 1933.

Review of Yarmolinsky, *Turgenev, The Man, His Art, and His Age*, in *City College Alumnus*, XXIII, 80.

"The Social and the Natural Sciences," in *The Social Sciences and Their Interrelations*. William Fielding Ogburn and Alexander Goldenweiser, eds. Boston: Houghton Mifflin Company. Reprinted in *Reason and Nature*, 1931.

"Spinoza, Prophet of Liberalism," *New Republic*, L, 164-166; reprinted in *Faith of a Liberal*, 1946.

1928

Foreword to Alvin Bruch, *Poems and Letters*. New York, privately printed.

"Law and Scientific Method," *American Law School Review*, VI, 231-239; reprinted in *Law and the Social Order*, 1933.

1930

"Atheism," *Encyclopedia of the Social Sciences*, II, 292-294. New York: The Macmillan Company.

"Belief," *Encyclopedia of the Social Sciences*, II, 500-502. New York: The Macmillan Company.

"F. H. Bradley," *Encyclopedia of the Social Sciences*, II, 672-673. New York: The Macmillan Company.

"The Faith of a Logician," in *Contemporary American Philosophy*. George F. Adams and William Pepperell Montague, eds. New York: The Macmillan Company.

"John Austin," *Encyclopedia of the Social Sciences*, II, 317-318. New York: The Macmillan Company.

Selected Readings in the Philosophy of Law. Morris R. Cohen and Felix S. Cohen, eds. New York: privately printed for students of St. John's Law School and the College of the City of New York.

"Vision and Technique in Philosophy," *Philosophical Review*, XXXIX, 127-152.

1931

"Fictions," *Encyclopedia of the Social Sciences*, VI, 225-228. New York: The Macmillan Company.

"In Dispraise of Life, Experience, Reality," *New Republic*, LXVI, 124-126; reprinted in *Reason and Nature*, 1931.

"Justice Holmes and the Nature of Law," *Columbia Law Review*, XXXI, 352-361; reprinted in *Law and the Social Order*, 1933.

"Possibility in History," in *Proceedings of the Seventh International Congress of Philosophy*. London: Humphrey Milford Company.

Reason and Nature. New York: Harcourt, Brace & Company, Inc.

"Reason, Nature and Professor Dewey" (a communication), *New Republic*, LXVII, 126-127.

"Rene Descartes," *Encyclopedia of the Social Sciences*, V, 106-107. New York: The Macmillan Company.

Review of Dabin, *La Philosophie de l'ordre positif dans les rapports de droit privé*, in *Yale Law Journal*, XL, 1336-1338.

Review of Fraenkel, *The Sacco-Vanzetti Case*, in *Nation*, CXXXIII, 702-703; reprinted in *Faith of a Liberal*, 1946.

Review of Frank, *Law and the Modern Mind*, in *Nation*, CXXXIII, 259-260; reprinted in *Law and the Social Order*, 1933.

Review of Parrington, *The Beginnings of Critical Realism in America* (Vol. III—1860-1920), in *New Republic*, LXV, 303-304; reprinted in *Faith of a Liberal*, 1946.

Review of Rueff, *From the Physical to the Social Sciences*, in *Harvard Law Review*, XLIV, 1149-1154.

"Thomas Davidson," *Encyclopedia of Social Sciences*, III, 10. New York: The Macmillan Company.

"What I Believe," *Nation*, CXXXIII, 128-131; reprinted in *Faith of a Liberal*, 1946.

"Why I Am Not a Communist," in *The Meaning of Marx: A Symposium*. New York: Farrar & Rinehart, Inc. Reprinted in *Modern Monthly*, VIII, 138. Reprinted in *Faith of a Liberal*, 1946.

1932

"Hegel," *Encyclopedia of the Social Sciences*, VII, 311-315. New York: The Macmillan Company.

"Hegel's Rationalism," *Philosophical Review*, XLI, 283-301.

"Intellectual Basis of Individualism," *L.I.D. Monthly*, X, no. 6, p. 3; reprinted in *Faith of a Liberal*, 1946.

"Philosophy and Legal Science," *Columbia Law Review*, XXXII, 1103-1127; reprinted in *Law and the Social Order*, 1933.

Review of Adams, *The Epic of America*, in *New Republic*, LXIX, 274; reprinted in *Faith of a Liberal*, 1946.

Review of Ayres, *Huxley*; Peterson, *Huxley—Prophet of Science*, in *New Republic*, LXXII, 182-185; reprinted in *Faith of a Liberal*, 1946.

Review of *Collected Papers of C. S. Peirce* (Hartshorne and Weiss, eds.), in *Nation*, CXXXV, 368-370; reprinted in *Faith of a Liberal*, 1946.

Review of Wright, *American Interpretations of Natural Law—A Study in the History of Political Thought*, in *Yale Law Journal*, XLI, 1102-1103.

"What I Owe to the Jewish Ghetto," *Jewish Standard*, VII, 138.

1933

"The Basis of Contract," *Harvard Law Review*, XLVI, 553-592; reprinted in *Law and the Social Order*, 1933.

"The Dark Side of Religion," in *Religion Today—A Challenging Enigma*. Arthur L. Swift, Jr., ed. New York: McGraw-Hill Book Company, Inc. Reprinted in *Faith of a Liberal*, 1946.

"The Jew in Science," *The Judaeans: Judaean Addresses*, IV, 79-89. New York: Bloch Publishing Company, Inc.

Law and the Social Order. New York: Harcourt, Brace & Company, Inc.

Review of Frankfurter, *Mr. Justice Brandeis*, in *Harvard Law Review*, XLVII, 165-170; reprinted in *Faith of a Liberal*, 1946.

Review of *Collected Papers of C. S. Peirce* (Hartshorne and Weiss, eds.), in *International Journal of Ethics*, XLIII, 220-226.

Review of Tugwell, *Industrial Discipline and the Governmental Arts*, in *Columbia Law Review*, XXXIII, 1273-1277; reprinted in *Faith of a Liberal*, 1946.

Review of Whitehead, *Adventures of Ideas*, in *Yale Review*, XIII, 173; reprinted in *Faith of a Liberal*, 1946.

"Scientific Method," *Encyclopedia of Social Sciences*, X, 389-395. New York: The Macmillan Company

1934

An Introduction to Logic and Scientific Method. Morris R. Cohen and Ernest Nagel. New York: Harcourt, Brace & Company, Inc.

"Jews in Commerce and the Professions," *Jewish Social Service Quarterly*, XI, 21.

Review of Hook, *Towards the Understanding of Karl Marx*, in *Student Outlook*, III, nos. 2-3, p. 31; no. 5, p. 13.

1935

"Fallacies about the Court," *Nation*, CXLI, 39-40; reprinted in *Congressional Digest*, XIV, 316.

Introduction to Goldberg and Levenson, *Lawless Judges*. New York: Rand School Press.

"Justice Holmes," *New Republic*, LXXXII, 206-209; reprinted in *Faith of a Liberal*, 1946.

1936

"How Shall I Vote," *New Republic*, LXXXVIII, 348.

"The Jews in Poland," in *Jews in Poland: Their History, Their Tragedy, Their Future* (a pamphlet). New York: Federation of Polish Jews in America.

Introduction to Hirsch Lazaar Silverman, *Random Thoughts*. New York: The Century House.

"On Absolutisms in Legal Thought," *University of Pennsylvania Law Review*, LXXXIV, 681-715

"Overruling the Supreme Court: A Plea for Abolishing the Judicial Veto," *New Leader*, XIX, 5.

Proposed Roads for American Jewry. M. Lowenthal, E. Gutkind and Morris R. Cohen. New York: National Council of Jewish Women.

Review of Arnold, *Symbols of Government*, in *Illinois Law Review*, XXXI, 411-418; reprinted in *Faith of a Liberal*, 1946.

Review of Einstein, *The World As I See It*, in *Menorah Journal*, XXIV, 107-122; reprinted in *Faith of a Liberal*, 1946.

Review of Morris, *Select Cases of the Mayor's Court of New York City, 1674-1784*, in *Columbia Law Review*, XXXVI, 1388-1390.

Review of Robinson, *Law and the Lawyers*, in *Cornell Law Quarterly*, XXI, 171-178.

Review of Robson, *Civilization and the Growth of Law*, in *Harvard Law Review*, L, 145.

"The Statistical View of Nature," *Journal of the American Statistical Association*, XXXI, 327-346; reprinted in *Preface to Logic*, 1944.

1937

"A Critical Sketch of Legal Philosophy in America," in *Law—A Century of Progress, 1835-1935*. New York: New York University Press.

The Work of the Conference on Jewish Relations. New York: Conference on Jewish Relations, Inc.

1938

"Antisemitic Drives Endanger Democracy," *New Leader*, XXI, No. 9.

"Benjamin Nathan Cardozo," *National Lawyers Guild Quarterly*, I, 283-286; reprinted in *Faith of a Liberal*, 1946.

"Constitutional Rights and Natural Rights in 1789 and Since," *National Lawyers Guild Quarterly*, I, 92, reprinted in *Faith of a Liberal*, 1946.

Preface to Oscar Janowsky, *People at Bay: The Jewish Problem in East-Central Europe*. New York: Oxford University Press.

1939

"A Critique of Kant's Philosophy of Law," in *The Heritage of Kant*. G. T. Whitney and D. F. Bowers, eds. Princeton: Princeton University Press.

"Minimizing Social Conflicts," *Annals of the American Academy of Political Science*, CCIII, 114-123; reprinted in *Faith of a Liberal*, 1946.

"Philosophies of Jewish History," *Jewish Social Studies*, I, 39-72.

"Philosophy and Scientific Methods," lecture mimeographed by the Department of Agriculture School, March 20, 1939.

"Publisher's Foreword," *Jewish Social Studies*, I, 3.

Review of Askenasi, *Contribution des Juifs à la fondation des écoles de médecine en France au Moyen-Age*, in *Jewish Social Studies*, I, 390.

Review of Birkeland, *Zum Hebräischen Traditionswesen*, in *Jewish Social Studies*, I, 390.

Review of Freud, *Moses and Monotheism*, in *Jewish Social Studies*, I, 469.

Review of Lods, *The Prophets and the Rise of Judaism*, in *Jewish Social Studies*, I, 373-376.

Review of Rees, *A Critique of the Jews*, in *Jewish Social Studies*, I, 257.

1940

"A Scandalous Denial of Justice," in *The Bertrand Russell Case*. John Dewey and Horace Kallen, eds. New York: The Viking Press, Inc. Reprinted in *Faith of a Liberal*, 1946.

"Discussion: American Literary Tradition and Economic Forces," *Journal of the History of Ideas*, I, 372-374; partially reprinted in *Faith of a Liberal*, 1946.

"Ebreo Leone: The Philosophy of Love," *Jewish Social Studies*, II, 96.

"Generalization in the Social Sciences," in *Eleven Twenty-Six, A Decade of Social Science Research*. Louis Wirth, ed. Chicago: University of Chicago Press.

"Moral Aspects of the Criminal Law," *Yale Law Journal*, XLIX, 987-1026.

Review of Parkes, *The Jew and His Neighbor—A Study of the Causes of Anti-Semitism;* Lewisohn, *The Answer—The Jew and the World, Past, Present and Future*, in *Jewish Social Studies*, II, 85-90.

Review of Smith, *Forces in American Criticism*, in *Journal of the History of Ideas*, I, 241-251; reprinted in *Faith of a Liberal*, 1946.

"Some Difficulties in Dewey's Anthropocentric Naturalism," *Philosophical Review*, XLIX, 196-228.

1941

"American Democracy in the Present Emergency," *The Jewish Center*, XIX, 5-8.

"Jewish Studies of Peace and Post-War Problems," *Contemporary Jewish Record*, IV, 110-125.

"My Philosophy of Law," in *My Philosophy of Law*. Boston: Boston Law Book Company.

Review of *American Jewish Yearbook, XLII, 5701, 1940-1941*, in *Jewish Social Studies*, III, 231-232.

Review of Anshen, *Freedom: Its Meaning*, in *Harvard Law Review*, LIV, 1424; reprinted in *Faith of a Liberal*, 1946.

Review of Bidney, *The Psychology and Ethics of Spinoza*, in *Jewish Social Studies*, III, 238.

Review of Bloom, *My Memories;* Frumkin, *In the Springtime of Jewish Socialism*, in *Jewish Social Studies*, III, 226.

Review of Fuller, *The Law in Quest of Itself*, in *Illinois Law Review*, XXXVI, 239

Review of Hochander, *The Priests and Prophets;* Finkelstein, *The Pharisees—The Sociological Background of Their Faith*, in *Jewish Social Studies*, III, 81-87

Review of *Judaism and Christianity* (Gillet, ed.), in *Jewish Social Studies*, III, 344-346.

Review of Kenyon, *The Bible and Archeology*, in *Jewish Social Studies*, III, 236.

Review of Montefiore and Loewe, *A Rabbinic Anthology*, in *Jewish Social Studies*, III, 237.

Review of Mosca, *The Ruling Class*, in *Columbia Law Review*, XLI, 177.

Review of Strickland, *Religion and the State in Georgia in the Eighteenth Century*, in *Jewish Social Studies*, III, 238-239.

1942

"Causation and Its Application to History," *Journal of the History of Ideas*, III, 12.

Review of Powell, *Spinoza and Religion*, in *Jewish Social Studies*, IV, 175.

1943

"The Background and Development of Legal Philosophy in the Americas," in *Proceedings of the Eighth American Scientific Congress*. Washington, D. C.: Department of State.

1944

Preface to Logic. New York: Henry Holt & Company, Inc.

1945

Foreword to Siegfried Goldschmidt, *Legal Claims against Germany*. New York: The Dryden Press, Inc.

1946

"Italian Contributions to the Philosophy of Law," *Harvard Law Review*, LIX, 577.

Faith of a Liberal. New York: Henry Holt & Company, Inc.

1947

The Meaning of Human History. Lasalle, Illinois: The Open Court Publishing Company.

1948

A Dreamer's Journey. Boston: The Beacon Press.

Source Book in Greek Science. New York: McGraw-Hill Book Company, Inc.

To Be Published

American Thought: A Critical Sketch.
Reflections of a Wondering Jew.
Studies in Juristic Philosophy.
Studies in Philosophy and Science.

INDEX